W9-BXF-184

BOWLING, BEATNIKS, AND BELL-BOTTOMS

Pop Culture of 20th- and 21st-Century America

BOWLING, BEATNIKS, AND BELL-BOTTOMS

Pop Culture of 20th- and 21st-Century America

VOLUME 6: 2000–2009

Cynthia Johnson, Editor
Lawrence W. Baker, Project Editor

U·X·L
A part of Gale, Cengage Learning

FEB 2 0 2013

Montante Family Library
D'Youville College

GALE
CENGAGE Learning·

Detroit • New York • San Francisco • New Haven, Conn • Waterville, Maine • London

GALE
CENGAGE Learning·

Bowling, Beatniks, and Bell-Bottoms: Pop Culture of 20th- and 21st-Century America, 2nd ed.

Cynthia Johnson, Editor

Project Editor: Lawrence W. Baker

Rights Acquisition and Management: Robyn Young

Composition: Evi Abou-El-Seoud

Manufacturing: Wendy Blurton

Imaging: John Watkins

Product Design: Kristine Julien

© 2012 Gale, Cengage Learning

ALL RIGHTS RESERVED. No part of this work covered by the copyright herein may be reproduced, transmitted, stored, or used in any form or by any means graphic, electronic, or mechanical, including but not limited to photocopying, recording, scanning, digitizing, taping, Web distribution, information networks, or information storage and retrieval systems, except as permitted under Section 107 or 108 of the 1976 United States Copyright Act, without the prior written permission of the publisher.

For product information and technology assistance, contact us at
Gale Customer Support, 1-800-877-4253.
For permission to use material from this text or product, submit all requests online at **www.cengage.com/permissions.**
Further permissions questions can be emailed to
permissionrequest@cengage.com

Front cover photographs: (Left to right) The Game of Life, © CameraShots-Concept/Alamy; Radio City Music Hall, © Sam Dao/Alamy; Slinky, © Garry Gay/Workbook Stock/Getty Images; Hollywood sign, © Gavin Hellier/Alamy. Back cover photographs: (Top to bottom) Nickelodeon, © Lewis Hine/Historical/Corbis; Bobbysoxers, © Bettmann/Corbis; Man bowling, © H. Armstrong Roberts/ClassicStock/Alamy.

While every effort has been made to ensure the reliability of the information presented in this publication, Gale, a part of Cengage Learning, does not guarantee the accuracy of the data contained herein. Gale accepts no payment for listing; and inclusion in the publication of any organization, agency, institution, publication, service, or individual does not imply endorsement of the editors or publisher. Errors brought to the attention of the publisher and verified to the satisfaction of the publisher will be corrected in future editions.

LIBRARY OF CONGRESS CATALOGING-IN-PUBLICATION DATA

Bowling, beatniks, and bell-bottoms : pop culture of 20th- and 21st-century America / Cynthia Johnson, editor ; Lawrence W. Baker, project editor. —2nd ed.
 v. cm.
 Contents: v. 1. 1900s-1910s — v. 2. 1920s-1930s — v. 3. 1940s-1950s — v. 4. 1960s-1970s — v. 5. 1980s-1990s — v. 6. 2000-2009.
  ISBN-13: 978-1-4144-1165-1 (set : alk. paper)
  ISBN-10: 1-4144-1165-0 (set : alk. paper)
  ISBN-13: 978-1-4144-1166-8 (v. 1 : alk. paper)
  ISBN-10: 1-4144-1166-9 (v. 1 : alk. paper)
  [etc.]
 1. United States—Civilization—20th century—Miscellanea—Juvenile literature. 2. United States—Civilization—21st century—Miscellanea—Juvenile literature. 3. Popular culture—United States—History—20th century—Miscellanea—Juvenile literature. 4. Popular culture—United States—History—21st century—Miscellanea—Juvenile literature. I. Johnson, Cynthia, 1969– II. Baker, Lawrence W.
 E169.1.B7825 2012
 306.097309'04—dc23   2012002579

Gale
27500 Drake Rd.
Farmington Hills, MI, 48331-3535

978-1-4144-1165-1 (set)   1-4144-1165-0 (set)
978-1-4144-1166-8 (vol. 1)   1-4144-1166-9 (vol. 1)
978-1-4144-1167-5 (vol. 2)   1-4144-1167-7 (vol. 2)
978-1-4144-1168-2 (vol. 3)   1-4144-1168-5 (vol. 3)
978-1-4144-1169-9 (vol. 4)   1-4144-1169-3 (vol. 4)
978-1-4144-1170-5 (vol. 5)   1-4144-1170-7 (vol. 5)
978-1-4144-1171-2 (vol. 6)   1-4144-1171-5 (vol. 6)

This title is also available as an e-book.
ISBN-13: 978-1-4144-1181-1   ISBN-10: 1-4144-1181-2
Contact your Gale, a part of Cengage Learning sales representative for ordering information

Printed .   ı
1 2 3 4 5 ϲ   15 14 13 12

E
169.1
.B7825
2012
vol.6

Contents

Print Culture

Sports and Games

The Way We Lived

The Way We Lived

VOLUME 5
1980s

VOLUME 6
2000S

Entries by Alphabetical Order

Entries by Topic Category

Sports and Games

TV and Radio

First-edition Contributors

Timothy Berg. Visiting assistant professor, Western Michigan University. Ph.D., History, Purdue University, 1999.

Charles Coletta, Ph.D. Instructor, Department of Popular Culture, Bowling Green State University. Contributing writer, *St. James Encyclopedia of Popular Culture* (2000).

Rob Edelman. Instructor, State University of New York at Albany. Author, *Baseball on the Web* (1997) and *The Great Baseball Films* (1994). Co-author, *Matthau: A Life* (2002); *Meet the Mertzes* (1999); and *Angela Lansbury: A Life on Stage and Screen* (1996). Contributing editor, *Leonard Maltin's Movie & Video Guide, Leonard Maltin's Movie Encyclopedia,* and *Leonard Maltin's Family Viewing Guide.* Contributing writer, *International Dictionary of Films and Filmmakers* (2000); *St. James Encyclopedia of Popular Culture* (2000); *Women Film-makers & Their Films* (1998); *The Political Companion to American Film* (1994); and *Total Baseball* (1989). Film commentator, WAMC (Northeast) Public Radio.

Tina Gianoulis. Freelance writer. Contributing writer, *World War I Reference Library* (2001–2); *Constitutional Amendments: From Freedom of Speech to Flag Burning* (2001); *International Dictionary of Films and Filmmakers* (2000); *St. James Encyclopedia of Popular Culture* (2000); and mystories.com, a daytime drama Web site (1997–98).

Sheldon Goldfarb. Archivist, Alma Mater Society of the University of British Columbia. Ph.D., English, University of British Columbia. Author, *William Makepeace Thackeray: An Annotated Bibliography, 1976–1987* (1989). Editor, *Catherine,* by William Makepeace Thackeray (1999).

Jill Gregg Clever, A.A., B.A., M.L.I.S. Graduate of Michigan State University, Thomas Edison State College, and Wayne State University. Business-technology specialist, Toledo–Lucas County Public Library.

Justin Gustainis. Professor of communication, State University of New York at Plattsburgh. Author, *American Rhetoric and the Vietnam War* (1993).

Audrey Kupferberg. Film consultant and archivist. Instructor, State University of New York at Albany. Co-author, *Matthau: A Life* (2002); *Meet the Mertzes* (1999); and *Angela Lansbury: A Life on Stage and Screen* (1996). Contributing editor, *Leonard Maltin's Family Viewing Guide.* Contributing writer, *St. James Encyclopedia of Popular Culture* (2000); *Women Filmmakers & Their Films* (1998); and *The American Film Institute Catalog of Feature Films.*

Edward Moran. Writer of American culture, music, and literature. Associate editor, *World Musicians* (1999); *World Authors* (1996); and *Random House Dictionary of the English Language* (1987; 1991). Contributing writer, *St. James Encyclopedia of Popular Culture* (2000). Editor, *Rhythm,* a magazine of world music and global culture (2001).

Sara Pendergast. President, Full Circle Editorial. Vice president, Group 3 Editorial. Co-editor, *St. James Encyclopedia of Popular Culture* (2000). Co-author, *World War I Reference Library* (2001), among other publications.

Tom Pendergast. Editorial director, Full Circle Editorial. Ph.D., American studies, Purdue University. Author, *Creating the Modern Man: American Magazines and Consumer Culture* (2000). Co-editor, *St. James Encyclopedia of Popular Culture* (2000).

Karl Rahder. M.A., University of Chicago Committee on International Relations. Author, several articles on international history and politics.

Chris Routledge. Freelance writer and editor. Ph.D., American literature, University of Newcastle upon Tyne (UK). Author, "The Chevalier and the Priest: Deductive Method in Poe, Chesterton, and Borges," in *Clues: A Journal of Detection* (2001). Editor, *Mystery in Children's Literature: From the Rational to the Supernatural* (2001).

Robert E. Schnakenberg. Senior writer, History Book Club. Author, *The Encyclopedia Shatnerica* (1998).

Steven Schneider. Ph.D. candidate, philosophy, Harvard University; Ph.D. candidate, cinema studies, New York University. Author, *An Auteur on Elm Street: The Cinema of Wes Craven* (forthcoming). Co-editor, *Horror International* (forthcoming) and *Dark Thoughts: Philosophic Reflections on Cinematic Horror* (forthcoming). Contributing writer, *British Horror Cinema* (2002); *Car Crash Culture* (2001); and numerous film journals.

Robert C. Sickels. Assistant professor of American film and popular culture, Whitman College. Ph.D., English, University of Nevada. Author, "A Politically Correct Ethan Edwards: Clint Eastwood's The Outlaw Josey Wales" in *Journal of Popular Film & Television* (forthcoming); "'70s Disco Daze: Paul Thomas Anderson's Boogie Nights and the Last Golden Age of Irresponsibility" in *Journal of Popular Culture* (forthcoming). Contributor, *St. James Encyclopedia of Popular Culture* (2000).

Reader's Guide

Popular culture—as we know it—was born in America, though historians disagree as to exactly when. Was it in 1893, when magazine publishers used new technologies to cut the costs of their magazines to a dime and sell hundreds of thousands of copies? Or was it in 1905, when the invention of the nickelodeon brought low-cost films to people all across the nation? Or was it back in 1886, when Richard Sears and Alvah Roebuck sent out their first catalog, which allowed people from all over to choose from among hundreds and then thousands of the same goods?

No matter the exact date, by the turn of the twentieth century, American magazine publishers, retailers, moviemakers, and other entertainers were bringing their goods before larger numbers of Americans than ever before. These magazines, movies, advertisements, shopping experiences, sports teams, and more were what we know as "popular culture," because they could be enjoyed firsthand by masses of Americans.

The story of America as revealed by its popular culture is complex and fascinating. Readers of *Bowling, Beatniks, and Bell-Bottoms: Pop Culture of 20th- and 21st-Century America* will discover, for example, that the comedic forms first developed by vaudeville comedians at the turn of the twentieth century lived on in film, radio, and finally television. They will learn that black musicians created the musical forms that are most distinctly American: blues and jazz. And they will realize that popular culture reacted to things like war and economic depressions in ways that were surprising and unexpected. The study of popular culture has a great deal to teach the student who is interested in how people use entertainment and consumption to make sense of their lives and shape their experience.

Bowling, Beatniks, and Bell-Bottoms gathers together essays that reflect the variety, diversity, and excitement of American popular culture of the twentieth and twenty-first centuries. This collection focuses more on events, fads, programs, performances, and products than on biographies of people, which are well documented in other sources. Even so, brief biographies of notables are sprinkled throughout. With approximately 850 essays on individual topics and dozens of overviews of pop culture trends, *Bowling, Beatniks, and Bell-Bottoms* covers a great deal of American popular culture, though not nearly enough. There are hundreds more people, bands, TV programs, films, and products that were worthy of mention but were left out due to space consideration. Our advisory board of media specialists, however, helped assure that the most prominent and studied subjects were included.

Have you ever wondered how the Slinky was invented, what Velveeta cheese is made of, or what people danced to before rock and roll? Those answers are in *Bowling, Beatniks, and Bell-Bottoms,* along with many others. It is our hope that this collection will bring both information and pleasure to all students of American culture.

Organization

Bowling, Beatniks, and Bell-Bottoms is arranged chronologically by decade over six volumes (two decades per volume for the twentieth century, and one volume covering the first decade of the twenty-first century). The approximately 850 entries are grouped into nine topic sections: Commerce, Fashion, Film and Theater, Food and Drink, Music, Print Culture, Sports and Games, TV and Radio, and The Way We Lived (though not all topics appear in every decade). Many subjects can easily appear in several different decades, so those essays are placed in either the decade in which the product was invented or the fad initiated, or in the decade in which the subject was most prominent or popular. In addition, several of the essays could have appeared under different topics (such as a book that was made into a movie), so those essays appear under the topic where it was best known. Users should make frequent use of the index or the two additional tables of contents (arranged alphabetically by entry name and by topic category) to locate an entry.

Essays range in length from 150 to 1000 words, with the majority averaging less than 500 words. Every essay aims to describe the topic and analyze the topic's contribution to popular culture. Each essay lists additional sources on the topic, including books, magazine or journal articles, and Web sites. Whenever possible, references to books are geared to younger readers. The editor and writers have personally visited every Web site mentioned and believe that these sites contain content that will assist the reader in understanding the subject. Due to the nature of the World Wide Web, it is possible that not all Web links will still function at the time of publication.

Bowling, Beatniks, and Bell-Bottoms also provides these features:

- A timeline that highlights key historic and pop culture events of the twentieth and twenty-first centuries
- A general overview of each decade
- A multipaged "At a Glance" box that breaks down "What We Said," "What We Read," "What We Watched," "What We Listened To," and "Who We Knew"
- An overview of each topic section in each decade
- Approximately 450 photos and illustrations
- Extensive use of cross references (pointing to decade, topic, and volume)

Acknowledgments

A thank-you encore goes to the advisors of this publication (their professional affiliation at the time of the publication of the first edition is noted): Catherine Bond, Department Chair, Library and Media Services, Conestoga High School, Berwyn, Pennsylvania; Cathy Chauvette, Assistant Regional Branch Manager, Fairfax County Public Library, Fairfax County, Virginia; Nancy Schlosser Garabed, Library Media Specialist, Council Rock High School, Newtown, Pennsylvania; Ann West LaPrise, Junior High/Elementary Media Specialist, Huron School District, New Boston, Michigan; and Nina Levine, Library Media Specialist, Blue Mountain Middle School, Cortlandt Manor, New York. Their input during the preparation of the first edition remains valuable.

The contributions of the writers from the first edition are noted on the contributors page (which reprints their background at the time of the first edition). For this second edition, much gratitude is given to writers David Larkins, Annette Petrusso, Maureen Reed, Patrick Walsh, and Greg Wilson.

Much appreciation goes to copyeditor Maxwell Valentine, proofreader Rebecca Valentine, indexer Theresa Murray, and typesetter

PreMediaGlobal. Additional thanks to Scott Rosen at the Bill Smith Group for permissions and imaging selection and Barry Puckett for image processing assistance.

Comments and Suggestions

We welcome your comments on *Bowling, Beatniks, and Bell-Bottoms.* Please send correspondence to: Editors, *Bowling, Beatniks, and Bell-Bottoms,* U•X•L, 27500 Drake Rd., Farmington Hills, MI 48331-3535; call toll-free: 800-877-4253; fax to 248-414-5043; or send e-mail via www.cengage.com.

Cynthia Johnson, Editor

1900 On January 29, Ban Johnson forms the American League to compete against baseball's National League.

1900 In February, Eastman Kodak introduces the Brownie Camera.

1900 In March, the Good Roads Campaign tries to build support for better roads. At the time, there are only ten miles of paved roads in the nation.

1900 On March 31, the first ad for an automobile appears in the *Saturday Evening Post.*

1900 On April 23, Buffalo Bill Cody's *Wild West Show* opens at Madison Square Garden in New York City.

1900 On November 6, Republican William McKinley is reelected U.S. president, with New York governor Theodore Roosevelt as his vice president.

1900 On November 12, *Floradora,* one of the most popular theatrical musicals of the decade, premieres in New York. It runs for more than five hundred performances.

1901 On February 25, U.S. Steel is formed out of ten companies and becomes the world's largest industrial corporation.

1901 On March 13, steel tycoon Andrew Carnegie donates $2.2 million to fund a New York public library system.

1901 On September 6, President William McKinley is shot by an assassin in Buffalo, New York, and dies eight days later from complications from gangrene due to improperly dressed wounds. Theodore Roosevelt becomes president.

1901 On October 16, President Theodore Roosevelt starts a national controversy when he dines with black leader Booker T. Washington in the White House.

1902 The Teddy Bear is introduced, named after President Theodore Roosevelt.

1902 On January 1, in the first Rose Bowl football game, the University of Michigan defeats Stanford 49–0.

1902 On March 18, Italian opera singer Enrico Caruso produces his first phonographic recording.

1902 On April 16, Tally's Electric Theater, the first theater solely devoted to presenting motion pictures, opens in Los Angeles, California.

1902 On December 21, Guglielmo Marconi transmits the first wireless signals across the Atlantic Ocean.

1903 *Redbook* magazine is founded.

1903 The Portage Lakers of Houghton, Michigan—the first professional hockey team from the United States—win the International Hockey League championship.

1903 On January 22, the United States signs a 99-year lease on what will become the Panama Canal Zone, where it will build a canal that connects the Caribbean Sea to the Pacific Ocean.

1903 In February, the *Ladies' Home Journal* becomes the first American magazine to reach one million paid subscriptions.

1903 On May 23, two men make the first transcontinental automobile trip from San Francisco to New York in sixty-four days. Upon returning home, one driver is ticketed for exceeding the speed limit of six miles per hour.

1903 On August 14, Jim Jeffries defeats James J. "Gentleman Jim" Corbett to retain the world heavyweight boxing title.

1903 On September 12, Scott Joplin's ragtime opera *A Guest of Honor* begins a midwest tour.

1903 In October, the Boston Pilgrims defeat the Pittsburgh Pirates in the first World Series to pit an American League team against a National League team.

1903 On December 1, Edwin S. Porter's film *The Great Train Robbery* is considered the first Western and the first American film with a plot.

1903 On December 17, Wilbur and Orville Wright make the first sustained flight at Kitty Hawk, North Carolina.

1904 The Ford Motor Company sells fourteen hundred of its Model A cars.

1904 On April 20, the World's Fair opens in St. Louis, Missouri.

1904 On May 5, Cy Young pitches baseball's first perfect game.

1904 On November 8, Theodore Roosevelt is reelected president.

1905 The German navy launches the first submarine.

1905 African American leader W. E. B. Du Bois helps found the Niagara Movement, an organization to advance African American issues.

1905 On May 5, the *Chicago Defender,* the first major black newspaper, begins publication.

1905 In June, the era of the nickelodeon begins when Harry Davis's Pittsburgh, Pennsylvania, movie theater offers continuous movie showings. By the end of the decade, more than eight thousand nickel-admission movie theaters are in operation.

1905 On June 18, the Twentieth Century Limited begins train service between Chicago, Illinois, and New York City and boasts a travel time of only eighteen hours.

1906 Kellogg's Corn Flakes breakfast cereal is introduced.

1906 In February, Upton Sinclair publishes *The Jungle,* a novel depicting the horrible conditions in the meat-packing industry. The work prompts the passage of the Meat Inspection Act.

1906 On April 14, President Theodore Roosevelt coins the term "muckraking" when he criticizes journalists who expose abuses and corruption and miss the larger social picture.

1906 On April 18, a major earthquake and fire destroy much of San Francisco, California.

1906 On May 3, the First Annual Advertising Show in New York City heralds the beginning of an important American industry.

1906 On November 21, the first voice radio transmission travels eleven miles from Plymouth to Brant Rock, Massachusetts.

1907 Work begins on the Panama Canal.

1907 On January 23, in what newspapers call the "trial of the century," millionaire Harry K. Thaw is tried for the murder of world-famous architect Stanford White over the honor of Thaw's wife, showgirl Evelyn Nesbit.

1907 On June 10, French motion picture pioneers Auguste and Louis Lumière announce they have developed a method for producing color film.

1907 On July 8, Florenz Ziegfeld's musical revue, the *Ziegfeld Follies,* opens in New York.

1907 On December 3, actress Mary Pickford makes her stage debut in *The Warrens of Virginia.*

1908 The world's first skyscraper, the forty-seven-story Singer Building, is completed in New York City.

1908 The General Motors Corporation is formed and soon becomes the biggest competitor of the Ford Motor Company.

1908 In March, the Original Independent Show, organized in New York, includes works by American painters Edward Hopper, George Bellows, and Rockwell Kent.

1908 On September 6, Israel Zangwill's play *The Melting Pot* opens in New York City; the title becomes an internationally recognized description of the United States.

1908 On October 1, the Ford Motor Company unveils its Model T with a price tag of $825. It soon becomes the best-selling automobile of its time.

1908 On November 3, former U.S. secretary of war William Howard Taft is elected president.

1908 On December 26, Jack Johnson defeats Tommy Burns to become the first black world heavyweight boxing champion. His victory is considered an outrage by white racists.

1909 The fifty-story Metropolitan Life Insurance Tower in New York City becomes the world's tallest building.

1909 The Ford Motor Company manufactures nineteen thousand Model T cars.

1909 On March 16, the Federal Bureau of Investigation is created as a federal law enforcement agency.

1909 On March 23, former president Theodore Roosevelt leaves for a safari in Africa. He is paid $50,000 by *Scribner's Magazine* for his account of the trip.

1909 On April 6, U.S. Navy commander Robert Peary reaches the North Pole.

1909 On May 3, the first wireless press message is sent from New York City to Chicago, Illinois.

1909 On July 12, the U.S. Congress asks the states to authorize a national income tax.

1910 Western novelist Zane Grey's book *Heritage of the Desert* becomes a huge commercial success, starting his career of bringing the American West to the reading world.

1910 Levi Strauss and Company begins making casual play clothes for children.

1910 The Boy Scouts of America are founded in Chicago, Illinois.

1910 On February 28, Russian ballerina Anna Pavlova makes her American debut at the Metropolitan Opera House in New York City.

1910 On March 28, the first one-man show by artist Pablo Picasso opens at photographer and editor Alfred Stieglitz's 291 Gallery in New York City.

1910 In November, the National Association for the Advancement of Colored People (NAACP) publishes the first issue of the *Crisis* magazine, edited by W. E. B. Du Bois.

1910 On November 3, the Chicago Grand Opera opens with a production of *Aida,* by Giuseppe Verdi.

1911 Irving Berlin composes "Alexander's Ragtime Band," the song that popularized ragtime music.

1911 Air conditioning is invented.

1911 *Photoplay,* the first movie fan magazine, is published.

1911 On March 25, in New York City, 146 female workers are killed in the Triangle Shirtwaist Factory fire, alerting Americans to the dangers women face in industrial labor.

1911 On May 23, President William Howard Taft dedicates the New York Public Library.

1911 On May 30, the first Indianapolis 500 auto race is won by Ray Harroun with an average speed of 74.59 mph.

1911 On August 8, *Pathé's Weekly,* the first regular newsreel to be produced in the United States, is released to motion picture theaters.

1911 On December 19, the Association of American Painters and Sculptors is founded.

1912 New Mexico and Arizona become the forty-seventh and forty-eighth states.

1912 The Little Theater in Chicago, Illinois, and the Toy Theater in Boston, Massachusetts, the first influential little theaters in the United States, are founded.

1912 Dancers Irene and Vernon Castle start a craze for ballroom dancing.

1912 On April 15, the *Titanic* sinks on its maiden voyage from Ireland to the United States, killing 1,517.

1912 In August, photographer and editor Alfred Stieglitz devotes an entire issue of his periodical *Camera Work* to the modern art movement.

1912 On August 5, former president Theodore Roosevelt is nominated as the presidential candidate of the newly formed Progressive Party.

1912 On October 31, *The Musketeers of Pig Alley*, a film by D. W. Griffith that points out the social evils of poverty and crime on the streets of New York, is released.

1912 On November 5, New Jersey governor Woodrow Wilson is elected president.

1912 On December 10, the Famous Players Film Company registers for copyright of the five-reel feature film *The Count of Monte Cristo,* directed by Edwin S. Porter.

1913 The 792-foot-high Woolworth Building in New York City becomes the world's tallest building, a record it holds until 1930.

1913 The first crossword puzzle is published.

1913 The Jesse Lasky Feature Play Co., which later would become Paramount Pictures, is established in Hollywood, California.

1913 The Panama Canal is completed, and officially opens on August 15, 1914.

1913 On February 17, the International Exhibition of Modern Art, known as the Armory Show, opens in New York City. It is the first opportunity for many Americans to view modern art.

1913 On February 25, the Sixteenth Amendment to the Constitution is approved, authorizing a federal income tax.

1913 On March 24, the million dollar, eighteen-hundred-seat Palace Theatre opens in New York City.

1913 On May 31, the Seventeenth Amendment to the Constitution is approved, providing for the direct election of U.S. senators by citizens, rather than by state legislatures.

1914 On February 13, the American Society of Composers, Authors, and Publishers (ASCAP), an organization that seeks royalty payments for public performances of music, is founded in New York City.

1914 In March, comedian Charles Chaplin begins to evolve the legendary character of the Little Tramp in the film *Mabel's Strange Predicament.*

1914 On July 3, the first telephone line connects New York City and San Francisco, California.

1914 On August 3, World War I starts in Europe when Germany invades Belgium. Soon all of Europe is drawn into the conflict, though the United States remains neutral.

1914 On September 5, a German submarine scores its first kill, sinking the British cruiser *Pathfinder*, as World War I intensifies.

1914 In September, in the World War I Battle of the Marne, Germany's advance into France is halted.

1914 On November 3, the first American exhibition of African sculpture opens at the 291 Gallery in New York City.

1914 On December 3, the Isadorables, six European dancers trained by American dancer Isadora Duncan, perform at Carnegie Hall in New York City after escaping with Duncan from her war-torn Europe.

1915 The first taxicab appears on the streets of New York City.

1915 The first professional football league is formed in Ohio and is called simply the Ohio League.

1915 Modern dancers Ruth St. Denis and Ted Shawn found the Denishawn School of Dancing in Los Angeles, California.

1915 Five hundred U.S. correspondents cover World War I in Europe.

1915 On March 10, the Russian Symphony Orchestra plays the American debut performance of the symphony *Prometheus* by Aleksandr Scriabin at Carnegie Hall in New York City. Color images are projected onto a screen as part of the show.

1915 On December 10, the Ford Motor Company manufactures its one millionth Model T automobile.

1916 The Boeing Aircraft Company produces its first biplane.

1916 Newspaper publisher William Randolph Hearst inaugurates the *City Life* arts section as a supplement to his Sunday newspapers.

1916 In November, inventor and radio pioneer Lee De Forest begins to transmit daily music broadcasts from his home in New York City.

1916 On November 7, Woodrow Wilson is reelected president after campaigning on the pledge to keep the United States out of the war in Europe.

1917 The Russian Revolution brings communism to Russia, setting the stage for nearly a century of intermittent conflict with the United States.

1917 Showman George M. Cohan composes the song that was a musical call-to-arms during World War I: "Over There."

1917 Motion picture pioneer Cecil B. DeMille directs *The Little American,* a patriotic melodrama starring Mary Pickford.

1917 On April 6, the United States declares war on Germany after German submarines continue to attack U.S. merchant ships.

1917 On May 28, Benny Leonard wins the lightweight boxing championship, which he holds until his retirement in 1924 while building a record of 209–5; he makes a comeback in 1931.

1917 On August 19, the managers of the New York Giants and Cincinnati Reds are arrested for playing baseball on Sunday.

1917 On October 27, sixteen-year-old Russian-born violinist Jascha Heifetz makes his debut American performance at Carnegie Hall in New York City.

1918 The annual O. Henry Awards for short fiction are inaugurated in honor of short story writer O. Henry (a pseudonym for William Sydney Porter).

1918 On January 8, President Woodrow Wilson delivers his "Fourteen Points" address before Congress, outlining his plans for the shape of the postwar world.

1918 In March, *The Little Review* begins to serialize the novel *Ulysses,* by James Joyce, which features stream of consciousness techniques and a kind of private language.

1918 On November 11, Germany signs an armistice with the Allies, ending the fighting in World War I.

1918 In December, the Theatre Guild is founded in New York City.

1919 *Maid of Harlem,* an all-black-cast musical starring "Fats" Waller, Mamie Smith, Johnny Dunn, and Perry Bradford, draws enthusiastic crowds at the Lincoln Theatre in New York City.

1919 On January 29, Prohibition begins with the adoption of the Eighteenth Amendment to the Constitution, which bans the manufacture, sale, and transportation of intoxicating liquors.

1919 On February 5, United Artists, an independent film distribution company, is founded by Charles Chaplin, Douglas Fairbanks, D. W. Griffith, and Mary Pickford.

1919 On June 28, the Treaty of Versailles is signed by the Allied powers, officially ending World War I. Germany is forced to pay costly reparations for the damage it caused during the war.

1919 On July 4, Jack Dempsey defeats Jess Willard to win the world heavyweight boxing championship.

1919 On October 31, the Provincetown Players stage *The Dreamy Kid,* by Eugene O'Neill, with an all-black cast.

1919 On December 22, Attorney General A. Mitchell Palmer authorizes government raids on communists, anarchists, and other political radicals. These "Palmer raids" are part of a nationwide "red scare."

1920 Sinclair Lewis publishes the novel *Main Street.*

1920 Douglas Fairbanks stars in the film *The Mark of Zorro.*

1920 On January 5, the Radio Corporation of America (RCA) is founded and becomes a leading radio broadcaster.

1920 On February 12, the National Negro Baseball League is founded.

1920 On August 20, the first radio news bulletins are broadcast by station 8MK in Detroit, Michigan.

1920 On August 26, the Nineteenth Amendment to the Constitution gives women the right to vote.

1920 On September 28, eight Chicago White Sox players are charged with throwing the 1919 World Series in what becomes known as the "Black Sox Scandal." They are eventually banned from the game for life.

1920 On September 29, New York Yankee Babe Ruth breaks his own single-season home run record with 54 home runs.

1920 On November 1, Eugene O'Neill's play *The Emperor Jones* opens in New York City.

1920 On November 6, U.S. senator Warren G. Harding of Ohio is elected president.

1921 The Ford Motor Company announces a plan to produce one million automobiles a year.

1921 The Phillips Gallery in Washington, D.C., becomes the first American museum of modern art.

1921 In this year, 13 percent of Americans own telephones.

1921 On March 10, the first White Castle hamburger chain opens in Wichita, Kansas.

1921 On April 11, radio station KDKA in Pittsburgh, Pennsylvania, broadcasts the first sports event on radio, a boxing match between Johnny Ray and Johnny Dundee. Later that year, the World Series is broadcast.

1921 On May 23, *Shuffle Along* is the first black Broadway musical written and directed by African Americans.

1921 On July 29, Adolf Hitler is elected dictator of the Nazi Party in Munich, Germany.

1921 On September 8, the first Miss America pageant is held in Washington, D.C.

1921 On November 2, Margaret Sanger founds the American Birth Control League in New York City, raising the anger of many religious groups, especially Catholic groups.

1922 Robert Flaherty releases the documentary film *Nanook of the North*.

1922 Irish author James Joyce publishes *Ulysses,* which is banned in some countries for its alleged obscenity.

1922 F. Scott Fitzgerald publishes *Tales of the Jazz Age.*

1922 The American Professional Football Association changes its name to the National Football League (NFL).

1922 *Reader's Digest* magazine is founded.

1922 Al Jolson pens the popular song "Toot Toot Tootsie."

1922 On May 5, Coco Chanel introduces Chanel No. 5, which becomes the world's best-known perfume.

1922 On August 28, the first advertisement is aired on radio station WEAF in New York City.

1922 On December 30, the Union of Soviet Socialist Republics (USSR) is established with Russia at its head.

1923 Cecil B. DeMille directs the epic film *The Ten Commandments.*

1923 Charles Kettering develops a method for bringing colored paint to mass-produced cars.

1923 Bessie Smith's "Down Hearted Blues" is one of the first blues songs to be recorded.

1923 *Time* magazine begins publication.

1923 On April 6, trumpet player Louis Armstrong records his first solo on "Chimes Blues" with King Oliver's Creole Jazz Band.

1923 On August 3, President Warren G. Harding dies and Vice President Calvin Coolidge takes office.

1924 John Ford directs the Western film *The Iron Horse.*

1924 The Metro-Goldwyn-Mayer (MGM) film studio is formed in Hollywood, California.

1924 Evangelist Aimee Semple McPherson begins broadcasting from the first religious radio station, KFSG in Los Angeles, California.

1924 The stock market begins a boom that will last until 1929.

1924 On January 1, there are 2.5 million radios in American homes, up from 2,000 in 1920.

1924 On February 12, the tomb of King Tutankhamen, or King Tut, is opened in Egypt after having been sealed for four thousand years.

1924 On February 24, George Gershwin's *Rhapsody in Blue* is performed by an orchestra in New York City.

1924 On March 10, J. Edgar Hoover is appointed director of the Federal Bureau of Investigation.

1924 In June, the Chrysler Corporation is founded and competes with General Motors and Ford.

1924 On November 4, incumbent Calvin Coolidge is elected president.

1925 In one of the most famous years in American literature, F. Scott Fitzgerald publishes *The Great Gatsby,* Ernest Hemingway publishes *In Our Time,* and Theodore Dreiser publishes *An American Tragedy.*

1925 Lon Chaney stars in the film *The Phantom of the Opera.*

1925 The *WSM Barn Dance* radio program begins broadcasting from Nashville, Tennessee; the name is later changed to *Grand Ole Opry* and it becomes the leading country music program.

1925 The *New Yorker* magazine begins publication and features the prices paid for bootleg liquor.

1925 In February, the Boeing aircraft company builds a plane capable of flying over the Rocky Mountains with a full load of mail.

1925 On May 8, the Brotherhood of Sleeping Car Porters, founded by A. Philip Randolph, is one of the first black labor unions.

1925 In July, in the Scopes "Monkey" trial, a Tennessee teacher is tried and found guilty of teaching evolution in a trial that attracts national attention.

1925 On August 8, forty thousand Ku Klux Klan members march in Washington, D.C., to broaden support for their racist organization.

1926 Latin idol Rudolph Valentino stars in the film *The Son of the Sheik.*

1926 Ernest Hemingway publishes *The Sun Also Rises.*

1926 The Book-of-the-Month Club is launched to offer quality books to subscribers.

1926 On March 7, the first transatlantic radio-telephone conversation links New York City and London, England.

1926 On March 17, *The Girl Friend,* a musical with songs by Richard Rodgers and Lorenz Hart, opens on Broadway.

1926 On April 18, dancer Martha Graham makes her first professional appearance in New York City.

1927 Al Jolson stars in the film *The Jazz Singer,* the first film to have sound. Clara Bow—the "It" girl—stars in *It.*

1927 On January 1, the Rose Bowl football game is broadcast coast-to-coast on the radio.

1927 On April 7, television is first introduced in America, but investors are skeptical.

1927 On May 21, Charles Lindbergh completes his nonstop flight from New York City to Paris, France, and is given a hero's welcome.

1927 On May 25, the Ford Motor Company announces that production of the Model T will be stopped in favor of the modern Model A.

1927 On September 22, the heavyweight championship fight between Jack Dempsey and Gene Tunney becomes the first sports gate to top $2 million.

1927 On December 4, Duke Ellington's orchestra begins a long run at the Cotton Club nightclub in Harlem, New York.

1927 On December 27, the Jerome Kern and Oscar Hammerstein musical *Show Boat* opens on Broadway in New York City.

1928 On April 15, the New York Rangers become the first American team to win the National Hockey League Stanley Cup.

1928 On May 11, WGY in Schenectady, New York, offers the first scheduled television service, though the high price of televisions keeps most people from owning them.

1928 On July 30, the Eastman Kodak company introduces color motion pictures.

1928 On November 6, former U.S. secretary of commerce Herbert Hoover is elected president.

1928 On December 13, George Gershwin's *An American in Paris* opens at Carnegie Hall in New York City.

1928 On December 26, swimmer Johnny Weissmuller retires from competition after setting sixty-seven world records.

1929 Mickey Mouse makes his first appearance in *Steamboat Willie,* an animated film made by Walt Disney.

1929 Commercial airlines carry 180,000 passengers during the year.

1929 Ernest Hemingway publishes *A Farewell to Arms,* a novel set during World War I.

1929 Nick Lucas's "Tiptoe through the Tulips with Me" and Louis Armstrong's "Ain't Misbehavin'" are two of the year's most popular songs.

1929 On February 14, in the Saint Valentine's Day Massacre, gunmen working for Chicago, Illinois, mobster Al Capone gun down seven members of a rival gang.

1929 On October 29, the stock market collapses on a day known as "Black Tuesday," marking the start of what will become the Great Depression.

1930 Grant Wood paints *American Gothic.*

1930 The Continental Baking company introduces Wonder Bread to the nation, the first commercially produced sliced bread.

1930 Unemployment reaches four million as the economy worsens.

1930 On January 14, jazz greats Benny Goodman, Glenn Miller, Jimmy Dorsey, and Jack Teagarden play George and Ira Gershwin's songs, including "I've Got a Crush on You," in the musical *Strike Up the Band* at the Mansfield Theater in New York City.

1930 On March 6, General Foods introduces the nation's first frozen foods.

1930 On May 3, Ogden Nash, a poet who will become famous for his funny, light verse, publishes "Spring Comes to Murray Hill" in the *New Yorker* magazine and soon begins work at the magazine.

1930 On September 8, the comic strip *Blondie* begins.

1930 On October 14, *Girl Crazy,* starring Ethel Merman, opens at New York's Guild Theater. The musical features songs by George Gershwin, Walter Donaldson, and Ira Gershwin, including "I Got Rhythm" and "Embraceable You."

1931 The horror films *Dracula* and *Frankenstein* are both released.

1931 Nevada legalizes gambling in order to bring revenue to the state.

1931 On March 3, "The Star Spangled Banner" becomes the national anthem by congressional vote.

1931 On April 30, the Empire State Building, the tallest building in the world, opens in New York City.

1931 On June 3, brother-and-sister dancers Fred and Adele Astaire perform for the last time together on the first revolving stage.

1931 On July 27, *Earl Carroll's Vanities,* featuring naked chorus girls, opens at the three-thousand-seat Earl Carroll Theater in New York City.

1931 On October 12, the comic strip *Dick Tracy* begins.

1932 Edwin Herbert Land, a Harvard College dropout, invents Polaroid film.

1932 On May 2, *The Jack Benny Show* premieres as a variety show on radio and runs for twenty-three years and then another ten years on television.

1932 On July 30, the Summer Olympic Games open in Los Angeles, California, and feature record-breaking performances by Americans Babe Didrikson and Eddie Tolan.

1932 On July 31, in German parliamentary elections, the Nazi Party receives the most seats but is unable to form a government.

1932 On November 7, the radio adventure *Buck Rogers in the Twenty-Fifth Century* premieres on CBS and runs until 1947.

1932 On November 8, New York governor Franklin D. Roosevelt is elected president, promising to take steps to improve the economy. In his first one hundred days in office, Roosevelt introduces much legislation to use the government to aid those harmed by the Great Depression.

1932 On December 27, Radio City Music Hall opens at the Rockefeller Center in New York City.

1933 President Franklin D. Roosevelt presents the nation with his first radio address, known as a "fireside chat."

1933 Walt Disney releases the feature film *The Three Little Pigs.*

1933 On January 3, *The Lone Ranger* radio drama premieres on WXYZ radio in Detroit, Michigan.

1933 On January 30, Nazi leader Adolf Hitler becomes chancellor of Germany. Hitler soon seizes all power and sets out to attack his party's political enemies.

1933 On May 27, fan dancer Sally Rand attracts thousands with her performance at the Chicago World's Fair that celebrated the Century of Progress.

1933 On September 30, *Ah, Wilderness,* acclaimed American playwright Eugene O'Neill's only comedy, opens at the Guild Theater in New York City.

1933 On December 5, the Twenty-first Amendment to the Constitution puts an end to Prohibition.

1934 The first pipeless organ is patented by Laurens Hammond. The Hammond organ starts a trend toward more electrically amplified instruments.

1934 Dashiell Hammett publishes *The Thin Man,* one of the first hard-boiled detective novels.

1934 The Apollo Theater opens in Harlem, New York, as a showcase for black performers.

1934 German director Fritz Lang flees Nazi Germany to make movies in the United States.

1934 On May 5, bank robbers and murderers Bonnie Parker and Clyde Barrow are killed by lawmen in Louisiana.

1934 On July 1, the Motion Picture Producers and Distributors of America (MPPDA) association creates the Hay's Office to enforce codes that limit the amount and types of sexuality and other immoral behavior in films.

1934 On July 22, "Public Enemy No. 1" John Dillinger is shot and killed outside a Chicago, Illinois, theater by FBI agents and local police.

1934 On August 13, Al Capp's *Li'l Abner* comic strip debuts in eight newspapers.

1934 On August 19, Adolf Hitler is declared president of Germany, though he prefers the title Führer (leader).

1935 One out of four American households receives government relief as the Depression deepens.

1935 Twenty million Monopoly board games are sold in one week.

1935 The first Howard Johnson roadside restaurant opens in Boston, Massachusetts.

1935 The Works Progress Administration Federal Arts Projects, some of President Franklin D. Roosevelt's many New Deal programs, give work to artists painting post offices and other federal buildings.

1935 In April, *Your Hit Parade* is first heard on radio and offers a selection of hit songs.

1935 On April 16, the radio comedy-drama *Fibber McGee and Molly* debuts on NBC and runs until 1952.

1935 On May 24, the first nighttime major league baseball game is played in Cincinnati, Ohio.

1935 On October 10, *Porgy and Bess,* known as the "most American opera of the decade," opens in New York City at the Alvin Theater. The music George Gershwin wrote for the opera combined blues, jazz, and southern folk.

1936 American Airlines introduces transcontinental airline service.

1936 Ten African American athletes, including Jesse Owens, win gold medals in the Summer Olympics held in Berlin, Germany, embarrassing Nazi leader Adolf Hitler, who had declared the inferiority of black athletes.

1936 Dust storms in the Plains states force thousands to flee the region, many to California.

1936 Popular public-speaking teacher Dale Carnegie publishes his book *How to Win Friends and Influence People.*

1936 To increase feelings of nationalism, the Department of the Interior hires folksinger Woody Guthrie to travel throughout the U.S. Southwest performing his patriotic songs such as "Those Oklahoma Hills."

1936 In the Soviet Union, the Communist Party begins its Great Purge, executing anyone who resists the party's social and economic policies. By 1938, it is estimated that ten million people have been killed.

1936 Throughout Europe, countries scramble to form alliances with other countries for what seems to be a likely war. Germany and Italy join together to support the military government of Francisco Franco in Spain, while Great Britain and France sign nonaggression pacts with the Soviet Union.

1936 On July 18, the Spanish Civil War begins when Spanish military officers rise up against the Republican government of Spain.

1936 In October, the New York Yankees win the first of four World Series in a row.

1936 On November 3, Franklin D. Roosevelt is reelected as president of the United States.

1936 On November 23, the first issue of *Life* magazine is published.

1937 Dr. Seuss becomes a popular children's book author with the publication of *And to Think That I Saw It on Mulberry Street.*

1937 The Hormel company introduces Spam, a canned meat.

1937 A poll shows that the average American listens to the radio for 4.5 hours a day.

1937 *Porky's Hare Hunt,* a short animated cartoon by Warner Bros., introduces audiences to the Bugs Bunny character and the talents of Mel Blanc, the voice of both Bugs Bunny and Porky Pig.

1937 The first soap opera, *Guiding Light,* is broadcast. It continues as a radio program until 1956 and moves to television.

1937 British writer J. R. R. Tolkien publishes *The Hobbit.*

1937 On June 22, black boxer Joe Louis knocks out Jim Braddock to win the world heavyweight boxing championship.

1937 On December 21, *Snow White and the Seven Dwarfs,* the first feature-length animated film, is presented by Walt Disney.

1938 Glenn Miller forms his own big band and begins to tour extensively.

1938 On January 17, the first jazz performance at Carnegie Hall in New York City is performed by Benny Goodman and His Orchestra, with Duke Ellington, Count Basie, and others.

1938 In June, the character Superman is introduced in *Action Comics #1.* By 1939, he appears in his own comic book series.

1938 On August 17, Henry Armstrong becomes the first boxer to hold three boxing titles at one time when he defeats Lou Ambers at New York City's Madison Square Garden.

1938 On October 31, Orson Welles's radio broadcast of H. G. Wells's science fiction novel *The War of the Worlds* is believed by many listeners to be a serious announcement of a Martian invasion, resulting in panic spreading throughout the country.

1938 On November 11, singer Kate Smith's performance of "God Bless America" is broadcast over the radio on Armistice Day.

1939 Singer Frank Sinatra joins the Tommy Dorsey band, where he will soon find great success.

1939 Federal spending on the military begins to revive the economy.

1939 Pocket Books, the nation's first modern paperback book company, is founded.

1939 The National Collegiate Athletic Association (NCAA) holds it first Final Four championship basketball series, which is won by the University of Oregon.

1939 *Gone with the Wind,* David O. Selznick's epic film about the Civil War, stars Vivien Leigh and Clark Gable.

1939 *The Wizard of Oz* whisks movie audiences into a fantasyland of magic and wonder. The film stars Judy Garland and includes such popular songs as "Somewhere Over the Rainbow," "Follow the Yellow Brick Road," and "We're Off to See the Wizard."

1939 On May 2, baseball great Lou "The Iron Man" Gehrig ends his consecutive game streak at 2,130 when he removes himself from the lineup.

1939 On September 1, German troops invade Poland, causing Great Britain and France to declare war on Germany and starting World War II. Days later, the Soviet Union invades Poland as well, and soon Germany and the Soviet Union divide Poland.

1940 The radio program *Superman* debuts, introducing the phrases "Up, up, and away!" and "This looks like a job for Superman!"

1940 On February 22, German troops begin construction of a concentration camp in Auschwitz, Poland.

1940 The first issue of the comic book *Batman* is published.

1940 On May 10, German forces invade Belgium and Holland, and later march into France.

1940 On June 10, Italy declares war on Britain and France.

1940 On June 14, the German army enters Paris, France.

1940 On August 24, Germany begins bombing London, England.

1940 On November 5, President Franklin D. Roosevelt is reelected for his third term.

1940 On November 13, the Disney film *Fantasia* opens in New York City.

1941 "Rosie the Riveter" becomes the symbol for the many women who are employed in various defense industries.

1941 *Citizen Kane,* which many consider the greatest movie of all time, is released, directed by and starring Orson Welles.

1941 On January 15, A. Philip Randolph leads the March on Washington to call for an end to racial discrimination in defense-industry employment. President Franklin D. Roosevelt eventually signs an executive order barring such discrimination.

1941 On March 17, the National Gallery of Art opens in Washington, D.C.

1941 On July 1, CBS and NBC begin offering about fifteen hours of commercial television programming each week—but few consumers have enough money to purchase television sets.

1941 On October 19, German troops lay siege to the Russian city of Moscow.

1941 On December 7, Japanese planes launch a surprise attack on the U.S. naval and air bases in Pearl Harbor, Hawaii, and declare war against the United States.

1941 On December 11, the United States declares war on Germany and Italy in response to those countries' declarations of war.

1942 On January 1, the annual Rose Bowl football game is played in Durham, North Carolina, rather than the usual Pasadena, California, location, to avoid the chance of a Japanese bombing attack.

1942 Humphrey Bogart and Ingrid Bergman star in *Casablanca,* set in war-torn Europe.

1942 On February 19, President Franklin D. Roosevelt signs an executive order placing all Japanese Americans on the West Coast in internment camps for the rest of the war.

1942 On May 5, sugar rationing starts in the United States, followed by the rationing of other products.

1942 In June, American troops defeat the Japanese at the Battle of Midway.

1942 On December 25, the comedy team of Abbott and Costello is voted the leading box-office attraction of 1942.

1943 Gary Cooper and Ingrid Bergman star in *For Whom the Bell Tolls,* the film version of the novel by Ernest Hemingway.

1943 On January 25, the Pentagon, the world's largest office complex and the home to the U.S. military, is completed in Arlington, Virginia.

1943 On March 14, composer Aaron Copland's *Fanfare for the Common Man* premieres in Cincinnati, Ohio.

1943 On March 30, the musical *Oklahoma!* opens on Broadway in New York City.

1943 During the summer, race riots break out in Detroit, Michigan, and Harlem, New York.

1943 On September 8, Italy surrenders to the Allies.

1943 On November 9, artist Jackson Pollock has his first solo show in New York City.

1943 On December 30, *Esquire* magazine loses its second-class mailing privileges after it is charged with being "lewd" and "lascivious" by the U.S. Post Office.

1944 *Seventeen* magazine debuts.

1944 *Double Indemnity,* directed by Billy Wilder, becomes one of the first of a new genre of movies known as *film noir.*

1944 On March 4, American planes bomb Berlin, Germany.

1944 On June 6, on "D-Day," Allied forces land in Normandy, France, and begin the liberation of western Europe.

1944 On June 22, the Serviceman's Readjustment Act, signed by President Franklin D. Roosevelt, provides funding for a variety of programs for returning soldiers, including education programs under the G.I. Bill.

1944 On August 25, Allied troops liberate Paris, France.

1944 On November 7, Franklin D. Roosevelt is reelected for an unprecedented fourth term as president.

1945 Chicago publisher John H. Johnson launches *Ebony* magazine.

1945 The radio program *The Adventures of Ozzie and Harriet* debuts.

1945 On January 27, the Soviet Red Army liberates Auschwitz, Poland, revealing the seriousness of German efforts to exterminate Jews.

1945 On April 12, President Franklin D. Roosevelt dies of a cerebral hemorrhage and Vice President Harry S. Truman takes over as president.

1945 On April 21, Soviet troops reach the outskirts of Berlin, the capital of Germany.

1945 On April 30, German leader Adolf Hitler commits suicide in Berlin, Germany, as Allied troops approach the city.

1945 On May 5, American poet Ezra Pound is arrested in Italy on charges of treason.

1945 On May 8, Germany surrenders to the Allies, bringing an end to World War II in Europe.

1945 On August 6, the United States drops the first atomic bomb on the Japanese city of Hiroshima, killing more than fifty thousand people.

1945 On August 9, the United States drops a second atomic bomb on Nagasaki, Japan.

1945 On September 2, Japan offers its unconditional surrender onboard the U.S.S. *Missouri* in Tokyo Bay, bringing an end to World War II.

1946 The Baby Boom begins as the birthrate rises 20 percent over the previous year.

1946 *It's a Wonderful Life,* starring Jimmy Stewart and directed by Frank Capra, becomes one of the most popular Christmas movies of all time.

1946 On January 10, the first General Assembly of the United Nations meets in London, England.

1946 On June 19, Joe Louis retains his title by knocking out Billy Conn in the first heavyweight boxing match ever shown on television.

1946 On December 11, country singer Hank Williams cuts his first single, "Calling You."

1947 On January 29, Arthur Miller's play *All My Sons* opens in New York City.

1947 On March 12, President Harry S. Truman announces his "containment" policy aimed at stopping the spread of communism. It will later become known as the Truman Doctrine.

1947 On March 21, Congress approves the Twenty-second Amendment, which limits the president to two four-year terms in office. The amendment is ratified in 1951.

1947 On April 10, Jackie Robinson breaks the "color barrier" when he signs a contract to play for professional baseball's Brooklyn Dodgers. He is later named Rookie of the Year by the *Sporting News.*

1947 Beginning September 30, the World Series is televised for the first time as fans watch the New York Yankees defeat the Brooklyn Dodgers in seven games.

1947 On October 13, the Hollywood Ten, a group of film directors and writers, appears before the House Un-American Activities Committee (HUAC).

1947 On December 3, Tennessee Williams's *A Streetcar Named Desire* opens on Broadway in New York City.

1948 The Baskin-Robbins ice cream chain opens.

1948 On April 3, Congress approves $6 billion in Marshall Plan aid for rebuilding European countries.

1948 On May 14, the state of Israel is established.

1948 On May 29, the play *Oklahoma!* closes after a record 2,246 performances.

1948 On June 25, heavyweight boxing champion Joe Louis knocks out Joe Walcott for his twenty-fifth title defense; following the fight, he announces his retirement from boxing.

1948 On September 13, Margaret Chase Smith of Maine becomes the first woman elected to the U.S. Senate.

1948 On November 2, incumbent Harry S. Truman is elected president.

1949 Builder Abraham Levitt and his sons begin construction on a Long Island, New York, suburb called Levittown, which will become a symbol for the postwar housing boom.

1949 On February 10, Arthur Miller's *Death of a Salesman* opens on Broadway in New York City.

1949 On April 4, the North Atlantic Treaty Organization (NATO) is formed by the United States and twelve other mainly European countries to provide for mutual defense.

1949 On September 23, American, British, and Canadian officials reveal that the Soviet Union has successfully detonated an atomic bomb.

1949 On October 1, the Communist People's Republic of China is proclaimed.

1950 The first Xerox copy machine is produced.

1950 Miss Clairol hair coloring is introduced, making it easy for women to dye their hair at home.

1950 Desegregation continues when Charles Cooper becomes the first black player in the National Basketball Association and Althea Gibson becomes the first black woman to compete in a national tennis tournament.

1950 In March, the Boston Institute of Contemporary Art and New York's Metropolitan Museum and Whitney Museum release a joint statement on modern art opposing "any attempt to make art or opinion about art conform to a single point of view."

1950 On May 8, President Harry S. Truman sends the first U.S. military mission to Vietnam.

1950 On June 30, U.S. combat troops enter the Korean War.

1950 On October 2, *Peanuts,* the comic strip written and drawn by Charles Schulz, debuts in seven U.S. newspapers.

1951 *The Caine Mutiny,* a war novel by Herman Wouk, is published and soon becomes one of the longest lasting best-sellers of all time, holding its place on the *New York Times* list for forty-eight weeks.

1951 On April 5, Julius and Ethel Rosenberg receive death sentences for allegedly giving secret information to the Soviet Union.

1951 On June 25, CBS offers the first color television broadcast.

1951 On August 5, the soap operas *Search for Tomorrow* and *Love of Life* premiere on CBS.

1951 On October 15, the sitcom *I Love Lucy* premieres on CBS.

1951 On November 18, the news program *See It Now,* hosted by Edward R. Murrow, premieres on CBS.

1952 *Gunsmoke* debuts as a radio drama. In 1955, the Western drama moves to TV where it lasts until 1975. The show, which starred James Arness as Marshal Matt Dillon, becomes the longest running prime-time TV show with continuing characters.

1952 In January, *American Bandstand,* a popular teen-oriented music program, debuts as a local show in Philadelphia, Pennsylvania. Dick Clark, its most famous host, joins the show in 1956.

1952 On January 14, *The Today Show* debuts on NBC.

1952 In September, *The Old Man and the Sea,* a short novel by Ernest Hemingway, is printed in *Life* magazine and is the Book-of-the-Month Club's co-main selection.

1953 On October 5, the New York Yankees become the first team in history to win five consecutive World Series when they defeat the Brooklyn Dodgers.

1952 In November, *Bwana Devil,* the first 3-D movie, is released.

1952 On November 4, World War II general Dwight D. Eisenhower is elected president.

1953 *Playboy* becomes the first mass-market men's magazine and rockets to popularity when it publishes nude pictures of rising movie star Marilyn Monroe.

1953 IBM introduces its first computer, the 701.

1953 On January 1, Hank Williams, the father of contemporary country music, dies at age twenty-nine from a heart disease resulting from excessive drinking.

1953 On April 3, the first national edition of *TV Guide* is published.

1953 On July 27, the Korean War ends.

1953 On September 13, Nikita Khrushchev is named first secretary of the Soviet Union's Communist Party.

1953 In November, an eleven-day photoengravers strike leaves New York City without a daily newspaper for the first time since 1778.

1954 U.S. senator Joseph McCarthy of Wisconsin leads hearings into the presence of communists in the U.S. Army; his actions are later condemned by the Senate.

1954 *Sports Illustrated* becomes the first glossy weekly magazine about sports.

1954 Swanson Foods introduces the first TV dinners.

1954 On April 4, legendary conductor Arturo Toscanini makes his final appearance conducting the NBC Symphony Orchestra. The concert is broadcast on the radio live from New York City's Carnegie Hall.

1954 On April 4, Walt Disney signs a contract with ABC to produce twenty-six television films each year.

1954 On May 14, the Soviet Union joins with seven Eastern European countries to form the Warsaw Pact, a union of nations pledged to mutual defense.

1954 On May 17, with its *Brown v. Board of Education* decision, the U.S. Supreme Court ends segregation in public schools.

1954 In July, the Newport Jazz Festival debuts in Newport, Rhode Island.

1954 On July 19, "That's All Right, Mama" and "Blue Moon of Kentucky," the first professional records made by Elvis Presley, are released on Sun Records.

1954 On September 27, *The Tonight Show* debuts on NBC.

1954 In October and November, Hungary tries to leave the Warsaw Pact but is attacked and reclaimed by the Soviet Union.

1955 Velcro is invented.

1955 *The $64,000 Question* debuts and soon becomes the most popular game show of the 1950s.

1955 In January, Marian Anderson becomes the first black singer to appear at the Metropolitan Opera.

1955 On January 19, President Dwight D. Eisenhower holds the first televised presidential news conference.

1955 In March, *The Blackboard Jungle,* the first feature film to include a rock and roll song on its soundtrack—"Rock Around the Clock," by Bill Haley and The Comets—opens. The song becomes the country's number-one single in July.

1955 On April 12, large-scale vaccinations for polio are administered throughout the United States.

1955 On July 17, the Disneyland amusement park opens in Anaheim, California.

1955 On September 30, actor James Dean dies after his Porsche roadster slams into another car on a California highway.

1955 On October 13, poet Allen Ginsberg gives the first public reading of *Howl,* his controversial poem-in-progress.

1955 On December 5, Rosa Parks refuses to give up her seat to a white man on a bus in Montgomery, Alabama, sparking a bus boycott that will become a key moment in the Civil Rights Movement.

1956 On June 20, Loew's Inc. releases MGM's pre-1949 film library—excluding *Gone with the Wind* (1939)—for television broadcast.

1956 On November 6, President Dwight D. Eisenhower is reelected.

1956 On November 30, videotape is first used commercially on television, during the broadcast of CBS's *Douglas Edwards with the News.*

1957 On September 26, the landmark musical *West Side Story,* a modern-day adaptation of *Romeo and Juliet* by William Shakespeare, opens on Broadway at the Winter Garden Theatre in New York City.

1957 On October 5, the Soviet Union launches the satellite *Sputnik,* the first man-made satellite in space.

1958 On October 2, Leonard Bernstein begins his first season as director of the New York Philharmonic.

1958 On October 16, sponsors drop the NBC quiz show *Twenty-One* after a grand jury investigation determines that contestants were provided with pre-show answers.

1959 On January 2, revolutionary leader Fidel Castro assumes power in Cuba.

1959 On January 3, Alaska becomes the forty-ninth state.

1959 On February 3, rock and roll legends Buddy Holly, Ritchie Valens, and J. P. Richardson (known as "The Big Bopper") die in a plane crash outside Clear Lake, Iowa.

1959 On August 21, Hawaii becomes the fiftieth state.

1959 On October 21, the Solomon R. Guggenheim Museum, designed by architect Frank Lloyd Wright, opens in New York City.

1960 Designer Pierre Cardin introduces his first fashion designs for men.

1960 On January 3, the Moscow State Symphony begins a seven-week tour at New York City's Carnegie Hall, becoming the first Soviet orchestra to perform in the United States.

1960 On February 11, Jack Paar, host of *The Tonight Show,* walks off the show when an NBC censor deletes a joke from his performance without his knowledge.

1960 On February 20, black students in Greensboro, North Carolina, stage sit-ins at local lunch counters to protest discrimination.

1960 In April, the New York state legislature authorizes the City of New York to purchase Carnegie Hall, which was scheduled for demolition.

1960 On April 1, Lucille Ball and Desi Arnaz appear for the last time as Lucy and Ricky Ricardo on *The Lucy-Desi Comedy Hour.*

1960 On May 5, the Soviet Union announces the capture of American pilot Francis Gary Powers, whose U-2 spy plane was shot down over the Soviet Union.

1960 On September 26, U.S. senator John F. Kennedy of Massachusetts and Vice President Richard M. Nixon appear in the first televised presidential debate.

1960 On October 13, jazz trumpeter Louis Armstrong begins a goodwill tour of Africa, partially sponsored by the U.S. State Department.

1960 On November 8, U.S. senator John F. Kennedy of Massachusetts is elected president.

1961 On January 20, Robert Frost reads his poem "The Gift Outright" at the inauguration of President John F. Kennedy.

1961 On January 27, soprano Leontyne Price first performs at New York's Metropolitan Opera.

1961 In April, folk singer Bob Dylan makes his debut at Gerde's Folk City in New York City's Greenwich Village.

1961 On April 12, Soviet cosmonaut Yuri Gagarin becomes the first man to orbit the Earth.

1961 During the summer, Freedom Rides across the South are aimed at desegregating interstate bus travel.

1961 On August 15–17, East Germany constructs the Berlin Wall, separating communist East Berlin from democratic West Berlin.

1961 On October 1, Roger Maris sets a new single-season home run record with 61 homers.

1962 On February 10, Jim Beatty becomes the first person to run a mile in less than four minutes with a time of 3:58.9.

1962 On May 30, jazz clarinetist Benny Goodman begins a six-week, U.S. State Department–arranged tour of Russia.

1962 On July 10, the *Telstar* satellite is launched and soon brings live television pictures to American television viewers.

1962 On August 5, actress Marilyn Monroe dies from an overdose of barbiturates.

1962 On September 25, Philharmonic Hall, the first completed building of New York's Lincoln Center for the Performing Arts, is inaugurated by Leonard Bernstein and the New York Philharmonic.

1962 On September 29, *My Fair Lady* closes on Broadway after 2,717 performances, making it the longest-running show in history.

1962 In October, the United States and the Soviet Union clash over the presence of Soviet missiles in Cuba.

1962 On October 1, James Meredith becomes the first black person to enroll at the University of Mississippi as federal troops battle thousands of protesters.

1963 On January 8, *Mona Lisa,* by Leonardo da Vinci, is shown at Washington's National Gallery, the first time the painting ever has appeared outside the Louvre in Paris, France.

1963 On May 7, the Guthrie Theatre in Minneapolis, Minnesota, the first major regional theater in the Midwest, opens.

1963 On November 22, President John F. Kennedy is assassinated in Dallas, Texas, and Vice President Lyndon B. Johnson assumes the presidency.

1963 On November 24, the murder of alleged presidential assassin Lee Harvey Oswald is broadcast live on television.

1964 Ford introduces its Mustang, a smaller sporty car.

1964 On February 9, the Beatles make their first live appearance on American television, on *The Ed Sullivan Show.*

1964 On February 25, Cassius Clay (who later changes his name to Muhammad Ali) beats Sonny Liston to become the heavyweight boxing champion of the world.

1964 In May, the just-remodeled Museum of Modern Art in New York City reopens with a new gallery, the Steichen Photography Center, named for photographer Edward Steichen.

1964 On July 2, President Lyndon B. Johnson signs the Civil Rights Act of 1964, which bans racial discrimination in public places and in employment.

1964 On August 7, in the Gulf of Tonkin Resolution, Congress gives President Lyndon B. Johnson the power to use military force to protect U.S. interests in Vietnam.

1964 On November 3, incumbent Lyndon B. Johnson is elected president.

1965 In January, Bob Dylan plays an electric guitar on his new single, "Subterranean Homesick Blues."

1965 On February 21, black leader Malcolm X is murdered in Harlem, New York.

1965 On March 8, the first U.S. combat troops are sent to Vietnam.

1965 On April 26, *Symphony No. 4* by Charles Ives is performed in its entirety for the first time by the American Symphony Orchestra, conducted by Leopold Stokowski.

1965 On May 9, piano virtuoso Vladimir Horowitz returns to the Carnegie Hall stage after a twelve-year "retirement."

1965 On June 2, in a letter to President Lyndon B. Johnson, Pulitzer Prize–winning poet Robert Lowell declines an invitation to attend a White House arts festival, citing his "dismay and distrust" of American foreign policy.

1965 In July, Bob Dylan and his electric guitar are booed off the Newport Folk Festival stage.

1965 On September 29, President Lyndon B. Johnson signs into law the Federal Aid to the Arts Bill.

1965 On October 15, demonstrations against the Vietnam War occur in forty U.S. cities.

1965 On December 9, *A Charlie Brown Christmas* becomes the first *Peanuts* special to air on TV.

1966 The National Organization for Women (NOW) is established.

1966 On June 8, the National Football League and the American Football League merge.

1966 On July 12, rioting by blacks breaks out in twenty U.S. cities over racial discrimination.

1966 On August 29, the Beatles play their last live concert.

1966 On December 8, philanthropist, horse breeder, and art collector Paul Mellon donates his collection of British rare books, paintings, drawings, and prints, valued at over $35 million, to Yale University.

1967 On January 15, in the first Super Bowl, the Green Bay Packers defeat the Kansas City Chiefs, 35–10.

1967 On February 18, the National Gallery of Art arranges to purchase Leonardo da Vinci's *Ginevra dei Benci* for between $5 million and $6 million, the highest price paid to date for a single painting.

1967 In June, the Monterey International Pop Festival, an important early rock music event, is held in California.

1967 On June 20, Muhammad Ali is stripped of his boxing titles after being found guilty of tax evasion.

1967 On July 23, federal troops are called in to put a stop to rioting in Detroit, Michigan. Forty-three people are killed in the rioting, which lasts a week.

1967 On November 9, the first issue of *Rolling Stone* magazine is published. On the cover is a portrait of the Beatles' John Lennon.

1967 In December, Universal News, the last of the movie newsreel companies, closes because it is unable to compete with television news.

1968 On January 30, North Vietnam launches the Tet Offensive, escalating the war in Vietnam.

1968 On April 4, civil rights leader Martin Luther King Jr. is murdered in Memphis, Tennessee.

1968 On April 19, *Hair* opens on Broadway, at New York City's Biltmore Theatre.

1968 On June 5, presidential candidate and U.S. senator Robert F. Kennedy of New York is murdered in Los Angeles, California.

1968 On September 16, presidential candidate and former vice president Richard Nixon appears as a guest on TV's *Rowan and Martin's Laugh-In* and delivers one of the show's signature lines: "Sock it to me."

1968 On November 1, the Motion Picture Association of America inaugurates its film ratings system.

1968 On November 5, former vice president Richard Nixon is elected president.

1969 Hot pants make their first appearance.

1969 On July 20, U.S. astronaut Neil Armstrong becomes the first man to walk on the moon when the *Apollo 11* mission succeeds.

1969 On August 15–17, the Woodstock Music and Art Fair is held on a six-hundred-acre hog farm in upstate New York.

1969 On November 15, a quarter million Vietnam War protesters march in Washington, D.C.

1969 On December 6, a fan is murdered during the Altamont Rock Festival in California.

1970 Soviet cosmonauts spend seventeen days in space, setting a new record for space longevity.

1970 Across the nation, protests continue over the ongoing Vietnam War.

1970 Rock stars Jimi Hendrix and Janis Joplin die within three weeks of each other, both as a result of drug overdoses.

1970 In March, three women—Elizabeth Bishop, Lillian Hellman, and Joyce Carol Oates—win National Book Awards.

1970 On May 4, National Guard members shoot antiwar protesters at Kent State University in Ohio, killing four students.

1970 On April 10, the Beatles disband.

1970 On April 30, U.S. and South Vietnamese troops invade Cambodia, which has been sheltering North Vietnamese troops.

1970 On September 6, four airliners bound for New York are hijacked by Palestinian terrorists, but no passengers are harmed.

1970 On September 19, *The Mary Tyler Moore Show* debuts on CBS.

1970 On September 21, *Monday Night Football* debuts on ABC.

1970 On October 2, the Environmental Protection Agency (EPA) is created to regulate environmental issues.

1971 Disney World opens in Orlando, Florida.

1971 Hot pants become a fashion sensation.

1971 On January 2, cigarette advertising is banned from television and radio.

1971 On February 6, British troops are sent to patrol Northern Ireland.

1971 On February 9, the European Economic Community, a precursor to the European Union, is established.

1971 On March 8, Joe Frazier defeats Muhammad Ali to retain the world heavyweight boxing title.

1971 On April 20, the U.S. Supreme Court rules that students can be bused to end racial segregation in schools.

1971 In June, the Twenty-sixth Amendment to the Constitution lowers the legal voting age to eighteen.

1971 On June 13, the *New York Times* publishes the "Pentagon Papers," which reveal Defense Department plans for the Vietnam War.

1971 In September, a prison uprising in Attica, New York, ends with forty-three people killed, including ten hostages.

1971 On October 12, the rock musical *Jesus Christ Superstar* opens on Broadway in New York City.

1971 On October 13, the Pittsburgh Pirates and the Baltimore Orioles play in the first World Series night game.

1971 On December 25, "Christmas bombing" occurs in North Vietnam.

1972 In a sign of the cooling of Cold War tensions, East and West Germany and North and South Korea each enter into negotiations to normalize relations.

1972 *Ms.* magazine begins publication.

1972 *Pong*, the first video game available to play at home, becomes popular, as does the first video game machine, Odyssey, introduced by Magnavox.

1972 On February 14, the musical *Grease* opens on Broadway in New York City.

1972 On February 21, President Richard Nixon begins a seven-day visit to Communist China.

1972 On May 22, President Richard Nixon begins a nine-day visit to the Soviet Union.

1972 On June 17, the Watergate scandal begins with the arrest of five men caught trying to bug the Democratic National Committee headquarters at the Watergate building in Washington, D.C. The investigation soon reveals deep corruption in the Nixon administration.

1972 On July 24, the United Nations asks the United States to end its bombing of North Vietnam.

1972 On August 12, the last American combat troops leave Vietnam.

1972 On November 8, cable TV network HBO premieres in Pennsylvania with 365 subscribers.

1973 Three major American cities—Los Angeles, California; Atlanta, Georgia; and Detroit, Michigan—elect a black mayor for the first time.

1973 Investigations into the Watergate affair capture the public attention and shatter the Nixon administration.

1973 The Sears Tower (now known as the Willis Tower), at the time the world's tallest building, is completed in Chicago, Illinois.

1973 Ralph Lauren designs the costumes for the film *The Great Gatsby*, helping build his reputation.

1973 Fantasy-adventure game Dungeons and Dragons is created by Dave Arneson and Gary Gygax.

1973 The first Internet is set up by the U.S. Department of Defense as a way of connecting all the department's computers.

1973 On January 14, the Miami Dolphins win the Super Bowl and become the first professional football team to finish a season undefeated.

1973 On October 16, the Organization of Petroleum Exporting Countries (OPEC) declares an embargo (ban) on the export of oil to the United States and other Western countries.

1973 On October 23, the House of Representatives begins impeachment proceedings against President Richard Nixon.

1974 The Ramones launch the American punk movement with their performances at the New York City club CBGB.

1974 The streaking fad sweeps the country.

1974 President Richard Nixon tours the Middle East and the Soviet Union.

1974 On January 18, Israel and Egypt sign a peace accord that ends their long armed conflict.

1974 On April 8, Hank Aaron of the Atlanta Braves breaks Babe Ruth's lifetime home run record when he hits his 715th career homer.

1974 In May, screenwriter Dalton Trumbo, who had been blacklisted in the 1950s during the anticommunist crusades of U.S. senator Joseph McCarthy of Wisconsin, receives an Academy Award for the 1957 film *The Brave One.*

1974 On August 8, Richard Nixon announces that he would become the first U.S. president to resign from office, amid evidence of a cover-up of the Watergate affair.

1974 On August 9, Vice President Gerald Ford replaces Richard Nixon as president. Less than a month later, he officially pardons Nixon.

1974 On September 8, motorcycle stunt rider Evel Knievel tries to jump a rocket over the Snake River Canyon in Idaho but falls short.

1974 On October 3, Frank Robinson joins the Cleveland Indians as major league baseball's first black manager.

1974 On October 30, boxer Muhammnad Ali regains his world heavyweight boxing title by defeating George Foreman.

1974 In December, unemployment hits 6.5 percent amid a prolonged economic slump and rises to 8.9 percent by May 1975.

1975 The video cassette recorder (VCR) is invented by Sony Corporation in Japan.

1975 The first personal computer, the Altair 8800, is sold in a kit form.

1975 The cult film *The Rocky Horror Picture Show* is released.

1975 Skateboarding becomes popular, and mood rings and pet rocks are popular fads.

1975 Rock star Bruce Springsteen appears on the cover of both *Time* and *Newsweek* thanks to his popular album *Born to Run*.

1975 The Soviet Union and the United States cooperate in the manned *Apollo-Soyuz* space mission.

1975 On January 5, the all-black musical *The Wiz* opens on Broadway in New York City. It eventually tallies 1,672 performances.

1975 On April 30, Saigon, the capital of South Vietnam, is invaded by the communist North Vietnamese, ending the Vietnam War.

1975 On October 1, the Organization of Petroleum Exporting Countries (OPEC) raises crude oil prices by 10 percent.

1975 On October 11, *Saturday Night Live* debuts on NBC.

1976 The first personal computer, the Apple, is developed by Steve Jobs and Steve Wozniak. The Apple II, introduced a year later, offers color graphics.

1976 Model and actress Farrah Fawcett-Majors sets a trend with her feathered haircut and appears on millions of posters in her tiny red bathing suit.

1976 On July 4, the United States celebrates its bicentennial.

1976 On November 2, former Georgia governor Jimmy Carter is elected president.

1976 On November 6, *Gone with the Wind* is broadcast on TV for the first time.

1977 The film *Saturday Night Fever* helps make disco music popular.

1977 Studio 54 becomes New York City's hottest nightclub featuring disco music.

1977 Egyptian artifacts from the tomb of King Tutankhamen, or King Tut, draw huge audiences across the nation.

1977 Alex Haley's book *Roots* becomes a best-seller after the airing of the TV miniseries based on the book.

1977 On January 21, President Jimmy Carter signs an unconditional pardon for most Vietnam-era draft evaders.

1977 On February 8, *Hustler* magazine publisher Larry Flynt is convicted of obscenity.

1977 In April, the Christian Broadcasting Network (CBN) makes its debut.

1977 On August 16, Elvis Presley, the king of rock and roll, dies at Graceland, his Memphis, Tennessee, mansion.

1978 The Walkman personal cassette player is introduced by Sony.

1978 On July 25, the first human test-tube baby is born in England.

1978 On September 17, U.S. president Jimmy Carter hosts negotiations between Israeli prime minister Menachem Begin and Egyptian president Anwar Sadat at Camp David, Maryland.

1978 On October 13, punk rock musician Sid Vicious of the Sex Pistols is arrested for the stabbing death of his girlfriend.

1978 On November 18, Jim Jones and over nine hundred followers of his People's Temple cult are found dead after a mass suicide in Jonestown, Guyana.

1978 On December 5, the Soviet Union and Afghanistan sign a treaty of friendship, and within a year U.S. support for the Afghan government disappears.

1979 Eleven people are trampled to death at a Who concert in Cincinnati, Ohio.

1979 Jerry Falwell organizes the Moral Majority to lobby politicians regarding the concerns of Christian fundamentalists.

1979 On January 1, the United States and the People's Republic of China establish formal diplomatic relations.

1979 On March 28, a major accident in the nuclear reactor at the Three Mile Island power plant near Harrisburg, Pennsylvania, raises concerns about nuclear power.

1979 On November 4, Iranian militants seize the U.S. embassy in Tehran, Iran, and take fifty-two hostages, whom they will hold for over a year.

1979 On December 27, the Soviet Union invades Afghanistan, beginning more than two decades of war and disruption in that country.

1980 Post-it notes are created by 3M chemist Arthur Fry.

1980 On February 22, the U.S. Olympic ice hockey team wins the gold medal, sparking national celebration.

1980 On April 12, the United States votes to boycott the Summer Olympics in Moscow to protest the Soviet presence in Afghanistan.

1980 On April 21, the Mariel boatlift begins, bringing 125,000 refugees from Cuba to Florida before being halted in September.

1980 In June, the all-news CNN cable TV network debuts.

1980 On August 19, a report issued by the *Los Angeles Times* indicates that 40 to 75 percent of NBA players use cocaine.

1980 On November 4, former California governor Ronald Reagan is elected president.

1980 On November 21, the "Who Shot J.R.?" episode of *Dallas* draws the largest television audience of all time.

1980 On September 4, Iraq begins an eight-year war with Iran.

1980 On October 2, in his last fight, heavyweight boxer Muhammad Ali is defeated by World Boxing Council champion Larry Holmes.

1980 On December 8, former Beatles musician John Lennon is shot and killed in New York City.

1981 Nintendo's *Donkey Kong* is the most popular coin-operated video game.

1981 NASA launches and lands the first reusable spacecraft, the space shuttle.

1981 On January 13, the National Collegiate Athletic Association (NCAA) votes to sponsor women's championships in twelve sports after the 1981–82 season.

1981 On January 20, American hostages held at the U.S. embassy in Tehran, Iran, are released on the day of President Ronald Reagan's inauguration.

1981 On January 23, the United States withdraws support for the Marxist government of Nicaragua and begins to support antigovernment rebels known as Contras.

1981 On March 26, comedian Carol Burnett wins a $1.6 million libel lawsuit against the tabloid *National Enquirer.*

1981 On March 30, President Ronald Reagan and three others are wounded in an assassination attempt in Washington, D.C.

1981 On July 29, Great Britain's Prince Charles marries Lady Diana Spencer in an event televised around the world.

1981 On August 1, the Music Television Network (MTV) starts offering music videos that soon become as important as the actual music.

1981 On September 21, Sandra Day O'Connor is confirmed as the first woman to serve on the U.S. Supreme Court.

1982 The compact disc is introduced.

1982 The popular movie *E.T.: The Extra-Terrestrial* sets box office records.

1982 Michael Jackson's album *Thriller* is the year's most popular recording.

1982 Americans frustrate themselves trying to solve Rubik's Cube, a popular puzzle.

1982 On April 2, Argentina invades the Falkland Islands off its coast, sparking a short war with Great Britain, which claims the islands.

1982 On June 7, Graceland, the late Elvis Presley's Memphis, Tennessee, home, is opened as a tourist attraction.

1982 On July 27, acquired immune deficiency syndrome (AIDS) is officially named.

1982 On September 15, *USA Today* becomes the first national newspaper.

1982 On October 7, *Cats* opens on Broadway in New York City and will become the decade's most popular musical.

1983 First lady Nancy Reagan announces a "War on Drugs."

1983 Sally Ride becomes the first woman astronaut in space when she joins the crew of the space shuttle *Challenger.*

1983 Actor Paul Newman introduces his own line of spaghetti sauces to be sold in grocery stores; he uses the proceeds to benefit charities.

1983 On February 28, the farewell episode of the sitcom *M*A*S*H* is seen by 125 million viewers.

1983 On March 23, President Ronald Reagan proposes a space-based antimissile defense system that is popularly known as "Star Wars."

1983 On April 18, terrorists bomb the U.S. embassy in Beirut, Lebanon, killing sixty-three.

1983 On September 1, the Soviet Union shoots down a Korean Air Lines flight that has strayed into its airspace, killing 269.

1983 On October 25, three thousand U.S. soldiers invade the Caribbean island nation of Grenada to crush a Marxist uprising.

1983 In November, Cabbage Patch Kids dolls, with their soft faces and adoption certificates, become the most popular new doll of the Christmas season.

1984 Trivial Pursuit becomes the nation's most popular board game.

1984 *The Cosby Show* debuts on NBC.

1984 Rap group Run-DMC is the first rap group to have a gold album.

1984 Apple introduces a new personal computer, the Macintosh, with a dramatic advertising campaign.

1984 On November 6, Ronald Reagan is reelected president.

1984 On December 3, a Union Carbide plant in Bhopal, India, leaks poison gas that kills two thousand and injures two hundred thousand.

1985 Nintendo Entertainment System, a home video game system that has brilliant colors, realistic sound effects, and quick action, is introduced to the United States.

1985 On March 16, U.S. journalist Terry Anderson is kidnapped in Lebanon; he will be held until December 4, 1991.

1985 In April, Coca-Cola changes the formula of its popular soft drink and the public reacts with anger and dismay, prompting the company to reissue the old formula as Classic Coke.

1985 On July 13, British rock star Bob Geldof organizes Live Aid, a charity concert and album to aid the victims of African famine.

1985 On October 2, the death of handsome movie star Rock Hudson from AIDS raises awareness about the disease.

1986 Country singer Dolly Parton opens a theme park in Tennessee called Dollywood.

1986 On January 28, the space shuttle *Challenger* explodes upon liftoff, killing the six astronauts and one teacher who were aboard.

1986 On February 26, Robert Penn Warren is named the first poet laureate of the United States.

1986 On April 26, a serious meltdown at the Chernobyl nuclear power plant near Kiev, Ukraine, releases a radioactive cloud into the atmosphere and is considered a major disaster.

1986 On May 1, in South Africa, 1.5 million blacks protest apartheid (the policy of racial segregation). Around the world, foreign governments place sanctions on South Africa.

1986 On June 10, Nancy Lieberman becomes the first woman to play in a men's professional basketball league when she joins the United States Basketball League.

1986 On July 15, the United States sends troops to Bolivia to fight against drug traffickers.

1986 On July 27, Greg LeMond becomes the first American to win France's prestigious Tour de France bicycle race.

1986 In October, it is discovered that members of the Reagan administration have been trading arms for hostages in Iran and illegally channeling funds to Contras in Nicaragua. This Iran-Contra scandal will eventually be investigated by Congress.

1986 On November 22, twenty-one-year-old Mike Tyson becomes the youngest heavyweight boxing champion when he defeats World Boxing Council champ Trevor Berbick.

1987 On March 19, televangelist Jim Bakker resigns after it is revealed that he has been having an adulterous affair with church secretary Jessica Hahn.

1987 On June 25, Soviet leader Mikhail Gorbachev announces *perestroika,* a program of sweeping economic reforms aimed at improving the Soviet economy.

1987 On October 3, Canada and the United States sign a free-trade agreement.

1987 On October 17, the stock market experiences its worst crash in history when it drops 508 points.

1987 On November 11, Vincent van Gogh's painting *Irises* is sold for $53.9 million.

1988 McDonald's opens twenty restaurants in Moscow, Russia.

1988 Singer Sonny Bono is elected mayor of Palm Springs, California.

1988 On February 5, former Panamanian dictator General Manuel Noriega is charged in a U.S. court with accepting bribes from drug traffickers.

1988 On February 14, Ayatollah Khomeini of Iran calls author Salman Rushdie's book *The Satanic Verses* offensive and issues a death sentence on him. The author goes into hiding.

1988 On April 14, Soviet forces withdraw from Afghanistan after ten years of fighting in that country.

1988 On July 3, believing it is under attack, a U.S. warship shoots down an Iran Air passenger liner, killing 290 passengers.

1988 On November 8, Vice President George Herbert Walker Bush is elected president.

1988 On December 21, Pan Am Flight 747 explodes over Lockerbie, Scotland, killing 259 on the flight and 11 on the ground. Middle Eastern terrorists are eventually charged with the crime.

1989 On March 24, the Exxon *Valdez* oil tanker runs aground in Alaska, spilling 240,000 barrels of oil and creating an environmental disaster.

1989 In May, more than one million Chinese demonstrate for democracy in Beijing.

1989 In June, Chinese troops crack down on demonstrators in Tiananmen Square, drawing attention to the repressive government.

1989 On August 9, Colin R. Powell becomes the United States' first black chairman of the Joint Chiefs of Staff.

1989 On August 23, the Soviet states of Lithuania, Latvia, and Estonia demand autonomy from the Soviet Union. Later, across the former Soviet-dominated region, Soviet republics and satellite countries throw off communist control and pursue independence.

1989 On August 24, former baseball star Pete Rose is banned from baseball for life because it is believed that he bet on games in which he was involved.

1989 On October 15, Wayne Gretzky of the Los Angeles Kings becomes the National Hockey League's all-time leading scorer with his 1,850th point.

1989 On October 17, a major earthquake hits the San Francisco, California, area.

1989 On December 16, American troops invade Panama and seize dictator General Manuel Noriega. Noriega will later be convicted in U.S. courts.

1989 On December 22, the Brandenburg Gate in Berlin is officially opened, allowing people from East and West Berlin to mix freely and signaling the end of the Cold War and the reunification of Germany.

1990 The animated sitcom *The Simpsons* debuts on the FOX network.

1990 Ken Burns's documentary *The Civil War* airs on PBS.

1990 British scientist Tim Berners-Lee invents the World Wide Web.

1990 On April 25, the Hubble Space Telescope is deployed in space from the space shuttle *Discovery.*

1990 On July 26, President George Herbert Walker Bush signs the Americans with Disabilities Act, which provides broad protections for those with disabilities.

1990 On August 2, Iraq invades Kuwait, prompting the United States to wage war on Iraq from bases in Saudi Arabia. Much of this conflict, called the Persian Gulf War, is aired live on television and makes CNN famous for its coverage.

1990 On October 3, East and West Germany are reunited.

1991 Mass murderer Jeffrey Dahmer is charged with killing fifteen young men and boys near Milwaukee, Wisconsin.

1991 On March 3, U.S. general Norman Schwarzkopf announces the end of the Persian Gulf War.

1991 In October, confirmation hearings for U.S. Supreme Court justice nominee Clarence Thomas are carried live on television and feature Anita Hill's dramatic accusations of sexual harassment. Despite the charges, Thomas is confirmed.

1991 On November 7, Los Angeles Lakers basketball star Earvin "Magic" Johnson announces that he has contracted the HIV virus.

1991 On December 8, leaders of Russia and several other former Soviet states announce the formation of the Commonwealth of Independent States.

1992 On April 29, riots erupt in Los Angeles, California, following the acquittal of four white police officers in the beating of black motorist Rodney King. The brutal beating had been filmed and shown widely on television.

1992 On May 21, Vice President Dan Quayle criticizes the CBS sitcom *Murphy Brown* for not promoting family values after the main character has a child out of wedlock.

1992 In August, the Mall of America, the nation's largest shopping mall, opens in Bloomington, Minnesota.

1992 On August 24, Hurricane Andrew hits Florida and the Gulf Coast, causing a total of over $15 billion in damage.

1992 On October 24, the Toronto Blue Jays become the first non-U.S. team to win baseball's World Series.

1992 On November 3, Arkansas governor Bill Clinton is elected president, defeating incumbent George Herbert Walker Bush and strong third party candidate H. Ross Perot.

1992 On December 17, the United States, Canada, and Mexico sign the North American Free Trade Agreement (NAFTA).

1993 Jack "Dr. Death" Kevorkian is arrested in Michigan for assisting in the suicide of a terminally ill patient, his nineteenth such action.

1993 On February 26, six people are killed when terrorists plant a bomb in New York City's World Trade Center.

1993 On April 19, more than eighty members of a religious cult called the Branch Davidians are killed in a mass suicide as leaders set fire to their compound in Waco, Texas, following a fifty-one-day siege by federal forces.

1993 In July and August, the Flood of the Century devastates the American Midwest, killing forty-eight.

1994 Tiger Woods becomes the youngest person and the first black to win the U.S. Amateur Golf Championship.

1994 Special prosecutor Ken Starr is appointed to investigate President Bill Clinton's involvement in a financial scandal known as Whitewater. The investigation will ultimately cover several scandals and lead to impeachment proceedings against the president.

1994 In January, ice skater Nancy Kerrigan is attacked by associates of her rival, Tonya Harding, at the U.S. Olympic Trials in Detroit, Michigan.

1994 On May 2, Nelson Mandela is elected president of South Africa. The black activist had been jailed for decades under the old apartheid regime and became the country's first black president.

1994 On August 11, major league baseball players go on strike, forcing the cancellation of the playoffs and World Series.

1994 On November 5, forty-five-year-old boxer George Foreman becomes the oldest heavyweight champion when he defeats Michael Moorer.

1995 On April 19, a car bomb explodes outside the Alfred P. Murrah Federal Office Building in Oklahoma City, Oklahoma, killing 168 people. Following a manhunt, antigovernment zealot Timothy McVeigh is captured, and later he is convicted and executed for the crime.

1995 On September 1, the Rock and Roll Hall of Fame opens in Cleveland, Ohio.

1995 On September 6, Cal Ripken Jr. of the Baltimore Orioles breaks the long-standing record for most consecutive baseball games played with 2,131. The total reaches 2,632 games before Ripken removes himself from the lineup in 1998.

1995 On October 3, former football star O. J. Simpson is found not guilty of the murder of his ex-wife and her friend in what many called the "trial of the century."

1996 Three years after the introduction of H. Ty Warners's Beanie Babies, the first eleven toy styles are retired and quickly become collector's items.

1996 On September 26, American astronaut Shannon Lucid returns to Earth after spending 188 days in space—a record for any astronaut.

1996 On November 5, Bill Clinton is reelected to the presidency.

1997 Researchers in Scotland successfully clone an adult sheep, named Dolly.

1997 The Hale-Bopp comet provides a nightly show as it passes by the Earth.

1997 Actress Ellen DeGeneres becomes the first openly gay lead character in her ABC sitcom *Ellen*.

1997 On January 23, Madeleine Albright becomes the first woman sworn in as U.S. secretary of state.

1997 On March 27, thirty-nine members of the Heavens Gate religious cult are found dead in their California compound.

1997 On April 13, Tiger Woods becomes the youngest person and the first black to win a major golf tournament when he wins the Masters with the lowest score ever.

1997 On June 19, the play *Cats* sets a record for the longest-running Broadway play with its 6,138th performance.

1997 On June 20, four major tobacco companies settle a lawsuit with states that will cost companies nearly $400 billion.

1997 On June 28, boxer Mike Tyson is disqualified when he bites the ear of opponent Evander Holyfield during a heavyweight title fight.

1997 On July 5, the *Pathfinder* spacecraft lands on Mars and sends back images and rock analyses.

1997 On August 31, Britain's Princess Diana is killed in an auto accident in Paris, France.

1998 Mark McGwire of the St. Louis Cardinals sets a single-season home run record with seventy home runs.

1998 The final episode of the popular sitcom *Seinfeld* is watched by an estimated audience of seventy-six million.

1998 On January 22, Unabomber Ted Kaczynski is convicted for a series of mail bombings and sentenced to life in prison.

1998 On March 24, the movie *Titanic* wins eleven Academy Awards, tying the record set by *Ben-Hur* in 1959.

1998 On April 10, a new drug for male impotence known as Viagra hits the market and is a popular sensation.

1998 On August 7, terrorists explode bombs outside the U.S. embassies in Nairobi, Kenya, and Dar es Salaam, Tanzania.

1998 In November, former professional wrestler Jesse "The Body" Ventura is elected governor of Minnesota.

1998 On December 19, the House of Representatives initiates impeachment proceedings against President Bill Clinton, but the U.S. Senate acquits Clinton on two charges in early 1999.

1999 The U.S. women's soccer team wins the World Cup by defeating China.

1999 On March 24, NATO launches a bombing campaign against Serbia to stop its actions in Kosovo.

1999 On March 29, the Dow Jones Industrial Average closes above 10,000 for the first time in history thanks to a booming stock market dominated by high-tech companies.

1999 On April 20, in Littleton, Colorado, two students go on a vicious shooting spree, killing themselves and twelve other students.

1999 On September 24, *IKONOS,* the world's first commercial, high-resolution imaging satellite, is launched into space; it can detect an object on Earth as small as a card table.

2000 The world wakes up on January 1 to find that the so-called "Y2K" computer bug had failed to materialize.

2000 In May, Eminem releases his *Marshall Mathers LP,* which sells 1.76 million copies in its first week, becoming the fastest-selling album by a solo artist of all time.

2000 The fourth Harry Potter book, *Harry Potter and the Goblet of Fire,* is released in July and sets new publishing sales records.

2000 Tiger Woods becomes the youngest golfer to win all four Grand Slam golf tournaments.

2000 The first inhabitants of the International Space Station take up residence in orbit over the Earth.

2000 In November, outgoing First Lady Hillary Rodham Clinton wins a seat in Congress as a senator representing New York state.

2000 On December 12, over a month after Election Day, Texas governor George W. Bush is declared the winner of the presidential race against Vice President Al Gore after contentious vote recounting in Florida is ordered stopped by the Supreme Court. Bush takes Florida by a margin of 527 votes and edges Gore in the Electoral College by only four votes.

2000 On December 28, squeezed by "big box" retailers like Wal-Mart, Montgomery Ward announces it will be closing its doors after 128 years in business.

2001 Wikipedia is launched.

2001 On April 1, a U.S. spy plane collides with a Chinese fighter jet and is forced to land on Chinese soil, causing an international incident.

2001 The first draft of the human genome, a complete sequence of human DNA, is published.

2001 The "dot com bubble" bursts, leading to widespread bankruptcies in the software and Internet industries.

2001 On September 11, nineteen terrorists hijack four planes, flying two into the twin towers of the World Trade Center in New York City and one into the Pentagon in Arlington, Virginia. The fourth plane goes down in a field in Pennsylvania during a fight over the controls and fails to reach its intended target, believed to be the White House.

2001 In October, Afghanistan, accused of harboring terrorist training camps and 9/11 mastermind Osama bin Laden, is invaded by the United States and its allies, initiating the so-called War on Terror.

2002 Europe introduces its first universal currency, the Euro, initially accepted in twelve countries.

2002 The U.S. State Department issues its report on state sponsors of terrorism, singling out seven countries: Cuba, Iran, Iraq, Libya, North Korea, Sudan, and Syria.

2002 The United States begins detaining suspected terrorists without trial at its military base in Guantanamo Bay, Cuba.

2002 Halle Berry wins the Academy Award for best actress, becoming the first African American to win the honor.

2002 Bulgaria, Estonia, Latvia, Lithuania, Romania, Slovakia, and Slovenia, all former Soviet bloc nations, are invited to join the North Atlantic Treaty Organization (NATO).

2003 On February 1, the space shuttle *Columbia* disintegrates during reentry, scattering the craft's debris across the United States and killing all seven astronauts aboard.

2003 SARS, a new respiratory disease, first appears in Hong Kong before spreading around the world.

2003 In the face of mass global protests, the United States invades Iraq on March 19 as part of its continuing war on terror. By April 9, the capital city of Baghdad is taken. The weapons of mass destruction that were reported to be harbored by Iraqi dictator Saddam Hussein and were the publicly stated reason behind the invasion are never found.

2003 On December 13, Saddam Hussein is found hiding in a bolt hole in an Iraqi village.

2004 Online social network Facebook is founded.

2004 On March 11, Madrid, Spain, is the target of the worst terrorist attacks since September 11, 2001; 191 people are killed and 2,050 wounded in a series of coordinated train bombings.

2004 George W. Bush is elected to a second term by a wider margin than in 2000.

2004 On December 26, a tsunami caused by an earthquake measuring 9.3 on the moment magnitude scale in the Indian Ocean kills over three hundred thousand people across eleven countries in Southeast Asia and Sri Lanka.

2005 The video-sharing Web site YouTube is launched.

2005 Prince Charles, the heir to the throne of Great Britain, marries his longtime love, Camilla Parker Bowles.

2005 In June, pop star Michael Jackson is acquitted of child molestation charges.

2005 On July 7, coordinated bombings on three trains and a bus kill fifty-six people in London, England.

2005 On July 26, American cyclist Lance Armstrong wins his record seventh-straight Tour de France.

2005 On August 29, Hurricane Katrina makes landfall on America's Gulf Coast. The resulting destruction, largely centered on New Orleans, Louisiana, after the city's levee system fails, leads to billions of dollars in damage and over eighteen hundred deaths. The federal government is widely criticized for its slow reaction to the disaster, with rapper Kanye West famously declaring on live television, "George Bush doesn't care about black people."

2005 In November, French surgeons perform the world's first face transplant.

2006 The issue of global warming becomes a mainstream subject of discussion with the release of former vice president Al Gore's film *An Inconvenient Truth* and the accompanying book of the same name.

2006 The *Oxford English Dictionary* adds the verb "google" to its pages.

2006 Online social network Twitter is launched.

2006 The United States reaches a population of three hundred million only thirty-two years after hitting the two hundred million mark.

2006 Pluto is downgraded from planetary status, reducing the number of planets in the solar system to eight.

2006 On February 22, the one billionth digital song is downloaded from Apple's iTunes store.

2006 Riding a backlash against the ongoing wars in Iraq and Afghanistan and dissatisfaction with the George W. Bush administration, the Democratic Party wins back majorities in both houses of Congress for the first time in twelve years.

2006 On December 30, Iraqis execute former president Saddam Hussein.

2007 President George W. Bush announces that 21,500 more troops will be sent to Iraq as part of a "surge" to stem the ongoing guerrilla attacks being carried out against U.S. troops and Iraqi civilians by Iraqi dissidents and Arab terrorists.

2007 On the night of February 17, pop star Britney Spears, increasingly under media scrutiny for her erratic behavior, shaves her head and lashes out against paparazzi and reporters who had been tailing her.

2007 Apple introduces the iPhone.

2007 In the wake of Barry Bonds setting a new home run record amongst whispers of his use of performance-enhancing drugs, the Mitchell Report is released, detailing a year-long investigation into the widespread abuse of steroids in major league baseball.

2008 The Iraq troop surge is judged largely a success by July, eighteen months after it was implemented.

2008 On August 17, swimmer Michael Phelps sets a new Olympic record when he wins his eighth gold medal.

2008 With the September 15 collapse of lending firm Lehman Brothers, a major panic sweeps the world financial markets. Along with the collapse of the housing bubble, these are the first clear signals of the onset of the Great Recession, the worst global economic crisis since the Great Depression.

2008 On November 4, U.S. senator Barack Obama of Illinois becomes the first African American elected president of the United States.

2009 Barack Obama's historic inauguration on January 20 draws over one million people to the National Mall in Washington, D.C.

2009 Upon assuming office, President Barack Obama orders the closing of the Guantanamo Bay detention center and passes a $75 billion economic stimulus package.

2009 On April 15 (tax day), protests break out across the country, marking the beginning of the loosely affiliated Tea Party movement. Although lacking a single guiding organization or national leader, the conservative, ostensibly grassroots, movement is united by its concern over certain types of government spending and increasing federal deficit levels.

2009 On June 25, pop star Michael Jackson is found dead of an apparent prescription drug overdose. His passing ignites worldwide mourning and an outpouring of grief from hundreds of millions of fans, despite the singer's legal and personal troubles through the 1990s and the first decade of the 2000s.

2009 On October 31, jobless claims break the 10 percent barrier for the first time since the Great Recession began.

2009 With the situation in Iraq less dire and attacks by the Afghan Taliban on the rise, President Barack Obama announces a surge of thirty thousand more troops in Afghanistan.

BOWLING, BEATNIKS, AND BELL-BOTTOMS

Pop Culture of 20th- and 21st-Century America

2000s

A New Millennium

At midnight on January 1, 2000, the clock ticked over into not only a new decade but also a new millennium, and the world wondered what lay in store for this new age. During the 1990s, new trends in business and entertainment had emerged to feed America's unprecedented prosperity. The first decade of the 2000s would see continual development of these trends to the point that they exerted a major—and in some cases, negative—influence on people's lives. Though the end of the Cold War (1945–91) had left the United States as the world's only superpower, the decade would also see a new threat—foreign terrorism—emerge in place of communism.

As January 1, 2000, approached, computer programmers had warned of the possibility of a bug in old computer code causing mass breakdowns in computer mainframes around the world. Thanks to the diligent effort of thousands of programmers working hard to fix the problem, the so-called "Y2K" bug failed to emerge, but it left its mark on popular culture.

As it turned out, worries about a major shift in the global political climate were not far off the mark. On September 11, 2001, the real bogeymen of the decade emerged, and they were all too human. A group of nineteen religious extremists, acting on plans masterminded by al-Qaeda terrorist leader Osama bin Laden (1957–2011), hijacked four domestic passenger planes and flew them into the World Trade Center,

2000s At a Glance

WHAT WE SAID:

Bling: This term for flashy jewelry or accessories made its way from a 1999 hip-hop song called "Bling Bling" into widespread use by the middle of the first decade of the 2000s.

Bounce: To leave, as in "I've gotta bounce!"

Hella: This uniquely San Francisco Bay Area term (a contraction of "hell of a lot") went national and international in the first decade of the 2000s thanks to the 2001 No Doubt hit song "Hella Good." It was used as an adjective to express positive or superlative opinion.

My precious: Catch phrase uttered repeatedly by the creature Gollum in the blockbuster *Lord of the Rings* films, this quickly became a cultural touchstone, often parodied and spoofed.

OMG: The first decade of the 2000s saw the use of Internet acronyms enter the mainstream, not only online but in conversation. "OMG" is one such example and is short for "oh my god," used to express surprise.

Shock and awe: A military doctrine first advanced in the late 1990s, the phrase gained major attention when it was applied to the United States' invasion of Iraq. Products from video games to shampoos adopted the phrase in their marketing and country singer Toby Keith (1961–) released an album playing off the term, *Shock'n Y'all*, in November 2003.

Showmance: Appropriately for the decade that spawned the reality television explosion, this word blend of (TV) "show" and "romance" was coined to describe two reality television contestants meeting and falling in love over the course of the season, a surprisingly common phenomenon.

Whale tail: During the low-rise jeans fad of the first decade of the 2000s, some women made a fashion statement by wearing thong underwear in such a way that it would rise above the low waistband, resulting in a visual that looked not unlike a breaching whale's tail.

WHAT WE READ:

***The Da Vinci Code* (2003):** Reviled by critics, Dan Brown's (1964–) conspiratorial pot boiler was a smash hit among casual readers, residing comfortably on the best-seller list for years after its release and leading to a blockbuster film adaptation. The novel, with its focus on murder and conspiracy in the Catholic church, stirred up controversy among religious groups who claimed the book was both anti-Catholic and anti-Christian.

***The Kite Runner* (2003):** Khaled Hosseini's (1965–) thoughtful and intense portrait of life in Afghanistan became an instant smash among a Western reading public who found themselves hungry for a glimpse into a part of the world suddenly made relevant by the War on Terror.

the Pentagon, and a Pennsylvania field. The events of 9/11, as that dark day came to be called, scarred America and its allies deeply. Within days of the attacks, President George W. Bush (1946–) had announced a new War on Terror, an international effort to wipe out terrorism.

Domestically, the trend towards globalizing business operations that had begun in the 1990s continued at a rapid pace. The Internet came

The *Harry Potter* and *Twilight* series: The first decade of the 2000s was one in which young adult fiction came into its own. J. K. Rowling's (1965–) seven book *Harry Potter* series sold millions of copies during the run-up to its final installment, *Harry Potter and the Deathly Hallows* (2007), one of the most hotly anticipated and hyped publishing events in decades. Stephenie Meyer's (1973–) *Twilight* series did for gothic horror what *Harry Potter* did for fantasy, redefining the genre for a whole new generation. What was truly remarkable about both series was their crossover appeal to adult audiences; never before had grown-up readers embraced fiction aimed at middle schoolers with such enthusiasm.

WHAT WE WATCHED:

Anime: The "Japanese invasion" continued with Japanese cartoons (called anime) making solid inroads among young viewers. Series like *InuYasha, Yu-Gi-Oh!,* and *Naruto* redefined the aesthetic of television animation and launched a bevy of marketing tie-ins.

***Avatar* (2009):** The first decade of the 2000s was in many ways one when spectacular computer-generated special effects trumped story, and nowhere was this more evident than with James Cameron's (1954–) 3-D sci-fi masterpiece. Not just the highest grossing film of the decade but the highest grossing film of all time to date, *Avatar,* despite criticisms of weak plot and lack of character development, proved enormously popular and spawned a new fad for 3-D movies.

***CSI: Crime Scene Investigation* (2000–):** Another show to set the trend for the remainder of the decade, *CSI* and its spin-offs reinvigorated the police procedural drama, one of television's oldest dramatic formats, with flashy and lurid presentation of forensic investigation. The series stirred controversy for its graphic violence and sexual content, but these elements are largely what made the series and its imitators such a success. The impact of the series on popular culture can be seen in the so-called "CSI effect" observed in courtrooms, in which jurors in the first decade of the 2000s began expecting to see more forensic evidence presented by prosecutors.

The *Harry Potter* and *Lord of the Rings* movies: The eight *Harry Potter* movies (2001–2011) and three *Lord of the Rings* films (2001–2003) were the unquestioned blockbuster movie events of the decade, and together they brought legitimacy to the long-neglected fantasy genre, particularly in the case of the *Lord of the Rings* films, which earned critical accolades and recognition, netting a total of seventeen Academy Awards.

***Survivor* (2000–):** The reality show that launched a thousand imitators, *Survivor* was an immediate hit upon its summer 2000 premiere. The first decade of the 2000s saw an explosion of so-called "reality television" in the form of *Survivor*-clones and talent competitions such as *American Idol* (2002–).

into its own during the first decade of the 2000s, speeding the process of globalization as it no longer became necessary for employees to gather together in the same location in order to conduct business. China and India in particular benefited from the outsourcing of American business overseas, and it soon became commonplace to hear an Indian accent on the phone when calling a corporation's technical support or

2000s At a Glance (continued)

WHAT WE LISTENED TO:

Eminem (1972–): Dubbed "The King of Hip-Hop," Marshall Mathers III, better known as Eminem, became the most successful rapper of all time in the 2000s and helped lead the genre to a dominant position in the music industry. In between turning in a succession of multi-platinum albums throughout the decade—*The Marshall Mathers LP* (2000), *The Eminem Show* (2002), *Encore* (2004), and *Relapse* (2009)—he turned actor in 2002's *8 Mile*; the song "Lose Yourself" from the movie's soundtrack became the first hip-hop song to win an Oscar.

Get Rich or Die Tryin' **(2003):** The major label debut of rapper 50 Cent (Curtis James Jackson III; 1975–), this Eminem-produced album became one of the biggest hits of the decade, selling over six million copies by the end of 2003 and spawning the worldwide hit "In da Club."

Indie rock: Growing out of the do-it-yourself, low-fidelity ethics of punk and the emotional earnestness of emo, so-called "indie" music emerged towards the end of the first decade of the 2000s as rock's next big thing. Thanks to digital downloads and viral videos, indie bands were increasingly able to bypass the traditional music industry channels and market themselves directly to their audiences. By decade's end, in fact, so many indie bands were competing for attention that some critics complained of the glut of sound-alike acts, dubbing them "the indie landfill."

"Jesus, Take the Wheel" (2005): Carrie Underwood (1983–) was the winner of the fourth season of the reality show *American Idol,* the first country singer to win the show and by far the show's most commercially successful winner of the decade. Her 2005 debut album, *Some Hearts,* from which this hit single was taken, was the best-selling debut country album on record, going on to earn recognition from *Billboard* magazine as the fourteenth best-selling album of all time.

Beyoncé Knowles (1981–): After getting her start in the pop-R&B group Destiny's Child, Beyoncé became an international superstar with the release of her 2003 solo album *Dangerously in Love.* Her 2008 single "Single Ladies (Put a Ring on It)" quickly became a cultural anthem, with over four million downloads. The accompanying video was noted for its choreography, starting an "Internet dance craze" based on its distinctive J-Setting choreography.

Britney Spears (1981–): In the late 1990s, Spears, who had gotten her start as a Mouseketeer on the Disney Channel, broke out among a new pack of teen pop superstars. In the first decade of the 2000s, she rebranded herself, moving from "pop tart" to superstar.

customer service phone number—there was even a TV show, *Outsourced* (2010–11), based on the premise.

The rise of the Internet also heralded massive changes in the ways Americans sought their entertainment and even communicated with one another. E-retailers like Amazon.com and the Apple iTunes Store offered consumers the ability to shop from the comfort of their home. In the

After the 2003 release of her *In the Zone* album, however, she became more notable for a series of tabloid scandals and personal meltdowns. Her career seemingly over, in 2009 Spears launched one of music's most remarkable comebacks.

White Stripes: The early part of the first decade of the 2000s saw an explosion of back-to-basics rock that music critics dubbed the "garage rock revival." Detroit two-piece band the White Stripes were among this field, producing primal rock with just a guitar and drum kit. Notable for their red and white wardrobe and the rumor that the two members were brother and sister (they were actually ex-spouses), the White Stripes managed to rise above the other garage rockers and enjoy continuing success throughout the decade thanks to guitarist Jack White's (1975–) eclectic understanding of American music, melding blues, folk, country, and punk into a seamless whole.

WHO WE KNEW:

Osama bin Laden (1957–2011): Sworn enemy of the Western world and what he perceived as its meddling in the affairs of the Islamic world, bin Laden became the most infamous terrorist in the world when he coordinated the September 11, 2001, attacks on the United States that resulted in the destruction of the two towers of the World Trade Center and the deaths of nearly three thousand people. This led to U.S. military action in Afghanistan and Iraq, part of the so-called "War on Terror." He was eventually found and killed by a team of U.S. Navy SEALS in 2011.

George W. Bush (1946–): Through his two terms as President of the United States (2001–2009), the son of the forty-first president, George H. W. Bush (1924–), set policies for America both at home and abroad that for better or for worse defined the country's role in the first decade of the twenty-first century. Beginning with the contentious and extremely close-run 2000 election against incumbent vice president Al Gore (1948–), Bush became a majorly divisive figure, ushering in an increasingly partisan and bitter era in American politics. It will be some years before Bush's legacy can be fully measured, but there is little doubt that his War on Terror became the defining event of the first decade of the 2000s.

Barack Obama (1961–): Fifty years after the Civil Rights Movement got under way in America, the United States elected its first black president, once an unthinkable proposition. Obama's race was the least of America's worries, however; the Democratic senator from Illinois was elected in November 2008 on a platform of "hope and change" amidst the worst economic crisis in America since the Great Depression.

case of digital music, book, and movie downloads, consumers could even enjoy instant access to their purchases. Digital music, in particular, had a major impact on the music industry and how people listened to music. With the ability to download selected songs individually, the age of the album came to a close. MP3 players allowed people to carry around libraries of thousands of songs in their pockets. Up-and-coming artists

2000s At a Glance (continued)

Jon Stewart (1962–): The first decade of the 2000s marked a time of increasing political fractiousness and cynicism. Stewart, as host of Comedy Central's *The Daily Show* (1999–), became an unlikely political pundit during the 2000s. The show provided a wry and satirical overview of American politics but despite its comedic bent, it soon became considered a legitimate source for political news among its young demographic and many politicians and media personalities began appearing on the show for humorous interviews with Stewart.

Mark Zuckerberg (1984–): At just twenty years of age, Zuckerberg co-founded the social networking site Facebook. He went on to serve as the company's president and chief executive officer through the rest of the decade, amassing billions of dollars in his personal fortune. The Web site he helped create and helm fundamentally changed the way people communicated with each other.

also no longer needed to resort to seeking out the support of major labels in order to get their music heard.

Similarly, the advent of blogging sites and micro-blogs like Twitter gave people the ability to quickly and easily post their thoughts to the Internet with little to no knowledge of computer code required. As with the music and book industries, the world of journalism was rocked by this new technology. Suddenly amateur bloggers were scooping veteran reporters and helping to drive the news cycle.

These new technological changes may have made life easier for the consumer, but they heralded difficult times for the businesses that found their models suddenly outdated. Newspapers, book and music stores, and even major publishers and record labels could see that they needed to adapt rapidly to the new ways or perish. By giving everyone a voice, it ironically became harder to get noticed among the other competing writers, artists, musicians, and bloggers. The rise of social networking sites like Facebook, which was founded in 2004, provided central meeting places online for people to interact and share bits of their personal lives. Social networking, blogging, and web shopping, though convenient, led some critics to wonder if Americans were becoming too disconnected and decadent.

Matters did not improve when the world slipped into its worst economic crisis since the Great Depression at the end of the decade. Costly wars in Iraq and Afghanistan, unregulated speculation in the housing market, and a variety of other factors combined to plunge the United States into economic crisis in 2008. Although Europe had been making strides towards a stronger economy, notably with the introduction of a continental currency called the Euro, the crisis hit certain countries like Greece and Iceland particularly hard. As if all the economic worries were not enough, the last years of the first decade of the 2000s also played host to intensified debate over the cause of and solution to the problem of climate change, popularly known as global warming. As the decade came to a close, many Americans began to question the impact their way of life was having on the world and started looking for ways to cut spending and living beyond their means.

In many ways, pop culture, as it had in the 1930s and 1970s, reacted to the tension and uncertainty of the 2000s decade by alternately focusing on spectacle and the brutal realities of life. The world of cinema was dominated by special effects blockbusters, starting with the *Lord of the Rings* trilogy (2001–2003) and culminating in the visually stunning 3D extravaganza, *Avatar* (2009). Documentaries like *Supersize Me* (2004), *Fahrenheit 9/11* (2004), and *An Inconvenient Truth* (2005) also drew large audiences and major awards, despite their dire critiques of consumer culture, American politics and the War on Terror, and the environmental crisis, respectively.

Dance and pop music enjoyed tremendous commercial success, as did gritty hip-hop and emotionally earnest rock music. Television continued reality TV, a type of programming that had debuted in the 1990s (it turned out it had very little to do with reality), while more traditional types of programs such as *Family Guy* (1999–2002, 2005–) and *CSI: Crime Scene Investigation* (2000–) pushed the boundaries of good taste with graphic violence, sexual situations, and crude humor. The first decade of the 2000s was a turbulent period fraught with great uncertainty. As always, popular culture reflected the spirit of the age.

2000s

Commerce

In the first decade of the twenty-first century, traditional commerce was transformed by the emergence of e-commerce (shopping via the Internet). Online shopping sites such as Amazon.com and eBay made shopping easier than ever. With just a few clicks of a computer mouse and the provision of a credit card, a shopper could purchase anything from books to clothing to food to an automobile from any location in the world without ever stepping out of the front door. Many "brick and mortar" stores suffered as a result of this new trend. For example, major bookstore chains such as Barnes & Noble and Borders saw stock prices and sales plummet in a matter of few years as they found themselves unable to compete with the vast selection and low prices offered by Amazon.com. Even as big chain stores struggled, many small, specialty businesses succeeded as never before thanks to the wide exposure and ease of doing business offered by the Internet. And eBay, the customer-to-customer online auction site, made it possible for average people to take their garage sales global.

The brick-and-mortar store did not become obsolete in the early twenty-first century, of course. However, smart retailers were pushed to reimagine the shopping experience in ways that made customers willing to forsake the comforts of their living rooms for something more exciting. Computer and consumer electronics giant Apple launched its first

Apple Stores in 2001. These sleekly designed, architecturally impressive stores sold beautifully displayed Apple products and offered enhanced customer service options that made shopping a pleasure rather than a chore. By the end of 2010, there were about three hundred stylish Apple Stores worldwide, and the opening of each new location continues to serve as a highly anticipated event.

While the Internet was the hero of commerce in the first decade of the 2000s, corruption was the villain. Multiple, massive, high-level business scandals seized headlines at the beginning of the decade. In 2001, the world was stunned when the massive energy and commodities company Enron Corporation declared bankruptcy. Within a period of mere weeks, Enron stock plummeted from $90 per share to less than $1, costing shareholders billions of dollars and many company employees their savings. Enron's financial success, it was revealed, was a fraud knowingly and intentionally perpetrated by the company's top executives. Similar scandals emerged at WorldCom telecommunications and Tyco International, a toy company. Such incidents shook public faith in business leaders and prompted Congress to pass legislation, including the Sarbanes-Oxley Act of 2002, to reform corporate accounting and reporting practices.

As the second decade of the twenty-first century began, all commerce, to some degree, had been affected by the Internet. The world of e-commerce still had a frontier feel, where the innovative, clever, or unscrupulous businessman could make a fortune and the unwary could find themselves fleeced. As always, lawmakers scrambled, albeit slightly too slowly, to bring order to the chaotic marketplace.

Amazon.com

Amazon.com is the world's largest online retail business. The company was launched in 1994 by Princeton-educated entrepreneur Jeff Bezos (1964–) after he came up with the idea during a cross-country trip. The company was named after the largest river in the world, an early indication of the grand ideas that Bezos envisioned. Amazon.com began as an online bookstore; according to Bezos, book sales are ideally suited for an online store because the seller can offer a far more extensive collection than any physical store could possibly hold. In its early years, Amazon.com billed itself as "the world's largest bookstore."

After finding great success with books, Bezos expanded upon his "ship directly from the warehouse" strategy to include other products as well. In 2005, Amazon.com sold over one hundred million items to customers around the world, with a single-day sales record of 3.6 million items during the Christmas shopping season. During the first half of 2011, Amazon.com averaged around seventy-five million unique visitors per month. This does not include regional domains that the company uses for other parts of the world, such as amazon.co.uk (Great Britain) and amazon.ca (Canada).

In 2007, Amazon expanded its domination of the virtual retail world. First, the company launched its own music download store to compete with **Apple Computer**'s (see entry under 1970s—The Way We Lived in volume 4) successful iTunes store. Instead of offering music in a proprietary, digitally protected format, Amazon offers its music downloads in the popular MP3 format. Also in 2007, Amazon debuted its own electronic book reader, known as the Kindle. The handheld Kindle quickly became a key player in the growing realm of digital publishing, selling an estimated six million units worldwide by 2011—amounting to nearly half of all e-readers sold. In May 2011, the company announced that e-book sales on its site had surpassed those of traditional printed books.

In 2011, Amazon debuted its own Cloud-based storage service for digital media. In addition to storing any digital purchases made from Amazon, users can upload their own digital content—including music, photos, and videos—and have it stored on Amazon's servers. Users can then access the content through digital streaming to any computer in any location with **Internet** (see entry under 1990s—The Way We Lived in volume 5) access.

The virtual nature of Amazon.com has led to criticism from brick-and-mortar retailers, who argue that they cannot compete against a company that is not required to charge customers state sales tax. Some states have passed laws requiring Amazon to maintain a physical presence in

A screen shot from Amazon.com, one of the top forty retailers in the world. © GARY LUCKEN/ALAMY.

the state, mainly due to the presence of third-party affiliates that sell goods on the Amazon Marketplace. Because of this, the states argue, Amazon is responsible for collecting sales tax from customers within those states. Some of the states in which Amazon charges sales tax are New York, Kansas, Kentucky, and Washington. Despite the controversy over sales tax, Amazon.com easily ranks among the top forty retail companies in the world, with revenues of more than $34 billion in 2010.

Greg Wilson

For More Information

"Amazon Gets Christmas Wish." *CNN Money* (December 27, 2005). http://money.cnn.com/2005/12/27/technology/holiday_amazon/index.htm (accessed on July 18, 2011).

Brandt, Richard L. *One Click: Jeff Bezos and the Rise of Amazon.com.* New York: Portfolio Penguin, 2011.

"Site Profile For: Amazon.com." *Compete.* http://siteanalytics.compete.com/amazon.com/ (accessed on July 18, 2011).

Solomon, Deborah. "Book Learning." *The New York Times Magazine* (December 2, 2009). http://www.nytimes.com/2009/12/06/magazine/06fob-q4-t.html (accessed on July 18, 2011).

Spector, Robert. *Amazon.com: Get Big Fast.* New York: HarperBusiness, 2000.

Apple Store

The Apple Store is a retail electronics franchise located in many major urban areas around the world. Unlike typical electronics stores, the Apple Store sells only **Apple Computer**–brand (see entry under 1970s—The Way We Lived in volume 4) devices, such as the iPad and iPhone. In addition to selling Apple devices and accessories, the Apple Store also acts as a support center for existing customers. Each store contains a "Genius Bar," where employees knowledgeable about Apple products can assist customers with questions or problems. The employees that staff the Genius Bar—known collectively as Geniuses—must complete a special certification program to ensure their technical knowledge of Apple products. The Apple Store also offers workshops and tutorials to help customers get the most out of their Apple devices.

The first Apple Store opened in Tysons Corner, Virginia, in 2001. Within ten years, the chain expanded to include more than three hundred locations in eleven different countries. Most Apple Stores feature a modern design that includes glass storefronts and clean, minimalist decor. The popular Apple brand has long been the subject of knockoffs and imitations, and the Apple Store is no exception. In 2011, more than twenty Apple Store imitators were discovered in Kunming, China—a city that contains no official Apple Store franchises. The locations featured similar decor, but were easily spotted as fakes by savvy customers familiar with the real thing. At least some employees at these imitation stores reportedly believed that they were working in genuine Apple Store locations.

Greg Wilson

For More Information

"At a Glance." *ifoAppleStore.com.* http://www.ifoapplestore.com/db/at-a-glance/ (accessed on August 28, 2011).

eBay

The largest online auction site in the world, eBay was created in 1995 by Pierre Omidyar (1967–), an Iranian American computer programmer. It began as a free service named Auction Web, but as the site grew in popularity, Omidyar came up with the new brand name as a shortened version of "echobay." The site allows users from around the world to bid on a wide variety of items, ranging from yachts to Pez dispensers. The user that places the highest bid before the auctions ends is considered the winner, and must pay the bid price to complete the transaction. The site is free for buyers; eBay earns profits from its sellers based on the starting and ending prices of each item won. The site also offers bidders the option of buying an item outright instead of bidding, as well as the ability to submit a lower offer on an item listed for a fixed price.

In addition to its selection of typical auction items, eBay has become famous for many oddball, stunt, or illicit listings. For example, a grilled cheese sandwich that allegedly bore the image of the Virgin Mary sold for around $28,000 in 2004. Other attempted sales—which violated either eBay policy or local laws—included organs for transplant and the entire country of New Zealand.

In 2002, eBay bought the popular online payment service PayPal. PayPal allows users to make secure purchases over the **Internet** (see entry under 1990s—The Way We Lived in volume 5) without having to provide credit card or bank account information to different online stores.

Paypal became a preferred payment method of eBay sellers, many of whom were not equipped to accept credit cards for auction payments. The payment service became even more popular when eBay began to require PayPal as a payment option—sometimes the only option—for some product categories. In 2010, more than $60 billion worth of goods and services were sold on eBay, and nearly one hundred million users held active PayPal accounts.

Greg Wilson

For More Information

Cohen, Adam. *The Perfect Store: Inside eBay.* Boston: Little, Brown, 2002.
Collier, Marsha. *eBay for Dummies.* 7th ed. Hoboken, NJ: Wiley, 2011.
"History." *eBay, Inc.* http://www.ebayinc.com/history (accessed August 28, 2011).

Enron Scandal

Enron was an energy company based in Houston, Texas, that became infamous in 2001 for its deceptive accounting practices, which made the company appear to be far more successful than it actually was. The company, which boasted revenue of more than $100 billion at its peak, went bankrupt just one year later in the largest American corporate bankruptcy in history up to that time. The company became a symbol of an era of short-term corporate thinking and out-of-control executive compensation.

Enron was created in 1985 through the merger of two companies focused mainly on natural gas. The company's chief executive officer (CEO) was Kenneth Lay (1942–2006), who had worked previously as an economist and an energy regulator and who was eager to take advantage of gradually relaxing standards in energy regulation. Lay built Enron into the largest natural gas seller in the United States and multiplied the company's success through commodities-trading and other energy enterprises.

In 1997, Jeffrey Skilling (1953–) was promoted to chief operating officer (COO) for his innovative accounting strategies, which allowed the company to claim profits on contracts not yet fulfilled. This meant that, on paper, Enron appeared more successful than it was in reality. The company's value became based on projected earnings reported as real earnings. These positive earnings reports helped Enron's stock price remain high. If a planned contract ended up being canceled or failed to show the reported profit, this created a problem, since the expected profits had already been claimed. The company would then be required to report the shortfall as a loss, which could drive the stock price back down—a problem for the company's executives, who held large quantities of Enron stock.

In 1998, Andrew Fastow (1961–) was hired as chief financial officer (CFO) of Enron. He came up with his own signature method for hiding company losses. He invented other companies (known as special purpose entities) to "do business" with Enron on paper in a complex web of financial transactions. Fastow shifted massive amounts of Enron's debt over to these companies, which were technically real though they existed solely to benefit Enron and its executives. It worked. Enron stock reached its peak of around $90 per share in 2000, and Lay became one of America's best-paid executives with more than $40 million in earnings. These corporate shenanigans appeared legitimate to investors because one of the country's largest and most prestigious accounting firm, Arthur Andersen, maintained that Enron's financial dealings were sound.

However, Enron's mounting debts could not be hidden forever. By 2001, some financial analysts had begun to question the stock value of Enron, which peaked at about seventy times the company's stated earnings. As the stock price began to drop, several Enron executives and their family members sold off large amounts of stock for tens of millions of dollars. When the company's financial fabrications finally came to light in late 2001, its stock value plummeted, leaving investors with billions in losses and sending the company into total liquidation bankruptcy.

Lay, Skilling, and Fastow were all convicted on various counts, including fraud, money laundering, and insider trading. Skilling and Fastow were sentenced and sent to federal prison. Just months before his scheduled sentencing, Lay died of a heart attack at the age of sixty-four. Lay's conviction was abated as a result of his death, making it difficult for the government to lay claim to the millions in his estate that were obtained through fraud.

Although Enron became the most notorious example of shady accounting practices and corporate greed gone unchecked, it was not the last. In 2002, two executives of Tyco International were charged with stealing approximately $100 million from the company by claiming personal purchases as company expenses and approved bonuses. Both executives were found guilty and sentenced to prison.

Greg Wilson

For More Information

Duffy, Michael. "By the Sign of the Crooked E." *Time* (January 19, 2002). http://www.time.com/time/business/article/0,8599,195268,00.html (accessed on September 27, 2011).

Fox, Loren. *Enron: The Rise and Fall.* Hoboken, NJ: Wiley, 2003.

McLean, Bethany, and Peter Elkind. *The Smartest Guys in the Room: The Amazing Rise and Scandalous Fall of Enron.* Updated ed. New York: Portfolio, 2004.

Swartz, Mimi, with Sherron Watkins. *Power Failure: The Inside Story of the Collapse of Enron.* New York: Doubleday, 2003.

2000s

Fashion

Fashion took the entire 1990s decade to recover from the outlandish exuberance of the 1980s. When it did, however, it produced styles and looks that will always be remembered as uniquely twenty-first century. The decade's styles were characterized by the democratization of high fashion. From the hit reality television show *Project Runway,* which presented a first-hand glimpse into the fashion design process, to designer knock-offs (and frequent counterfeits) appearing in stores immediately, to the phenomenon of major fashion designers creating lower-priced lines for chain stores such as Target and H&M, fashion was suddenly available to everyone.

Throughout the decade, the style-conscious revived utilitarian classics, repurposing them for rugged or sporty looks. Ray-Ban aviator sunglasses, which were rebranded as a luxury brand in 1999, became the crowning accessory for a sleek, sporty look, while cargo pants became a wardrobe staple for actresses known for their fit and healthy lifestyles, such as Jennifer Aniston (1969–). The hoodie and the puffy vest, no longer just for athletes and mountaineers, became menswear classics. Fuzzy, shapeless UGGs—sheepskin boots that starlets wore with miniskirts—became must-haves for fashionable women in all climates.

While fashion embraced this kind of rugged gear, it also trended toward the body-conscious. By the end of the decade, the lower halves of many young women—and even some men—were on display thanks to skinny jeans, which took popular low-rise jeans to a newly revealing level by hugging the body from hips to ankles. Leggings, which appeared mid-way through the decade under dresses and tunics, eventually came to replace pants altogether for some wearers, despite the objections of the self-appointed "style police" of the media and the blogosphere. Women's shoes reached great heights with the arrival of the ultra-sexy power platform in 2008—as much as eight inches high—and body piercings became increasingly common.

Some style-makers went in the opposite direction, prizing quirky, unexpected looks such as trucker hats (worn ironically), vintage printed tees, and big, chunky glasses on both men and women. This so-called "hipster" fashion found a style icon in actress Chloé Sevigny (1974–) and an affordable retail outlet in the socially responsible chain American Apparel. Casual style reigned, but shoppers were consuming more fashion than ever before.

Body Piercing

As a form of body modification, an expression of personal style, and a cultural tradition, body piercing has been a phenomenon around the world for millennia. In early cultures as well as in contemporary tribal societies that still practice body modification, piercings tended to have social meaning. For example, all women who are married wear a ring or stud in their left nostril in contemporary Hindu society, and all men of the government class wore ear plugs in stretched lobes in pre-Columbian Inca society. In the 1970s, body piercing began to signify rejection of a mainstream Western culture and membership in the youthful **punk** (see entry under 1970s—Music in volume 4) subculture. In the decades that followed, a large variety of styles and locations of body piercings proliferated. Eyebrows, septums, ear cartilage, lips, cheeks, tongues, navels, nipples, and genitals became popular sites for the rings and bars of surgical steel and other high-quality metals adorning people's bodies.

Achieved with a hollow needle rather than the guns associated with jewelry store ear piercings, body piercings diverged into two distinct phenomena in the 1990s and 2000s. On the one hand, piercings trended toward the extreme. Earlobe piercings, which by then had come to seem innocuous even on men, began to be stretched by some wearers

A woman displays her pierced tongue. © BRAND X PICTURES/JUPITERIMAGES/GETTY IMAGES.

through a process called "gauging," at times resulting in an opening large enough for a fist to fit through. Gauging is accomplished through the use of large or heavy earrings in the earlobe piercing. Others applied dermal implants, which consist of studs placed in holes in the skin, which then grows over the metal and creates the illusion of horns or a pattern of raised dots. Such piercings gave rise in the 2000s to media reports warning of their associated health risks, including Hepatitis C and other infections.

At the same time, other kinds of facial piercing once considered countercultural became thoroughly mainstream. As many as one in ten people had body piercings (not including earlobes) in 2008, and three-fourths of them were women. Unconventional piercings were no longer equated with acts of rebellion. For example, a stud piercing on the upper lip, known as a Monroe, for its placement near **Marilyn Monroe**'s (1926–1962; see entry under 1950s—Film and Theater in volume 3) famous mole, began to appear in the late 2000s on young women with otherwise mainstream looks. Even navel piercings—once the epitome of rebellion as sported by Alicia Silverstone's (1976–) character in the chart-topping 1993 Aerosmith music video "Cryin'"—are common enough that they are unlikely to raise any eyebrows, pierced or not.

Rachel Hertz Cobb

For More Information

Angel, Elayne. *The Piercing Bible: The Definitive Guide to Safe Body Piercing.* Berkeley, CA: Crossing Press, 2009.

Pitts, Victoria. *In the Flesh: The Cultural Politics of Body Modification.* New York: Palgrave Macmillan, 2003.

"Tattoos and Piercings Go Mainstream, but Risks Continue." *Northwestern University News Center* (June 12, 2006). http://www.northwestern.edu/newscenter/stories/2006/06/tattoos.html (accessed on August 12, 2011).

"Warnings over Body Piercing Boom." *BBC News* (June 12, 2008). http://news.bbc.co.uk/2/hi/health/7451580.stm (accessed on August 12, 2011).

Carpenter Pants

Carpenter pants, high-waisted, wide-legged trousers with a fabric loop on the outer thigh originally meant as a hammer holder, are one of the classic utilitarian garments revisited by the fashion world again and again. The original carpenter pants were born in the early twentieth century, when several companies—including Dickies and Carhartt—began to industrialize the manufacture of work wear. Using sturdy fabrics with a dense weave, such as cotton duck, and pioneering the use of reinforced seams and rivets for strength, these industrial designers created shirts, overalls, and jackets that tolerated a lot of physical activity. Mass-producing work-wear quickly led to its standardization, and soon the unofficial uniform for manual laborers was established. Chief among this wardrobe were carpenter pants or, as they are also called, painter's pants.

Carpenter pants first became a fashion statement rather than merely a practical choice in the 1970s, when they started appearing in the closets and on the slim figures of young women. Freed by feminism to adopt menswear, young women enjoyed the comfort and casual style of carpenter pants. The look was even safe for less adventurous dressers. The pants' wide leg was in keeping with the flare, **bell-bottom** (see entry under 1960s—Fashion in volume 4), and "elephant" styles that dominated the 1970s trouser silhouette. While the pants were initially worn in their original color—off-white—designers were quick to pick up on the trend, and the pants became available in a wide range of colors and fabrics.

Carpenter pants passed out of style with the narrowing of trouser legs in the 1980s. They stayed out of fashion until the 1990s, when the rise of **hip-hop** (see Rap and Hip-hop entry under 1980s—Music in volume 5) culture brought a revival of utilitarian chic; one of its major trends, the baggy **jeans** (see entry under 1950s—Fashion in volume 3), effectively resurrected carpenter pants. Versions of the classic appeared under popular urban labels such as Phat Farm and Sean John alongside standard-issue Dickies and Carhartt, anchoring a look that also came to include parkas, work boots, and button-down shirts. Beyond hip-hop fashion, carpenter pants have also ridden a twenty-first-century revival of classic clothing in the world of high fashion. As late as 2008, designer Isabel Toledo (1961–) was quoted in the *New York Times* raving about the one article of clothing she cannot do without: carpenter pants.

Rachel Hertz Cobb

For More Information

Stalder, Erika. *Fashion 101: A Crash Course on Clothing.* San Francisco: Zest Books, 2008.

Trebay, Guy. "The Fashion Report of 1920." *New York Times* (October 22, 2008). http://www.nytimes.com/2008/10/23/fashion/23CLASSICS .html?scp=1&sq=the%20fashion%20report%20of%201920&st=cse (accessed July 9, 2011).

Crocs

Within four years of the birth of the Croc, the brightly colored, holey plastic shoe became a staple in the wardrobes of kids, restaurant chefs, hospital workers, and all kinds of casual dressers, whether or not they spent a lot of time on their feet. The bulb-toed clogs, made of a non-porous resin that molds to the wearer's feet, were introduced to the market in 2002 by a trio of friends from Colorado who had gone in search of the perfect boating shoe. Their research resulted in a popular product, and ultimately an empire of shoe lines, accessories, and retail outlets all based on the patented material out of which the shoes are made, Croslite.

A pair of Croc shoes. © FINNBARR WEBSTER/ALAMY.

The original Crocs shoe, with its $30 price tag, appealed to a wide spectrum of wearers despite—or perhaps because of—their quirky appearance. Celebrity chef Mario Batali (1960–) gave the product an early boost with his unofficial endorsement. (Batali later introduced his own line of Crocs, with extra-slip-resistant soles and a closed top for kitchen safety.) It was not long before health claims were added to comfort as a benefit of wearing the shoes. Though critics of the brand deemed such health claims to be fraudulent, both the American Podiatric Medical Association and United States Ergonomics certified the shoes. One podiatric surgeon went on the record in the *Washington Post* recommending them for people suffering from various foot ailments.

Nearly a decade after their invention, Crocs have endured despite the appearance of entire groups and Web sites dedicated to trashing them. The malice of such critics is based purely on the shoes' purported ugliness—ugliness that the brand itself has incorporated into marketing campaigns. When hospitals banned Crocs due to the static electricity they generated, the company introduced a new product, CrocsRx, that were safe for hospital wear. Crocs also expanded its product line to include fashion-forward styles, which have even been spotted on first lady Michelle Obama (1964–), known for her elegant and edgy dress sense. While the shoes' popularity dropped off after their peak in 2006–7, the company has continued to do brisk business in subsequent years.

Rachel Hertz Cobb

For More Information

Huget, Jennifer. "Not Such a Croc." *Washington Post* (August 1, 2006). http://www.washingtonpost.com/wp-dyn/content/article/2006/07/31/AR2006073100890.html (accessed July 15, 2011).

"Michelle Obama Style Evolution." *StyleList.com* (October 8, 2008). http://main.stylelist.com/2008/10/08/michelle-obama-style-evolution/ (accessed July 18, 2011).

Hoodies

The first hooded sweatshirts—or, as they are now almost universally known, hoodies—were made in the 1930s to keep factory workers warm. The company that manufactured them, Champion, would go on to become a mainstay of athletic wear as would its signature garment. The hoodie did not achieve its iconic status until 1976, however, when Sylvester Stallone (1946–), in his grey, sweat-stained sweatshirt, trained his way to underdog triumph in the boxing blockbuster ***Rocky*** (see entry under 1970s—Film and Theater in volume 4). Hooded sweatshirts became campus staples, emblazoned with school logos front and back, and worn oversized.

Through the 1980s and 1990s, hoodies made their way into the uniforms of numerous subcultures. **Hip-hop** (see entry Rap and Hip-hop entry under 1980s—Music in volume 5) embraced the look, and zippered varieties—the more tattered, the better—were taken up by the closely related **skateboarding** (see entry under 1950s—Sports and Games in volume 3) and **punk** (see entry under 1970s—Music in volume 4) rock cultures. Worn most often by young men who lived, played, and sometimes misbehaved on the fringes of society, or were at least perceived to, hoodies came to represent the shady character up to no good, with a reason to hide his face.

In the twenty-first century, hoodies underwent a transformation in both meaning and style. The **t-shirt** (see entry under 1910s—Fashion in volume 1) company American Apparel recreated the hoodie for a new generation interested in ironic repurposing of classics from the past—a generation of young people known as **hipsters** (see entry under

2000s—The Way We Lived in volume 6). Cut slimmer and no longer necessarily decorated with patches or printed with logos, the hoodie made its way onto the bodies of people of all ages and from all walks of life. **Facebook** (see entry under 2000s—The Way We Lived in volume 6) founder Mark Zuckerberg (1984–), one of the richest and youngest corporate executives in the world, frequently sported a hoodie. Hoodies have even made their way into the world of high fashion, with designer labels such as Balenciaga sending them down the runway and Eileen Fisher dressing them up to appeal to well-to-do middle-aged women.

Rachel Hertz Cobb

For More Information

Onstad, Katrina. "The Hoodie Goes Corporate Chic." *Globe and Mail* (January 15, 2011). http://www.theglobeandmail.com/life/relationships/news-and-views/katrina-onstad/the-hoodie-goes-corporate-chic/article1867027/ (accessed July 18, 2011).

Wilson, Denis. "A Look under the Hoodie." *New York Times* (December 23, 2006). http://www.nytimes.com/2006/12/23/opinion/23wilson.html (accessed July 18, 2011).

Low-rise Jeans

Low-rise **jeans** (see entry under 1950s—Fashion in volume 3) are a type of cut of traditional denim jeans in which the distance between the crotch of the pants and the waistband is noticeably shorter than usual. The distance from crotch to waist is traditionally about twelve inches; low-rise jeans shorten this distance by at least four inches, sometimes going as far as shortening the distance to no more than three inches from crotch to waist.

Low-rise jeans first appeared in the 1960s as a fashion of the **hippie** (see entry under 1960s—The Way We Lived in volume 4) counterculture. Called "hip-huggers," they were worn by men and women alike. By the mid-1970s, the hip-hugger fashion had died out and low-rise jeans languished in fashion obscurity until designer Alexander McQueen (1969–2010) revived them in 1996. By 2000, low-rise jeans were becoming an increasingly mainstream fashion. They received a huge boost in popularity thanks to pop diva **Britney Spears** (1981–; see entry under 1990s—Music in volume 5), who adopted the fashion around this time.

Unlike hip-huggers, low-rise jeans in the twenty-first century were primarily a female fashion statement. They became so prevalent among young women during the first decade of the new century that associated slang terms began to appear. "Muffin top" described the visual effect of hip fat spilling out over the top of an overly tight pair of low-rise jeans while "whale tail" was the term applied to the appearance (intentionally or otherwise) of thong or G-string underwear above the low-rise waistband.

Because low-rise jeans were often worn by young women and teenage girls, there was some degree of public backlash against what was perceived as risqué fashion. Attempts were made in Louisiana and Virginia to outlaw low-rise jeans, but these legislative efforts met with failure. Across the country, some schools banned low-rise jeans and visible underwear.

Although the fashion for low-rise jeans began to wane about five years after its peak of popularity, it continued to find a niche into the 2010s. In particular, low-rise, tightly cut jeans became a signature look of the hipster youth culture.

David Larkins

For More Information

Brown, Janelle. "Here Come the Buns." *Salon.com* (May 28, 2002). http://www.salon.com/life/style/2002/05/28/booty_call/ (accessed July 26, 2011).

"Jeans Rising." *Newsweek* (March 27, 2006). http://www.newsweek.com/2006/03/26/jeans-rising.html (accessed July 26, 2011).

Thomas, Bethany. "Memo to Britney: Lose the Low-slungs." *MSNBC.com* (May 13, 2004). http://www.msnbc.msn.com/id/4963512/ (accessed July 26, 2011).

Metrosexual

Although it did not gain cultural traction until the first decade of the 2000s, the term "metrosexual" was first coined in 1994 by British writer and pop culture observer Mark Simpson. A combination of "metropolitan" (as in from a large city) and heterosexual, Simpson came up with the term to describe an emerging consumer group: young, urban, single men who spent a significant amount of their time and money on their clothing and appearance. This new type of man stood in marked contrast to the typical Western male stereotype as someone only concerned with sports, beer, and women. The metrosexual male was actually much closer to the stereotypical homosexual male in his preference for shopping for designer clothes, expensive haircuts, and visits to salons for manicures and pedicures.

By the first decade of the 2000s, several celebrities were emerging as icons of metrosexuality. Simpson identified British soccer star David Beckham (1975–) as the archetypal metrosexual. Actors Brad Pitt (1963–) and Dominic Monaghan (1976–) were often cited as other examples of the new metrosexual. The phenomenon came at a time when Western culture was becoming increasingly accepting of the gay male sub-culture. The television show *Queer Eye for the Straight Guy*, which aired in both British and American versions, featured a team of gay men "fixing up" a typically slovenly straight man, teaching him about flattering hairstyles, gels, trendy garments, gourmet cooking, interior decorating, and other lifestyle elements that would have at one time been rejected as embarrassingly feminine interests for heterosexual men.

The rise of the metrosexual was aided by increasingly lax attitudes regarding appearance. Metrosexuals could be seen as a reaction against the acceptability of wearing elastic-waisted sweatpants in public, the abandonment of dress codes at schools and businesses, and the scruffy, unkempt **grunge** (see entry under 1990s—Music in volume 5) look of the 1990s.

Metrosexuality was fundamentally a consumerist movement and so was eagerly promoted by marketers, who saw the opening of a whole new demographic to whom they could sell products. In the past, straight men had been largely ignored, as their role was seen as money earners rather than money spenders. Metrosexuals also represented the blurring of traditional gender roles and larger acceptance of alternative lifestyles that came about with the dawn of the twenty-first century.

David Larkins

For More Information

Colman, David. "Gay or Straight? Hard to Tell." *New York Times* (June 19, 2005).

Flocker, Michael. *The Metrosexual Guide to Style.* Cambridge, MA: Da Capo Press, 2003.

Salzman, Marian, Ira Matathia, and Ann O'Reilly. *The Future of Men.* New York: Palgrave Macmillan, 2005.

Simpson, Mark. "Meet the Metrosexuals." *Salon.com* (July 22, 2002). http://www.salon.com/entertainment/feature/2002/07/22/metrosexual/ (accessed July 26, 2011).

Plastic Surgery

Plastic surgery is the term used to describe medical procedures performed mainly to alter a person's physical appearance. In many cases, plastic surgery is performed to restore or reconstruct a body feature damaged by genetics, disease, or trauma. However, the late twentieth and early twenty-first century saw a dramatic increase in cosmetic plastic surgery, which focused on altering or improving physical appearance. More than a million Americans undergo cosmetic surgery procedures each year, with many more opting for nonsurgical cosmetic procedures. In the United States alone, the cosmetic surgery industry generates $10 billion per year in revenue.

The most common cosmetic surgeries include breast augmentation, rhinoplasty (altering the shape and/or size of the nose), and liposuction (the removal of fat cells, usually from the thighs or abdomen). Most cosmetic surgeries involve the removal of unwanted body material or the insertion of implants to provide additional shape. Some nonsurgical procedures work in different ways. For example, Botox injections involve the insertion of a potentially deadly neurotoxin into certain parts of the face such as the forehead; the toxin essentially paralyzes the muscle tissue, which lessens the appearance of wrinkles. The toxin wears off after several months, requiring the patient to seek additional treatments if he or she wishes to maintain a wrinkle-free appearance.

As the popularity of cosmetic surgery has increased, so too has the variety of people willing to go under the knife for an improved appearance. In 2011, males comprised almost ten percent of cosmetic surgery patients, and nearly one-third of all liposuction patients were under the age of thirty-five. Even as cosmetic surgery has become accepted in mainstream culture, the small risk of deformity or death remains all too real. In November 2007, the mother of famed **hip-hop** (see Rap and Hip-hop entry under 1980s—Music in volume 5) artist Kanye West (1977–), Donda West (1949–2007), died one day after undergoing a combination tummy tuck, liposuction, and breast surgery. Though the official cause of death was described as heart disease, factors relating to the surgery were also found to have played a role.

Greg Wilson

For More Information

Goudreau, Jenna. "The Hidden Dangers of Cosmetic Surgery." *Forbes* (June 16, 2011). http://www.forbes.com/sites/jennagoudreau/2011/06/16/hidden-dangers-of-cosmetic-surgery/ (accessed September 28, 2011).

Kotler, Robert. *The Essential Cosmetic Surgery Companion.* Beverly Hills, CA: Ernest Mitchell, 2005.

Loftus, Jean M. *The Smart Woman's Guide to Plastic Surgery.* 2nd ed. New York: McGraw-Hill, 2008.

"Statistics." American Society for Aesthetic Plastic Surgery. http://www.surgery.org/media/statistics (accessed September 28, 2011).

Skinny Jeans

A woman shows off the skinny jeans look.
© SHUTTERSTOCK.COM.

Skinny **jeans** (see entry under 1950s—Fashion in volume 3) are pants that are tailored to fit tightly along the wearer's body. While they are usually made of cotton denim, some skinny jeans include a small amount of spandex material, which gives the pants a form-fitting flexibility. Often, skinny jeans are tapered so tightly at the ankles that they contain **zippers** (see entry under 1910s—Fashion in volume 1) to allow the wearer's feet to pass through.

Tapered-leg jeans rose to popularity in the 1980s but largely fell out of fashion during the 1990s, when baggy clothing became a signature style of both the **grunge** (see entry under 1990s—Music in volume 5) and **hip-hop** (see Rap and Hip-hop entry under 1980s—Music in volume 5) musical movements. Skinny jeans mounted a resurgence in the early twenty-first century, with clothing retailer **the Gap** (see entry under 1960s—Commerce in volume 4) at the forefront of the movement. In 2006, the Gap created a commercial featuring a clip of film starlet Audrey Hepburn (1929–1993) dancing in black tapered jeans, taken from the 1957 film *Funny Face.* The commercial was a hit. Makers such as True Religion and J Brand began to offer their own high-end styles, and skinny jeans became a common sight on models and celebrities alike.

By 2009, the skinny jean trend had transcended genders. Musicians such as Justin Timberlake (1981–) and Kanye West (1977–) popularized the skinny jean look for men, and sales of the high-fashion jeans grew even as sales of more traditional jeans shrank. The skinny jean look for men has also increasingly become associated with the **hipster** (see entry under 2000s—The Way We Lived in volume 6) subculture.

Greg Wilson

For More Information

Smith, Ray A. "Tight Squeeze: Making Room for a New Men's Fashion." *Wall Street Journal* (July 6, 2009). http://online.wsj.com/article/SB124683780090998061.html (accessed July 18, 2011).

Snuggies

Several products have claimed to be the original "blanket with sleeves," but the brand name that has come to be most associated with the novelty item is the Snuggie. The Snuggie and its fellow sleeved blankets—the aptly named Slanket, the Freedom Blanket, and the Doojo—became a pop culture phenomenon in 2008 and 2009 as much for their unintentionally campy commercials and infomercials as for the actual comfort they afforded. While the Snuggie's competitors offered features such as higher-quality fleece (the Slanket) and even built-in gloves (the Doojo), it was the $15 Snuggie that achieved brand-name ubiquity, selling four million units in its first few months on the market.

The Snuggie's popularity was attributed by alternative newspaper *The Village Voice* to "American consumer ridiculousness," a mass delight in trends for either earnest or ironic purposes. While the Snuggie and its competitors were bestselling Christmas gifts for several years running, they were also the subject of numerous highly visible pranks, spoofs, and more or less gentle mocking by television personalities, comedians, and rock stars. Compared at times to a bathrobe worn backwards or a church choir robe, the slouchy garment soon became the theme of events such as pub crawls in major American cities and world record attempts at sporting events for the most people wearing them in one place (forty thousand).

Rachel Hertz Cobb

A woman cozies up with her Snuggie, a blanket with sleeves. © NEWSCOM.

For More Information

Schmidt, Mackenzie. "2009, The Year of the Snuggie: A Handy Timeline From 'The WTF Blanket' to Weezer's Wuggies." *Village Voice* (December 21, 2009). http://blogs.villagevoice.com/runninscared/2009/12/2009_year_of_th.php (accessed July 26, 2011).

Spanx

Before the explosive popularity of Spanx in the early twenty-first century, shapewear—called corsets, girdles, or foundation garments in earlier eras—was decidedly out of fashion. The 1960s women's rights movement liberated women from constricting social roles as well as constricting undergarments, and those who still felt the need for support around their waists and hips turned to control-top pantyhose in the 1970s. While foundation garments continued to be sold as specialty items, the appeal of shapewear to the mainstream market was almost unknown until 2000, when Sara Blakely (1971–), the founder of Spanx, introduced her first product, a patented footless pantyhose. The garment, designed to present a smooth, line-free surface under light-colored pants, was the result of years of experimentation. At least nine million pairs have since been sold.

The Spanx line then expanded to include more than two hundred products, including **bras** (see entry under 1910s—Fashion in volume 1), swimwear, men's undergarments, and activewear. In 2008, the company (which is not publicly traded) racked up $350 million in sales across thirty countries and ten thousand retail locations in the United States alone. While Spanx were initially sold in boutiques and high-end department stores, the company later developed lower-priced lines for sale at bargain department stores. The brand also stimulated a $750 million per year U.S. shapewear industry, with competitors at many price points.

Celebrity endorsement proved a major boon for Spanx early in their history: media queen Oprah Winfrey (1954–) named them one of her "favorite things" on her talk show in 2000. Since then, their popularity has only increased as more and more celebrities credit Spanx with their slim silhouettes during red-carpet interviews. While the designer wardrobes of Spanx enthusiasts such as Gwyneth Paltrow (1972–) and Kim Kardashian (1980–) may be out of the ordinary shopper's reach, their shapewear—available at around $70 per item—is not.

Rachel Hertz Cobb

For More Information

Dodes, Rachel. "Shapewear Has Women Bent Out of Shape." *Wall Street Journal* (November 5, 2009). http://online.wsj.com/article/SB10001424052748704 3281045745154818399338404.html (accessed July 25, 2011).

Jacobs, Alexandra. "Smooth Moves: How Sara Blakely Rehabilitated the Girdle." *New Yorker* (March 28, 2011): 60–68.

Moss, Wes. *Starting from Scratch: Secrets from 21 Ordinary People Who Made the Entrepreneurial Leap.* Chicago: Dearborn Trade, 2005.

UGGs

Known in Australia by its generic name, the ugg boot, and everywhere else by the brand name UGG, the popular sheepskin footwear became a must-have trend in the United States and, shortly, around the world

Originally from Australia, UGG sheepskin boots are strange to say but comfortable to wear. © PETER DENCH/ ALAMY.

in the middle of the first decade of the 2000s. Though the origins of the ugg boot's name are disputed, they have been made and worn by Australians since the early twentieth century. While they originally warmed the feet of sheep farmers, the shapeless, chunky, fleece-lined boots were adopted by surfers of the 1970s to warm their feet after emerging from the water in the winter. It would be decades, however, before ugg boots were seen as even remotely fashionable.

The ugg boot's reinvention as the height of all-American chic followed several years of low-key marketing in the United States under the brand name UGG Australia by the company that originally trademarked it. In 1995, the brand was purchased by Deckers Outdoor Corporation, which was then known as the maker of the functional yet unstylish Teva sandals. Following a deliberate campaign to rebrand them, UGGs were being sold in boutiques and high-end department stores by the late 1990s. By 2003, starlets such as Kate Hudson (1979–) were being photographed wearing their UGGs between takes on movie sets, Oprah Winfrey (1954–) touted them on her talk show, and stores were selling out shipments within days.

With an expanded product line that included outerwear and handbags in addition to boots of all shapes and colors, UGG Australia saw revenues of more than $700 million in 2009. The company's flagship line was forced to a stop in Australia, where its boots are no longer even made because production had shifted to China. When Deckers sued a number of Australian boot-makers for trademark infringement in 2005, some of them fought back, successfully arguing that the term ugg (also spelled "ugh" or "ug") was a generic term for the style, and trademark of the name should never have been granted in the first place.

Rachel Hertz Cobb

For More Information

Conley, Lucas. "The Golden Fleece." *Wall Street Journal* (September 9, 2010). http://magazine.wsj.com/features/behind-the-brand/the-golden-fleece/tab/print/ (accessed July 31, 2011).

Moore, Booth. "Ugly, Maybe, but Uggs Are All the Rage." *SFGate.com* (November 30, 2003). http://articles.sfgate.com/2003-11-30/living/17518711_1_becker-surf-sport-ugg-australia-boots (accessed July 31, 2011).

Ultra-high Heels

The original stiletto heel, four inches or more in height and tapering to a point no more than half an inch in diameter, first appeared in the early 1950s, as the new ideals of domesticated femininity took hold. Creating the illusion of a dainty, feminine foot and leg while restricting their wearers' comfort and movement, soaring heel heights were only possible thanks to post–World War II (1939–45) steel technology. Since then, heel height has risen and fallen with changing fashions, even falling to zero with the periodic popularity of flats. By the late 1990s, however, stilettos and other ultra-high-heeled shoes had returned to the forefront of fashion, thanks in part to the spectacular rise of the designer shoe brands Manolo Blahnik and Jimmy Choo, which in turn owed much of their success to the television show **Sex and the City** (see entry under 2000s—TV and Radio in volume 6).

The latest in women's shoes: a stiletto heel on one end and a power platform on the other add up to ultra-high heels.
© ADI GILAD/ALAMY.

In the first decade of the twenty-first century, heel heights rose even higher in the form of the so-called "power platform," a shoe that combined a platform under the toe with the classic narrow stiletto heel. These shoes allowed for heels as high as eight inches, and after their first appearance in the form of an Yves Saint Laurent sandal in 2008, quickly became a red-carpet staple. No longer saddled with its former reputation as clunky and retro, the platform was now the height of sex appeal.

Women suffered serious health problems from bunions to back pain to keep their feet in ultra-high heels, however, and some even went under the knife to narrow their feet or shorten their toes, just to fit into the shoes. Even runway models had a hard time staying upright while wearing them, and spectacular falls became the hallmarks of many fashion shows. While style-makers such as Victoria Beckham (1974–) and Kim Kardashian (1980–) were regularly photographed in their chic, leg-lengthening power platforms, other celebrities took the concept of the ultra-high heel to new levels. Pop singer/performance artist **Lady Gaga** (1986–; see entry under 2000s—Music in volume 6) wore Alexander McQueen's (1969–2010) "hoof" shoe, a ten-inch heeled platform with the silhouette of a cartoonish hoof, in her 2009 music video "Bad Romance," taking the shoes from costume to club-wear. With extreme versions such as these on the market, the classic stiletto never seemed tamer.

Rachel Hertz Cobb

For More Information

Cartner-Morley, Jess. "The Rise of the Power Platform." *Guardian* (May 10, 2011). http://www.guardian.co.uk/lifeandstyle/2011/may/10/power-platform-high-heel-shoe (accessed August 12, 2011).

Cox, Caroline. *Stiletto.* New York: Harper Design International, 2004.

"Heights of Fashion: A History of the Elevated Foot." *All About Shoes—The Bata Shoe Museum.* http://www.allaboutshoes.ca/en/heights_of_fashion/ (accessed August 1, 2011).

2000s

Film and Theater

The film industry in the first decade of the 2000s racked up some of the biggest box office successes in cinema history and launched several billion-dollar series. At the same time, there was an increasing tendency in Hollywood for producers to fall back on safe bets: "reboots" of existing movie series, movies based on already successful intellectual properties, or special effects extravaganzas. Broadway theater followed a similar path, with the revival of old classics and the rise of the "jukebox musical."

The 2000s decade in film was defined by computer-generated imagery (CGI). CGI came into its own in this decade, culminating with the visual spectacle of *Avatar* (2009), which quickly became the highest grossing film of all time. *Avatar* was also the flagship of an emerging trend in the 2000s, the return of 3-D to mainstream popularity. 3-D films, which carried higher ticket prices than 2-D films, were one of the leading factors in the record-high box office returns of the latter part of the first decade of the 2000s. Of the top fifty highest-grossing films of all time as of 2010, seven were from 2009, the highest number for any individual year.

The spread of CGI technology led to a resurgence of animated features, with films such as *Shrek* (2001), *Finding Nemo* (2003), *Wall-E* (2008), and *Up* (2009) transcending their traditional audience of families and children and garnering widespread praise and popularity.

Up even managed to garner a nomination for an Academy Award for best picture, only the second animated film so honored.

The decade also saw an explosion of popularity in genres that had long languished in Hollywood: the comic book superhero genre, the fantasy genre, and even the musical. Christopher Nolan's (1970–) Batman reboot and the Spider-Man movies were both tremendously successful and widely praised by critics, bringing longed-for legitimacy to the genre of comic book movies. Adaptations of fantasy novels both old (*Lord of the Rings*) and new (the *Harry Potter* series) made stunningly effective use of CGI and raked in billions of dollars, finally bringing the fantasy movie genre out of the shadow of its science fiction cousin. Musicals like *Moulin Rouge!* (2001) and *Chicago* (2002) temporarily revived the movie musical, although public interest had largely faded by the decade's end.

Although the movie musical revival quickly lost steam, Broadway musical theater remained the biggest money-maker in the world of stage production throughout the decade. Just as with Hollywood, Broadway producers remained reluctant to take major risks, relying on safe choices such as revivals of old hits or adaptations of existing properties such as *Wicked* (2003), which was based on *The Wizard of Oz.* A new development in musical theater that grew out of this desire to ensure surefire hits was the "jukebox musical." Such musicals featured an original musical score, and the productions were built around existing pop hits, usually by a single artist or act. Such musicals have centered around the songs of Billy Joel (1949–; *Movin' Out,* 2002), Queen (*We Will Rock You,* 2002), and the Four Seasons (*Jersey Boys,* 2006). *Mamma Mia!* (2008), featuring the music of 1970s pop sensation ABBA, was a particularly successful jukebox musical. Although these productions might have been seen as safe choices by critics, they paid off by earning Broadway record ticket sales.

Avatar

Avatar is a 2009 science fiction film written and directed by James Cameron (1954–) that earned astounding levels of popular and critical success. The film takes place primarily on a planet-like moon called Pandora, where a native humanoid species struggles to survive as humans attempt to gain control of the moon for its valuable natural resources. The focus of the story is Jake Sully (played by Sam Worthington,

1976–), a paraplegic former soldier who accepts an assignment to study and interact with Pandora's natives, ten-foot-tall, blue-skinned creatures known as Na'vi. To do this, Jake and other team members link their brains to remotely controlled Na'vi-like bodies known as avatars. As Jake learns the ways of the Na'vi, he becomes emotionally attached to Neytiri (played by Zoe Saldana, 1978–), the daughter of the local tribe's chief. When he discovers that the human expedition force intends to wipe out the Na'vi and their habitat, he rallies the natives to fight back against their human invaders.

Cameron spent years developing the technology required to film *Avatar,* which uses a seamless blend of live-action and computer-generated imagery to depict the lush alien world of Pandora. Cameron and his team also developed a **new 3-D** (see entry under 2000s—Film and Theater in volume 6) camera system and shot the film with the intention of showcasing the capabilities of **3-D movies** (see entry under 1950s—Film and Theater in volume 3). With production costs of more than $200 million, *Avatar* was considered to be one of the most expensive movies ever made at the time of its release. However, overwhelming critical and popular praise helped the movie earn triple its budget in the United States alone; worldwide, the film grossed nearly $2.8 billion during its original run and an "extended" re-release in 2010. This makes *Avatar* the highest-grossing film of all time, ahead of Cameron's previous blockbuster, *Titanic* (1997). The film was nominated for nine Academy Awards, winning three. When *Avatar* was released on DVD and Blu-ray in 2010, it quickly became the highest-selling Blu-ray film in history. In October 2010, Cameron confirmed plans to create two sequels to the film, which would include some of the characters introduced in the first film.

Greg Wilson

For More Information

Duncan, Jody, and Lisa Fitzpatrick. *The Making of "Avatar."* New York: Abrams, 2010.

Ebert, Roger. "*Avatar.*" *rogerebert.com* (December 11, 2009). http://rogerebert.suntimes.com/apps/pbcs.dll/article?AID=/20091211/REVIEWS/912119998 (accessed July 23, 2011).

Fitzpatrick, Lisa. *The Art of "Avatar."* New York: Abrams, 2009.

Goodyear, Dana. "Man of Extremes: The Return of James Cameron." *New Yorker* (October 26, 2009). http://www.newyorker.com/reporting/2009/10/26/091026fa_fact_goodyear (accessed July 23, 2011).

Crouching Tiger, Hidden Dragon

Crouching Tiger, Hidden Dragon (2000) is a martial arts film directed by Ang Lee (1954–). It is considered to be an example of the traditional Chinese storytelling genre *wuxia,* which focuses on the adventures of heroic **martial artists** (see entry under 1960s—The Way We Lived in volume 4) and often contains fantastical or magical elements. Although Taiwanese director Lee was already an experienced director of English-language films, including *Sense and Sensibility* (1995) and *The Ice Storm* (1997), *Crouching Tiger, Hidden Dragon* was filmed entirely in Mandarin Chinese, which was subtitled for English-speaking audiences.

Crouching Tiger, Hidden Dragon is a complex tale of love and honor set in China during the late eighteenth century. In preparation for retirement, martial arts master Li Mu Bai (played by Chow Yun-Fat, 1955–) entrusts his sword, Green Destiny, to his colleague and secret love, Shu Lien (played by Michelle Yeoh, 1962–), to be delivered as a gift to another friend. The sword is stolen, and the thief is later discovered to be Jen (played by Zhang Ziyi, 1979–), daughter of a wealthy governor. Jen wishes to become a martial arts master, but she is arranged to be married—destined for a life of nobility rather than a life of adventure. Another deadly female warrior from Li Mu Bai's past also appears, further complicating matters.

Lee's experience with both Chinese and Western filmmaking led *Crouching Tiger, Hidden Dragon* to great international success. The film won four Academy Awards, including best foreign language film, and earned more than $200 million in box-office revenues. It also exposed Western audiences to a film genre little-known outside of China, and prompted the development of several other successful *wuxia* films, including *Hero* (2002) and *House of Flying Daggers* (2004).

Greg Wilson

For More Information

Corliss, Richard. "Year of the Tiger." *Time* (January 15, 2001). http://www.time.com/time/world/article/0,8599,2047704,00.html (accessed August 8, 2011).

Wang, Huiling, et al. *"Crouching Tiger, Hidden Dragon": Portrait of the Ang Lee Film.* New York: Newmarket Press, 2000.

The Dark Knight

The Dark Knight (2008) is a film by director Christopher Nolan (1970–) that stars Christian Bale (1974–) as the DC Comics superhero **Batman** (see entry under 1930s—Print Culture in volume 2). The film is the second in a trilogy of *Batman* films directed by Nolan and starring Bale, following *Batman Begins* (2005) and preceding *The Dark Knight Rises* (scheduled for release in 2012). The trilogy is considered a cinematic "reboot" of the franchise, disregarding previous Batman films in favor of developing a uniquely gritty, realistic vision of the superhero and his world.

In *The Dark Knight,* Gotham City is terrorized by a new villain known as the Joker (played by Heath Ledger, 1979–2008). The Joker seizes control of criminal operations in the city and kidnaps Batman's first love, Rachel Dawes (played by Maggie Gyllenhaal, 1977–), as well as crusading district attorney Harvey Dent (played by Aaron Eckhart, 1968–). Batman saves Dent from a bomb planted by the Joker, but Dent suffers severe burns to half his face. This marks the beginning of Dent's transformation into the villainous vigilante known as Two-Face.

Six months prior to the film's release, Ledger died following an accidental overdose of prescription medication. Since shooting had already been completed, Ledger's performance as the Joker remained intact in the finished film. While the film drew nearly universal praise as a dark, complex tale of crime and vengeance, it was Ledger's brilliant performance in particular that won over critics and audiences alike. The film went on to earn more than $1 billion worldwide, making it the top-grossing release of 2008 and one of the highest-grossing films of all time. In 2009, Ledger became only the second actor in history to win a posthumous Academy Award, which was awarded for best supporting actor in recognition of his work on the film.

Greg Wilson

Heath Ledger as the Joker and Christian Bale as Batman in a scene from the 2008 film The Dark Knight. *Ledger won a posthumous Oscar for best supporting actor.* © WARNER BROS./DC COMICS/THE KOBAL COLLECTION/ART RESOURCE, NY.

For More Information

Beatty, Scott. *Batman: The Ultimate Guide to the Dark Knight.* Updated ed. New York: DK, 2005.

Gordon, Devin. "Bat Trick." *Newsweek* (July 12, 2008). http://www.newsweek.com/2008/07/11/bat-trick.html (accessed July 25, 2011).

White, Mark D., and Robert Arp, eds. *Batman and Philosophy: The Dark Knight of the Soul.* Hoboken, NJ: Wiley, 2008.

Youngs, Ian. "Obituary: Heath Ledger." BBC News. January 23, 2008. http://news.bbc.co.uk/2/hi/entertainment/7203904.stm (accessed July 25, 2011.)

Finding Nemo

Finding Nemo (2003) is a computer-animated film created by Pixar Studios and distributed by Walt **Disney** (see entry under 1920s—Film and Theater in volume 2) Pictures. The title character is a young clownfish (voiced by Alexander Gould, 1994–) who is captured by a scuba diver after wandering off from "school" to investigate a nearby shipwreck. Nemo's neurotic and overprotective father, Marlin (voiced by Albert Brooks, 1947–), then embarks on a quest to find and rescue his only son. Along the way, Marlin teams up with Dory (voiced by Ellen DeGeneres, 1958–), a tropical fish with a short-term memory loss problem. Meanwhile, Nemo is picked up by a diver and placed in a fish tank in a dentist's office near the ocean. He shares the tank with a varied group of other captives who hatch a plan to escape and make their way back to the sea.

Finding Nemo was an immediate hit upon its release, earning more than $800 million worldwide and winning an Academy Award for best animated feature. The film also had an impact on tourism to Australia and the Great Barrier Reef, which served as the setting for the tale. The widespread popularity of the main characters also drove sales of tropical fish, especially clownfish. This led to an unfortunate depletion of clownfish from some native areas such as Vanuatu. In addition, the complexity of caring for tropical fish led some new owners to "free" their pets into non-native ocean habitats, potentially causing environmental destruction—the exact opposite of the film's message of ecological awareness.

Greg Wilson

Marlin and Dory stay ahead of trouble in the 2003 computer-animated film Finding Nemo. © EVERETT COLLECTION.

For More Information

Brylske, Alex. "Invaders from Inner Space: Revealing Nemo's True Colors." *Dive Training* (October 2004). http://www.dtmag.com/Stories/Ocean%20 Science/10-04-feature.htm (accessed August 8, 2011).

Price, David A. *The Pixar Touch: The Making of a Company.* New York: Knopf, 2008.

Vaz, Mark Cotta. *The Art of "Finding Nemo."* San Francisco: Chronicle Books, 2003.

The Lord of the Rings Film Trilogy

J. R. R. Tolkien (1892–1973; see entry under 1950s—Print Culture in volume 3) published his epic fantasy, *Lord of the Rings,* in three volumes in 1954 and 1955, but the books did not enjoy mass popularity until the appearance of paperback editions a decade later. Since the initial publication of the trilogy, particularly after its explosion in popularity in the United States in the 1960s, there have been periodic attempts to adapt it to other media. The length and depth of the books combined with their fantastic subject matter proved a stumbling block to these efforts for decades. There were **radio** (see entry under 1920s—TV and Radio in volume 2) dramatizations and animated features, but due to the limitations of visual effects, no live-action adaptation was produced until nearly fifty years after the books' initial publication.

With the release of the movie ***Jurassic Park*** (see entry under 1990s—Print Culture in volume 5) in 1992, visual effects took a quantum leap forward. Peter Jackson (1961–), a New Zealander and director of several well-received independent films, began to think the time for a *Lord of the Rings* adaptation had arrived. With his wife Fran Walsh (1959–) and later a second writing partner, Philippa Boyens, he began to draft a treatment of an adaptation, simultaneously shopping his project around to major studios. The process of securing film rights and sufficient budgeting took several years, during which time the script went through several drafts, expanding from a two-film adaptation into a trilogy that roughly matched the three volumes of the original story.

Jackson took the helm as director of the trilogy and made the unusual decision to film all three films simultaneously. Principal photography took over a year, lasting from October 1999 to December 2000. Jackson filmed the entire trilogy far from **Hollywood** (see entry under 1930s—Film and Theater in volume 2) in his native New Zealand, another unusual decision. Jackson's instincts proved sound, however, as the New Zealand landscape and simultaneous filming gave the films a grandiose and unified appearance that contributed to their success.

The popularity of the films is difficult to exaggerate. They comprise the most financially lucrative film trilogy ever released, surpassing even the original ***Star Wars*** trilogy (see entry under 1970s—Film and Theater in volume 4). Ten years after the first volume in the trilogy, *The Fellowship of the Ring,* (2001) was released, the films had grossed nearly $3 billion together. The final installment in the trilogy, *The Return of the King* (2003), tied the record for most Academy Awards won by a single film by earning eleven Oscars.

The films also had a tremendous cultural impact. Along with the ***Harry Potter*** books and movies (see entry under 1990s—Print Culture in volume 5), which were released around the same time, the *Lord of the Rings* films greatly raised the visibility and credibility of the fantasy genre (similar to what *Star Wars* had done for science fiction) and revived interest in Tolkien's body of work. The visual look of the films and its use of computer-generated special effects spawned countless imitations for years to come. Jackson was established as a major creative player in Hollywood due to the strength of the films. Even New Zealand enjoyed a huge upsurge in popularity among tourists from around the world.

David Larkins

For More Information

Bogstad, Janice M., and Philip E. Kaveny, eds. *Picturing Tolkien: Essays on Peter Jackson's "The Lord of the Rings" Film Trilogy.* Jefferson, NC: McFarland, 2011.

Braun, J. W. *The Lord of the Films: The Unofficial Guide to Tolkien's Middle Earth on the Big Screen.* Toronto: ECW Press, 2009.

Croft, Janet Brennan. *Tolkien on Film: Essays on Peter Jackson's Lord of the Rings.* Albuquerque, NM: Mythopoeic Press, 2005.

Sibley, Brian. *"The Lord of the Rings": The Making of the Movie Trilogy.* New York: Houghton Mifflin, 2002.

Thompson, Kristen. *The Frodo Franchise: "The Lord of the Rings" and Modern Hollywood.* Berkeley: University of California Press, 2007.

Mamma Mia!

Mamma Mia! is a 2008 film based on a popular 1999 British musical. The musical was designed to showcase the songs of 1970s Swedish pop group ABBA, including such hits as "Dancing Queen" (1975), "SOS" (1974), "Take a Chance on Me" (1977), and the title song. The story was inspired by the lyrics of the various songs, in essence linking the group's most popular songs into a single narrative. The film, directed by Phyllida Lloyd (1957–), features actors Meryl Streep (1949–), Amanda Seyfried (1985–), and Pierce Brosnan (1953–).

In the film, which takes place on a Greek island, Seyfried plays a young woman named Sophie who is soon to be married. Her mother, Donna (played by Streep), has always kept the identity of Sophie's father a secret, but Sophie narrows down the possibilities to three men from Donna's past. Sophie invites all three men to her wedding, with the intention of discovering which of the three is her father.

Mamma Mia! includes performances of twenty of the most popular ABBA songs, as well as additional scoring by Benny Andersson (1946–), one of the original members of the band. Although the film received

Mamma Mia!, the 2008 ABBA-centric film, was based on a 1999 British stage production and was still playing at Broadway's Winter Garden Theatre in 2011. For the four thousandth performance on May 31, the cast took a curtain call: (L to R) Clarke Thorell, Judy McLane, John Dossett, Lisa Brescia, Patrick Boll, and Jennifer Perry. © BRUCE GLIKAS/FILMMAGIC/GETTY IMAGES.

a lukewarm critical reception—with some of the harshest reviews focused on the less-than-stellar vocal skills of its cast members—it became the top-grossing film in the United Kingdom for 2008. With a worldwide box office gross of more than $600 million, *Mamma Mia!* is one of the most successful musical films of all time.

Greg Wilson

For More Information

Andersson, Benny, et al. *Mamma Mia! How Can I Resist You?* London: Weidenfeld and Nicolson, 2006.

Hanser, Anders, and Carl Magnus Palm. *From ABBA to Mamma Mia!* Rev. ed. Stockholm: Premium, 2010.

Hornaday, Ann. "*Mamma Mia!*: Gotta Love It, Like It or Not." *Washington Post* (July 18, 2008). http://www.washingtonpost.com/wp-dyn/content/article/2008/07/17/AR2008071702998.html (accessed July 26, 2011).

Netflix

Netflix is a through-the-mail movie rental service launched in 1999. The service has fundamentally changed the nature of the movie rental industry by eliminating the need for brick-and-mortar locations. Netflix's "store-free" business model allowed the company to succeed as other rental services, such as Blockbuster, faltered. New subscribers start by visiting the Netflix Web site to create a virtual queue of DVDs and/or Blu-rays that they wish to rent, ranking them in order of desire. Netflix then mails out each subscriber's highest-ranked selection based on availability; some subscription plans allow customers to have two or three movies out at a time. After viewing, the subscriber places the film in its prepaid return envelope and drops it in the mail. Once Netflix receives the disc, it sends out the subscriber's next highest choice, and so on. Rather than charging a rental fee per film or disc, Netflix uses a monthly subscription fee. Subscribers who return discs quickly are able to rent more discs per month.

In addition to disc rentals, Netflix offers subscribers a streaming video option for some of its titles. This streaming service, which requires a high-speed **Internet** (see entry under 1990s—The Way We Lived in volume 5) connection, has proven very popular with subscribers, perhaps too much so. According to at least one Internet traffic watchdog, Netflix video-streaming in 2011 accounted for about a quarter of all Internet traffic in North America, where the company boasts more than twenty million subscribers. Although most users stream video to the computer, many other media devices—including the Xbox 360, the Wii, and the PlayStation 3—allow subscribers to stream movies instantly to their televisions.

Greg Wilson

For More Information

O'Brien, Jeffrey M. "The Netflix Effect." *Wired* (December 2002). http://www
.wired.com/wired/archive/10.12/netflix.html (accessed August 23, 2011).

New 3-D

The "Golden Age" of **three-dimensional (3-D) movies** (see entry under 1950s—Film and Theater in volume 3) came in the early 1950s and had largely passed by the time the 1960s came about. Due to the format's expense and technical limitations, 3-D was effectively dead until the mid-1980s, when it began to reappear in theme parks and specialty venues such as IMAX theaters. 3-D films remained a novelty throughout the 1990s and into the twenty-first century.

Beginning in 2003, 3-D films once again found a niche in mainstream movie theaters. Systems like IMAX and RealD offered the latest in 3-D technology, although it was fundamentally unchanged from the polarization projection systems in use since the mid-1950s. Long gone were the old red and blue cardboard glasses; newer systems used lenses that were closer in appearance to standard sunglasses. At first these releases were limited to children's films like *The Polar Express* (2004) or genre films like *My Bloody Valentine 3D* (2009). Though this 3-D technology came with a higher cost because theaters had to purchase more expensive specialty projectors and passed the cost on to ticket buyers with hefty surcharges, the format continued to expand and grow in popularity. Besides *My Bloody Valentine 3D,* six other major 3-D films were released in 2009. The final 3-D release of that year, **Avatar** (see entry under 2000s—Film and Theater in volume 6), would usher in a new era of mainstream 3-D entertainment.

Avatar, filmed in 3-D at a cost of $250 million, became the highest-grossing film to date, largely on the strength of its remarkable visuals. The film's success caused a veritable 3-D stampede among **Hollywood** (see entry under 1930s—Film and Theater in volume 2) producers and marketing executives, who rushed to put out as many 3-D movies as they could in 2010. Unlike *Avatar,* these films were converted to 3-D in post-production using a process that resulted in a dimmer picture quality and an underwhelming visual effect. The quantity of low-quality 3-D releases in 2010 guaranteed a lucrative year for Hollywood, but it left many industry insiders, critics, and movie fans questioning the long-term impact of 3D's widespread adoption.

Film critics like Roger Ebert (1942–) blasted 3-D as an unnecessary gimmick spawned by a movie industry feeling threatened by emerging media. Critics also expressed concerns that 3-D, like computer-generated special effects, was being used as a crutch to prop up increasingly formulaic, creatively bankrupt movies. Even supporters of the new 3-D technology like producer Jeffrey Katzenberg (1950–) noted that the market was becoming oversaturated with cheap 3-D films that would in the long term do more harm than good to the format and the movie industry's ultimate financial health.

The new 3-D technology was not limited to movie screens. Televisions with 3-D technology began to hit the market around the same time 3D films were experiencing their resurgence in popularity. In 2010, the world's first 3-D television channels began broadcasting. **ESPN** (see entry under 1970s—TV and Radio in volume 4), for instance, added a 3-D channel in 2010. Around the same time, the first 3-D monitors and game platforms that did not require special glasses began to hit the market. Several companies were also hard at work attempting to perfect glasses-free theater projection 3-D technology. Respected movie directors like Martin Scorsese (1942–) and Werner Herzog (1942–) announced plans to film their next projects in 3-D. George Lucas (1944–) also had plans in the offing to re-release the original *Star Wars* (see entry under 1970s—Film and Theater in volume 4) trilogy in 3-D. Despite the controversy surrounding 3-D movies, it seemed that the technology had managed to carve out a niche for itself beyond mere kids' films and documentaries.

David Larkins

For More Information

Browning, Skylar. "Two D's Better Than Three: Hank Green Finds a Place in Hollywood's Excesses." *Missoula Independent* (June 16, 2011): 8.

Ebert, Roger. "Why I Hate 3-D (And You Should Too)." *Newsweek* (May 10, 2010). http://www.newsweek.com/2010/04/30/why-i-hate-3-d-and-you-should-too.html (accessed July 26, 2011).

Hayes, R.M. *3-D Movies: A History and Filmography of Stereoscopic Cinema.* Jefferson, NC: McFarland, 1998.

Mendiburu, Bernard. *3D Movie Making: Stereoscopic Digital Cinema from Script to Screen.* Burlington, MA: Focal Press, 2009.

Zone, Ray. *3-D Filmmakers: Conversations with Creators of Stereoscopic Motion Pictures.* Lanham, MD: Scarecrow Press, 2005.

The Passion of the Christ

The Passion of the Christ (2004) is a controversial film co-written and directed by Mel Gibson (1956–) that depicts the last hours of the life of Jesus Christ. In Christian tradition, the Passion is a term that refers to Jesus's trial and death by crucifixion as described in the Gospels of the New Testament; it was often the subject of religious plays staged around the Easter holiday. In the film, Jesus (played by James Caviezel, 1968–) is shown undergoing his trial, sentencing, and execution. The

Jarreth Merz as Simon of Cyrene and Jim Caviezel as Jesus in Mel Gibson's controversial 2004 film The Passion of the Christ.
© NEWMARKET RELEASING/EVERETT COLLECTION.

dialogue is rendered in ancient Aramaic and Latin and accompanied by subtitles. Much of the film features graphic depictions of Jesus's torture and execution, and some have argued that its R rating was not sufficient for the level of violence shown. During a screening of the film in Wichita, Kansas, a member of the audience died of a heart attack during the intense crucifixion scene.

The Passion of the Christ also stirred up controversy for what some viewed as an anti-Semitic bias in the film. Historically, depictions of the Passion were sometimes used to disparage Jewish people by suggesting that Jews were responsible for the death of Jesus. Gibson has claimed that his film includes no such message, though some reviewers and activists have argued that the film relies upon negative stereotypes for its depiction of several Jewish characters. In spite of the controversies, *The Passion of the Christ*—which was funded solely by Gibson's own production company—earned more than

$600 million during its theatrical run and was nominated for three Academy Awards.

Greg Wilson

For More Information

Bartunek, John. *Inside "The Passion": An Insider's Look at "The Passion of the Christ."* West Chester, PA: Ascension Press, 2005.

Ebert, Roger. "The Passion of the Christ." *Rogerebert.com.* http://rogerebert .suntimes.com/apps/pbcs.dll/article?AID=/20040224/REVIEWS/402240301/1023 (accessed August 9, 2011).

"Mel Gibson's Great Passion." *Zenit* (March 6, 2003). http://www.zenit.org/article-6723?l=english (accessed August 9, 2011).

Pirates of the Caribbean

Pirates of the Caribbean is an adventure film franchise based loosely on a popular attraction found in Walt **Disney** (see entry under 1920s—Film and Theater in volume 2) **amusement parks** (see entry under 1950s—The Way We Lived in volume 3). The films take place roughly during the early eighteenth century and, as the name implies, focus on piracy in the New World; however, the films also rely heavily upon supernatural and fantasy elements. The series began in 2003 with *Pirates of the Caribbean: The Curse of the Black Pearl,* starring Johnny Depp (1963–), Keira Knightley (1985–), Orlando Bloom (1977–), and Geoffrey Rush (1951–). The story in the first film centers largely on Will Turner (played by Bloom), the blacksmith son of a pirate, and his budding relationship with Elizabeth Swann (played by Knightley), daughter of the governor of Jamaica. They are drawn into a plot to end a gruesome curse placed upon the crew of a pirate ship known as *The Black Pearl*—the same ship on which Turner's father had sailed.

The standout character of the series is Captain Jack Sparrow, played by Depp. Sparrow is the former captain of *The Black Pearl*. He was overthrown by mutiny and is determined to seek revenge. Depp's unusual mannerisms used to portray Sparrow were reportedly inspired by a mixture of cartoon character Pepé Le Pew and **Rolling Stones** (see entry under 1960s—Music in volume 4) guitarist Keith Richards (1943–), who appeared in the third and fourth films in the series as Captain Teague, Sparrow's father. Sparrow's distinctive "rock-star pirate" look became a popular Halloween costume for children and adults alike, and

Johnny Depp (left) as Capt. Jack Sparrow and Orlando Bloom as Will Turner find adventure on the high seas in the Pirates of the Caribbean *film franchise.* © WALT DISNEY PICTURES/THE KOBAL COLLECTION/ART RESOURCE, NY.

subsequent films in the franchise have focused on Sparrow as the main character. The first four *Pirates of the Caribbean* films earned more than $3.7 billion worldwide, making it one of the most successful film franchises in movie history. The second film, *Pirates of the Caribbean: Dead Man's Chest* (2006), won an Academy Award for best visual effects. In 2006, Disneyland Park in California added the character of Sparrow to the original *Pirates of the Caribbean* attraction that had inspired the films.

Greg Wilson

For More Information

Nashawaty, Chris. "Box Office Buccaneer." *Entertainment Weekly* (July 25, 2003). http://www.ew.com/ew/article/0,,465481,00.html (accessed August 7, 2011).

Singer, Michael. *Bring Me That Horizon: The Making of "Pirates of the Caribbean."* New York: Disney Editions, 2007.

Shrek

Shrek is an animated fantasy film that launched a highly successful franchise for the DreamWorks film studio beginning in 2001. The film focuses on the title character (voiced by Mike Myers, 1963–), an ogre whose wonderfully miserable existence is upended when his swamp is invaded by other fairy-tale creatures, banned from the rest of the kingdom by human tyrant Lord Farquaad (voiced by John Lithgow, 1945–). Accompanied by a persistent and energetic donkey (voiced by Eddie Murphy, 1961–), Shrek sets off on a quest to help the fairy-tale creatures and reclaim his solitude. To accomplish this, Shrek must rescue Princess Fiona (voiced by Cameron Diaz, 1972–) from a dragon and take her to Farquaad so that he can marry her. By placing an unpleasant ogre in the role of hero, *Shrek* pokes fun at fairy-tale clichés and well-known childhood stories.

The original film earned nearly $500 million worldwide and won the first-ever Academy Award for best animated feature, prompting three sequels that continued the story of Shrek, Donkey, and Fiona. The films feature numerous fairy-tale characters, including the Gingerbread Man,

Donkey (voiced by Eddie Murphy) and Shrek (voiced by Mike Myers) in the film franchise Shrek. © DREAMWORKS LLC/THE KOBAL COLLECTION/ ART RESOURCE, NY.

the Three Little Pigs, and Pinocchio. One of the most popular additions to the main cast was Puss in Boots, a swashbuckling feline voiced by Antonio Banderas (1960–). With the release of *Shrek Forever After* in 2010, the four-film series became the highest-grossing animated film franchise of all time, with nearly $3 billion in box-office revenue. The films also inspired a successful **Broadway** (see entry under 1900s—Film and Theater in volume 1) musical that opened in 2008, as well as several made-for-television holiday specials.

Greg Wilson

For More Information

Cole, Stephen. *"Shrek": The Complete Guide*. New York: DK, 2007.
"Is Shrek Bad for Kids?" *Time* (May 10, 2007). http://www.time.com/time/magazine/article/0,9171,1619573,00.html (accessed August 7, 2011).

Slumdog Millionaire

Slumdog Millionaire (2008) is an Academy Award–winning film directed by Danny Boyle (1956–). It was based on a novel by Indian diplomat and author Vikas Swarup. The film has been lauded for its predominantly Indian cast—a rarity in Western cinema.

Slumdog Millionaire tells the story of Jamal (played by Dev Patel, 1990–), a poor boy—or "slumdog"—from the streets of Mumbai who ends up as a contestant on the Indian version of the television quiz show **Who Wants to Be a Millionaire?** (see entry under 1990s—TV and Radio in volume 5). As Jamal correctly answers question after question, amassing enormous winnings, the show's producers and the local police accuse him of cheating. Jamal explains how he knew the answer to each question through flashbacks from his difficult but fascinating life.

The film was a worldwide success upon its release and earned an astounding eight Academy Awards, including best picture, best director, best cinematography, and best adapted screenplay. However, the film became the focus of controversy when it was discovered that two of the film's main child stars, recruited from the slums of Mumbai, had been paid a relatively small sum for their roles and continued to live in squalor. In response, Boyle revealed that the child actors had been given substantial trust funds that would be available to them when they reached adulthood.

Greg Wilson

For More Information

Gross, Terry. "Danny Boyle, from *Trainspotting* to *Slumdog*." *National Public Radio* (November 12, 2008). http://www.npr.org/templates/transcript/transcript.php?storyId=96905439 (accessed July 26, 2011).

Swarup, Vikas. *Slumdog Millionaire: A Novel (Originally Published as "Q&A")*. London: Black Swan, 2009.

2000s

Food and Drink

Though Americans' lives became more digital than ever during the first decade of the twenty-first century, many turned to "natural," choices when it came to food and drink. Grocery store chains increasingly offered healthy products for consumers interested in eating well. Shoppers also found new chains, specializing in gourmet or organic ingredients, being started in their upper-middle-class neighborhoods. Farmers' markets drew trend-conscious crowds interested in purchasing locally grown foods. Once stocked up on fine ingredients, these Americans turned to popular Food Network shows for inspiration on how to create magic in the kitchen.

Despite the growing availability of organic, gourmet, and locally grown food, many Americans could not afford the time or money to eat well all the time. Less expensive prepared and processed foods continued to dominate the American food marketplace. Busy Americans continued to rely on fast food chains or grocery store choices that they could eat straight from the package. Commuters dashed into Starbucks on their way to work in the morning, gulped down fast food for lunch, and picked up microwaveable family meals for dinner.

Such habits took their toll on American waistlines. Obesity remained a critical health concern, and doctors warned of the impact of poor eating habits on children. Celebrities including first lady Michelle Obama

(1964–) and renowned chef Alice Waters (1944–) drew attention to the need to reform school lunch and exercise programs to ensure better health. Adults seeking weight loss turned to reduced-fat foods and drinks, or, more drastically, to fad diets such as the low-carb craze. Under pressure from the medical community and governments, fast food restaurants began offering healthy choices such as salads alongside burgers and fries. Nutrition information began appearing on fast food menus, sometimes leading customers to think twice about what they ordered.

Options for food and drink continued to expand, but the choice of what to consume proved challenging. Americans juggled concerns about fitting mealtimes into their schedule, keeping food costs down, and eating well. Whether trying to cook like popular chef Rachael Ray (1968–), shopping at upscale markets, or zooming through McDonalds drive-thrus, Americans in the 2000s continued their ongoing quest for the perfect meal.

Farmers' Markets

Farmers' markets are places at which independent food producers, farmers, ranchers, bakers, and others sell their produce and products directly to the public. Usually outdoors and more common in the summer months, farmers' markets are gathering places for members of communities and have become vital to the health of the towns and cities they serve. Although such markets have been a feature of societies for centuries, farmers' markets have been growing swiftly in popularity in the United States during the 2000s. According to the U.S. Department of Agriculture, the number of farmers' markets in America rose from 1,755 to 7,175 between 1994 and 2011. With one thousand new markets appearing in 2010 alone and with total sales of over $1 billion, it is clear that farmers' markets represent an important new trend in the way Americans shop and eat. They correspond to a rising interest in fresh produce and humanely raised meats, contradicting the trend of increasingly processed foods and petroleum-based agriculture that characterized the American diet after World War II (1939–45).

Some criticisms of farmers' markets include complaints that they are too expensive and that they do not take food stamps, thereby excluding many low-income customers. In terms of price, it is true that produce and meats at farmers' markets are usually costlier than they are at supermarkets. However, the items for sale at a farmers' market offer other

Locavores support and promote farmers' markets because the farmer can sell directly to the customer.
© BALONCICI/DREAMSTIME.COM.

benefits, such as being organic and usually coming from local sources, or locavores. Thus, farmers' markets are considered an important part of the locavore movement, which prizes locally produced foods for environmental and cultural reasons. Places like farmers' markets, locavores believe, create deeper bonds between people and the places the live. They also reduce greenhouse gas emissions by shortening the distance food travels from producer to consumer. The farmer benefits as well by essentially "eliminating the middleman" and selling directly to the consumer. By doing so, farmers receive retail, rather than wholesale, prices for their goods. Still, only about 12 percent of farmers' markets participated in the food stamp–related Supplemental Nutrition Assistance Program (SNAP) in 2010, though this number was still rising at the decade's end. As it does, farmers' markets will likely continue to become ever more important in defining the way that all Americans eat.

Patrick J. Walsh

For More Information

Robinson, Jennifer Meta, and J. A. Hartenfeld. *The Farmers' Market Book: Growing Food, Cultivating Community.* Bloomington, IN: Quarry Books, 2007.

Stephenson, Garry. *Farmers' Markets: Success, Failure, and Management Ecology.* Ithaca, NY: Cambria Press, 2008.

United States Department of Agriculture Marketing Service. *Farmers Markets and Local Food Marketing.* http://www.ams.usda.gov/AMSv1.0/farmersmarkets (accessed August 16, 2011).

Gourmet Grocery Stores

During the first decade of the 2000s, consumers began flocking to grocery stores that were built on a different model from that of the traditional suburban supermarket. These so-called gourmet grocery stores offered less selection than supermarkets and sold more expensive products, yet they experienced a surge in popularity, moving from the world of hardcore "health nuts" into the commercial mainstream. By 2006, Whole Foods Market, the leading gourmet grocery store chain, was posting sales of $5.6 billion, a figure unthinkable for a store of its type just a decade earlier.

The grocery store is a twentieth-century development, having grown out of the general stores, trading posts, and neighborhood markets of the nineteenth century. Piggly Wiggly, the first self-service grocery store in which customers selected products off of shelves, placed them in a basket, and took them to a cashier for checking out, opened in 1916. After World War II (1939–45), as America's prosperity grew in leaps and bounds and urban populations moved out into the suburbs, the "supermarket" appeared. Supermarkets offered all the basic staple foods of a regular grocery store but in greater variety and at cheaper prices. They also offered more specialty foods and ingredients as well as non-food items such as books and magazines, alcohol, medical and hygiene products, and other household items.

In many ways, the supermarket was emblematic of post-war American prosperity, but there emerged from the 1960s counter-culture a movement against the supermarket model of food retailing. Although stores specializing in health food had been around for some time, they multiplied significantly throughout the 1970s as part of the "natural foods" movement. The crux of this movement was the belief that supermarkets and mainstream grocery stores sold food that was either overly processed and losing most of its nutritional value or treated with potentially harmful pesticides and growth hormones. Meats were the product of industrial farms that treated animals with mechanical indifference and kept them in unhygienic conditions, necessitating the injection of antibiotics. Health food stores, on the other hand, offered organic foods that were grown without any chemicals or additives. They also sold whole grain breads and other foodstuffs supplied by local, small farms.

Health food stores remained a marginal segment of the food supply industry through the 1980s, stereotypically patronized by aging **hippies** (see entry under 1960s—The Way We Lived in volume 4) and health nuts. This image was soon to change thanks to the ambitions of local stores in Texas and California. Whole Foods Market got its start as an Austin health food store in 1980. Through the 1980s, Whole Foods slowly expanded, buying existing health food stores and opening new stores outside Austin, first in Texas and then in other states. Whole Foods' growth exploded in the 1990s as the company bought out a number of local health food chains from North Carolina to New England to California. Trader Joe's, a California-based "specialty store," experienced similar levels of growth in the 1990s, expanding from its West Coast base to open stores across the country.

Both Whole Foods and Trader Joe's operate along a model markedly different from the standard supermarket. They offer organic foods and meats, pre-packaged meals with vegetarian ingredients, ethnic foods, and specialty wines. Of note is the fact that although the two chains appeal to a similar customer base, their business models are quite different. Trader Joe's sells a small range of products, many under its own brand name. Its stores are generally small and the company bills itself as "your neighborhood market." Whole Foods, on the other hand, could be called the world's first health food supermarket because its stores are as large as major grocery chains and offer as wide a selection. The key difference lies in Whole Foods' stated commitment to limit its product selection to "natural" foods—that is, foods with a limited number of additives or other "unacceptable ingredients."

Whole Foods has been the target of criticism over the apparent contradiction between its corporate policies and its commitment to the natural foods movement. In 2009, owner and founder John Mackey (1953–) admitted to a dip in quality of products and vowed to return to the company's organic roots. The rapid expansion of Whole Foods has even brought the attention of the U.S. government, which investigated potential abuses of anti-trust laws; the chain was cleared of suspicion in 2008. Despite such problems, Whole Foods and Trader Joe's ranked among the most successful grocery chains in the industry throughout the first decade of the 2000s. The limited selection and sometimes premium prices for organic goods was balanced out for consumers looking for a different shopping experience. In 2009, *Consumer Reports* ranked Trader Joe's as the second best grocery store in the United States. Its success lay in the appeal to the health-conscious, upwardly mobile consumer; in effect, it made health food stores "cool."

David Larkins

For More Information

Armstrong, Larry. "Trader Joe's: The Trendy American Cousin." *Bloomberg Business Week* (April 26, 2004). http://www.businessweek.com/magazine/content/04_17/b3880016.htm (accessed August 1, 2011).

Lewis, Len. *The Trader Joe's Experience.* Chicago: Dearborn Trade, 2005.

Maloney, Field. "Is Whole Foods Wholesome?: The Dark Secrets of the Organic-Food Movement." *Slate* (March 17, 2006). http://www.slate.com/id/2138176/ (accessed August 1, 2011).

Reed, Matthew. *Rebels for the Soil: The Rise of the Global Organic Food and Farming Movement.* New York: Routledge, 2010.

"Trader Joe's Targets 'Educated' Buyer." *Seattle Post Intelligencer* (August 29, 2003). http://www.seattlepi.com/business/article/Trader-Joe-s-targets-educated-buyer-1123007.php (accessed August 1, 2011).

Low-carb Diets

The Atkins Diet, created by Dr. Robert Atkins (1930–), made its debut in the 1972 book *Dr. Atkins' Diet Revolution.* This low-carbohydrate, high-protein **diet** (see entry under 1950s—The Way We Lived in volume 3) lay dormant during the successive dieting fads of the later twentieth century that stressed limiting fat intake at all costs. In contrast, the Atkins Diet and others like it encouraged eating high-fat foods such as meat and cheese, while limiting the consumption of carbohydrates like sugars and processed grains—exactly what made up most of the low-fat snack foods marketed to dieters.

When a new version of the Atkins Diet was featured in the book *Dr. Atkins' New Diet Revolution* (2002), it quickly changed North

America's attitude toward food. Grain-based foods like bread and pasta—staples of the Western diet for centuries—were now looked upon with suspicion, and food manufacturers scrambled to introduce low-carb versions of these classics. By mid-2003, 9 percent of Americans—or one in eleven—reported following the diet. Nearly four thousand food products were either introduced or remarketed to emphasize their low carbohydrate content.

At the height of the Atkins craze, American eaters found themselves in an upside-down food world, turning up their noses at bananas—long considered one of nature's finest health foods—while celebrating the virtues of the fat- and calorie-laden ten-ounce steak. Dieters were encouraged to eat fats of all kinds, and no meat (except for processed and breaded meat) was off-limits. The goal of the diet was to induce a process called ketosis, in which the body stops using the more readily available glucose (available from carbohydrates) and begins converting energy from stored body fat. Dieters who stuck to the plan often saw significant weight loss, but like most extreme diets, for many eaters it proved unsustainable.

By early 2004, followers of the Atkins Diet declined to less than 5 percent of American adults, and by 2005 the figure was down to just 2 percent. By mid-2005, Atkins Nutritionals, Inc., which marketed several hundred of its own low-carb foods, had filed for Chapter 11 bankruptcy protection. Dieters and the general public did not turn away completely from the low-carb trend, however. Some diets, such as the Zone, which called for a more even distribution of carbs, proteins, and fats, continued in popularity. Other diets, such as the South Beach Diet, stressed "good" carbs (such as beans and whole grains) and "good" fats (such as lean meats and nuts) while cutting out the "bad," allowing dieters a larger range of foods from which to choose.

Rachel Hertz Cobb

For More Information

Chauncey, Katherine B. *Low-carb Dieting for Dummies*. Hoboken, NJ: Wiley, 2004.

Greger, Michael. *Carbophobia: The Scary Truth about America's Low-carb Craze*. New York: Lantern Books, 2005.

Kaufman, Wendy. "Atkins Bankruptcy a Boon for Pasta Makers." *NPR* (August 3, 2005). http://www.npr.org/templates/story/story.php?storyId=4783324 (accessed August 13, 2011).

Rogak, Lisa. *Dr. Robert Atkins: The True Story of the Man Behind the War on Carbohydrates.* New York: Chamberlain Bros., 2005.

Warner, Melanie. "Is the Low-Carb Boom Over?" *New York Times* (December 5, 2004). http://www.nytimes.com/2004/12/05/business/yourmoney/05atki .html?pagewanted=1&_r=1&sq=low-carb&st=cse&scp=3 (accessed August 13, 2011).

Rachael Ray (1968–) and Celebrity Chefs

While sociologists noted a steep decline in home cooking and in the ritual of the family dinner, food culture was on the rise in the first decade of the twenty-first century. This was nowhere clearer during the decade than in the case of celebrity chefs, who built their personas (and their substantial wealth) on Food Network television shows, restaurant empires, magazine and cookbook sales, and lines of kitchenware and housewares. With salaries mounting into the multimillions, celebrity chefs made food into a glamorous, international pursuit. Riding the wave of reality television that made ordinary people household names, celebrity chefs also brought talent, charisma, and shrewd business sense to a once-tedious, unfashionable activity: cooking.

Of the many celebrity chefs to expand well beyond the kitchen, the most dazzling success story was that of Rachael Ray (1968–). Ray grew up in a family of restaurateurs, and though she never had any formal chef's training herself, she parlayed an interest in food and an appealing, down-to-earth persona into her own show on the Food Network, *30 Minute Meals,* in 2001. Ray's signature catch-phrases, such as "EVOO" (short for extra virgin olive oil, a staple of her cooking) and "yum-o," characterized her on-screen delivery, earning her millions of fans—and a large serving of mockery. Nevertheless, the success of her cooking show led to the publication of nearly twenty best-selling cookbooks, a magazine established in 2005 (*Every Day with Rachael Ray*), a second show on the Food Network (*Rachael Ray's Tasty Travels*), a syndicated daytime talk show (*Rachael Ray*), lines of kitchen and home products, and several lucrative endorsement deals. Ray's annual earnings reportedly topped $18 million.

Many of Ray's celebrity chef peers took similar routes, building their reputations through television work and cookbooks. Anthony Bourdain (1956–), Giada De Laurentiis (1970–), Paula Deen (1947–), Jamie

Oliver (1975–), and Nigella Lawson (1960–) all became known for their compelling personalities in writing and on screen. Other celebrity chefs, many of whom have developed television shows as well, began primarily as restaurateurs and professional chefs, and used television to promote their restaurant empires. Mario Batali (1960–), Gordon Ramsay (1966–), Emeril Lagasse (1959–), and Wolfgang Puck (1949–) are among the most dynamic and wealthy of the celebrity chefs of this type from the 2000s decade.

Rachel Hertz Cobb

For More Information

Abrams, Dennis. *Rachael Ray: Food Entrepreneur*. New York: Chelsea House, 2009.

Jacobs, Laura. "Just Say Yum-O!" *Vanity Fair* (September 11, 2007). http://www.vanityfair.com/culture/features/2007/10/rachaelray200710#gotopage6 (accessed August 12, 2011).

Keedle, Jayne. *Rachael Ray*. Pleasantville, NY: Gareth Stevens, 2010.

Rousseau, Signe. *Food Media: Celebrity Chefs and the Politics of Everyday Interference*. London: Berg, 2012.

Vorasarun, Chaniga. "Ten Top-Earning Celebrity Chefs." *Forbes* (August 8, 2008). http://www.forbes.com/2008/08/08/celebrity-chef-earners-forbeslife-cx_cv_0808food.html (accessed August 12, 2011).

2000s

Music

The first decade of the twenty-first century was a time of great turmoil and upheaval for the music industry. It marked a dramatic shift in how people accessed recorded music, as consumers moved from primarily buying physical albums to single-song digital downloads. The music industry's response to this shift was unsteady and often reactionary. By 2010, new business agreements between recording companies and musicians had begun to emerge to deal with the inevitable changes that the industry had at first resisted.

Although the way people bought music was changing, trends from the late 1990s continued to dominate the first years of the 2000s. Hip-hop claimed the crown as king of popular music, with Eminem (1972–) emerging as both the genre's greatest star and the first widely popular white rapper. New sub-genres of hip-hop such as crunk and southern hip-hop gained popularity, and acts such as T-Pain (1985–) and the Black Eyed Peas popularized the use of Auto-Tune recording software to create a unique vocal sound in their recordings. Pop artists also embraced Auto-Tune, although usually more for its intended purpose of correcting a singer's pitch. There was also a significant minority of rock acts that sought to return to the style's earlier, unpolished roots.

The early years of the first decade of the 2000s saw an explosion of popularity of "garage rock" bands such as the White Stripes, the Strokes, the Vines, the Hives, and the Yeah Yeah Yeahs that produced intentionally stripped-down, raw music. The garage rock revival was one of several such attempts in pop music to return to earlier musical roots. Another notable revival was the renewed interest in 1960s-style soul music, spearheaded by British acts such as Amy Winehouse (1983–2011), Joss Stone (1987-), and Adele (1988–).

Although pop-punk bands like Sum 41 and New Found Glory found success in the first years of the 2000s decade, their fan base had moved on to a genre of music known as emo by the middle of the decade. Emo had been around as a style since the 1980s, but bands like My Chemical Romance and Dashboard Confessional made it commercial, broadening the term to include fashion and lifestyle choices in the same way the word "punk" had been generalized in the 1970s. The style's lyrics, which focused on raw and dramatic emotional content, along with its equally raw sound appealed to the same "back to basics" sentiment that had spawned the garage rock revival.

As the decade came to a close, the emo and garage rock bands had been largely eclipsed and subsumed by so-called "indie" bands such as Death Cab for Cutie, Modest Mouse, and Arcade Fire that carried forward the raw, emotional, stripped-down aesthetics of the two styles. As the name of the genre suggests, they also added an independent, DIY (do it yourself) aesthetic to the process of producing and recording music.

Metal entered the decade riding a surge of popularity thanks to post-grunge bands and more traditional metal bands like Metallica, Slayer, and Megadeth. "Nu metal" and rap metal acts such as Linkin Park and Limp Bizkit also were popular. Country, the reigning popular music genre of the 1990s, was knocked off its throne by hip-hop. The country genre, although still popular, did not begin to enjoy a resurgence until the later years of the first decade of the 2000s, thanks to the recording efforts of American Idol winner Carrie Underwood (1983–) and, particularly, teen singer-songwriter Taylor Swift (1989–), who enjoyed massive crossover success on the pop and country charts. As the decade came to a close, hip-hop looked set to continue its popular music dominance, while rock's fortunes continued to dwindle.

Auto-Tune

Auto-Tune is among the latest music engineering technologies to have a profound effect on the sound of popular music. Developed in the mid-1990s and released to the public in 1997, the audio processor was initially intended to allow sound engineers to alter the pitch of recorded vocal tracks in order to correct off-key singing. Auto-Tune was first put to use as an in-studio "instrument" in and of itself with Cher's (1946–) song "Believe" (1998).

The vocoder, a kind of vocal synthesizer that gives the human voice an electronic, robotic sound, had been featured in musical recordings since the 1970s. For "Believe," producers utilized Auto-Tune as a sort of digital vocoder, taking Cher's recorded vocals and altering their pitch drastically until they achieved a distorted, digitized effect. The resulting sound was a novelty and contributed to the song's massive international success. The sound, dubbed "the Cher Effect," was widely copied over the next three years, but soon fell out of favor as the novelty wore off.

Unexpectedly, the use of Auto-Tune-distorted vocals enjoyed a comeback in the last years of the first decade of the twenty-first century. Credit for this revival rested with urban/**rhythm and blues** (see entry under 1940s—Music in volume 3) singer T-Pain (1985–), who used the distortion extensively in his work. Once again, the style was widely copied, most notably by **hip-hop** (see Rap and Hip-hop entry under 1980s—Music in volume 5) superstar Kanye West (1977–). The distinct sound quickly became synonymous with popular music, so much so that Auto-Tuned vocals had become the target of parody by 2010. Musical satirists the Gregory Brothers launched a video series on **YouTube** (see entry under 2000s—The Way We Lived in volume 6) called "Auto-Tune the News," in which they ran regular news stories, viral videos, and interview footage through Auto-Tune to produce songs. Their video "Bed Intruder Song" became the most-watched viral video on YouTube in 2010 and the resulting song, featuring the heavily distorted, Auto-Tuned vocals of news interviewee Antoine Dodson (1986–), actually cracked the *Billboard* Hot 100.

The use of Auto-Tune for its original intended purpose, meanwhile, had become so widespread as to become nearly standard within the recording industry. Its use spread beyond the studio as artists began to make use of the technology during live performances as well. This widespread pursuit of the "perfect" vocal had led to a backlash by 2010, as many musicians and fans protested against the increasingly bland, same-sounding vocals in pop music. Artists like **Bob Dylan** (1941–; see entry under 1960s—Music in volume 4), Death Cab for Cutie, Jay-Z (1969–), and Christina Aguilera (1980–) made statements, both public and musical, against the use of Auto-Tune. In 2010, *Time* magazine (see entry under 1920s—Print Culture in volume 2) named Auto-Tune one of the "50 Worst Inventions," noting, "It's a technology that can make bad singers sound good and really bad singers … sound like robots. And it gives singers who sound like West or Cher the misplaced confidence that they too can croon. Thanks a lot, computers."

David Larkins

For More Information

Fletcher, Dan. "The 50 Worst Inventions: Auto-Tune." *Time* (May 27, 2010). http://www.time.com/time/specials/packages/article/0,28804,1991915_1991909_1991903,00.html (accessed August 1, 2011).

Frere-Jones, Sasha. "The Gerbil's Revenge." *New Yorker* (June 9, 2008). http://www.newyorker.com/arts/critics/musical/2008/06/09/080609crmu_music_frerejones?currentPage=all (accessed August 1, 2011).

Lipshutz, Jason. "YouTube Remix Auteurs Turn Ordinary Videos into Pop Music Hits." *Billboard* (August 20, 2010). http://www.billboard.com/features/youtube-remix-auteurs-turn-ordinary-videos-1004107001.story (accessed August 1, 2011).

Tyrangiel, Josh. "Auto-Tune: Why Pop Music Sounds Perfect." *Time* (February 5, 2009). http://www.time.com/time/magazine/article/0,9171,1877372-1,00.html (accessed on August 1, 2011).

Sean "Diddy" Combs (1969–)

Sean Combs is a **hip-hop** (see Rap and Hip-hop entry under 1980s—Music in volume 5) artist and entrepreneur famous for his many nicknames, which include "P. Diddy" and "Puff Daddy." Combs began his music career as a promoter, but he quickly moved into producing. He launched his own record company, Bad Boy Records, in 1993, and scored several hits with artists such as the Notorious B.I.G. (Christopher George Latore Wallace; 1972–1997) and Faith Evans (1972–). In 1997, he released his own debut album under the name Puff Daddy and became an immediate success. Combs was a key player in the East Coast hip-hop scene and became entangled in an infamous rivalry with West Coast hip-hop performers like Tupac Shakur (1971–1996). Both Shakur and the Notorious B.I.G. were killed in drive-by shootings, which some believe were connected to this East Coast/West Coast rivalry. In 1999, Combs was arrested on weapons charges related to a shootout in a Manhattan night club; he was later acquitted.

In addition to his work in music, Combs enjoyed great success as an actor and a fashion designer. In 2001, Combs had small but important roles in two films: *Made,* in which he portrayed a drug dealer, and *Monster's Ball,* in which he played a murderer on death row. Combs also performed on **Broadway** (see entry under 1900s—Film and Theater in volume 1) and guest starred on television shows such as ***CSI: Miami*** (see entry under 2000s—TV and Radio in volume 6) and ***Hawaii Five-O*** (see entry under 1960s—TV and Radio in volume 4). In 1998, Combs launched the Sean John clothing line, which earned him the 2004 Men's Designer of the Year from the Council of Fashion Designers of America. In 2005, Combs decided to shorten his stage name to simply Diddy, though he often used his real name when working as an actor.

Greg Wilson

For More Information

Cable, Andrew. *A Family Affair: The Unauthorized Sean "Puffy" Combs Story.* New York: Ballantine Books, 1998.

Ro, Ronin. *Bad Boy: The Influence of Sean "Puffy" Combs on the Music Industry.* New York: Pocket Books, 2001.

Soriano, César G. "Nitty-gritty on Diddy." *USA Today* (August 16, 2005). http://www.usatoday.com/life/people/2005-08-16-p-diddy_x.htm (accessed August 29, 2011).

Traugh, Susan. *Sean Combs.* Detroit: Lucent, 2010.

Crunk

In the mid-1990s in Atlanta, Georgia, DJ Lil Jon (born Jonathan Smith, 1971–) developed an interest in a new style of **hip-hop** (see Rap and Hip-hop entry under 1980s—Music in volume 5) called southern hip-hop, or Dirty South. Lil Jon could tell there was room for progress in bass music. By combining a driving bass line and booming drums with rap lyrics shouted over the top, he created a new style that came to be known as crunk. The underground sound of crunk simmered for years before becoming a household word and hip-hop craze in the early 2000s.

Crunk was not solely the product of Lil Jon's imagination. Other southern hip-hop artists, such as Three 6 Mafia, DJ Paul (1977–), and Juicy J (1975–), had been toying with the style since the 1990s. However, it was Lil Jon and his group the East Side Boyz that became the faces of crunk when they released their debut, *Get Crunk: Who U Wit: Da Album* in 1997.

On that album, Lil Jon perfected crunk by deepening the bass and adding intricate musical details on top of the bass line. The cult success of *Get Crunk: Who U Wit: Da Album* went mainstream when Lil Jon was signed to the label TNT and released the crossover hit *Kings of Crunk* in 2002. With the single "Get Low," featuring the Ying Yang Twins, Lil Jon put crunk just one spot shy of the number one position on Billboard's Hot 100 chart.

Crunk was inescapable after "Get Low." The single launched the Ying Yang Twins to stardom and scored them a guest spot on a single from pop icon **Britney Spears** (1981– see entry under 1990s—Music in volume 5), "(I Got That) Boom Boom" from her hit album *In the Zone* (2003). Sister act Cherish experimented with a new offshoot called "crunk 'n' B," which blended the funky rhythms of crunk with the smooth harmonies of traditional **rhythm and blues** (see entry under 1940s—Music in volume 3). Lil Jon remained the king of crunk, however, helping R&B singer Usher (1978–) score an international hit by co-writing, producing, and lending his gritty voice to "Yeah!" and releasing his own hit album, *Crunk Juice,* in 2004.

In 2006, Three 6 Mafia brought crunk to the Oscars. The group became the first hip-hop act to perform at the Academy Awards ceremony, and their song "It's Hard Out Here for a Pimp" from the soundtrack of *Hustle and Flow* (2005) won an Academy Award for best original song in a motion picture.

Michael Segretto

For More Information

Green, Tony. "Punk Rap." *Today Music* (March 21, 2004). http://today.msnbc.msn.com/id/5015949 (accessed July 18, 2011).

Sanneh, Kelefa. "Lil Jon Crunks Up the Volume." *New York Times* (November 28, 2004). http://www.nytimes.com/2004/11/28/arts/music/28sann.html (accessed July 11, 2011).

Shepherd, Julianne. "Soul Bounce: Crunk 'n' B 101." *VH1.com* (August 18, 2006). http://www.vh1.com/news/articles/1538791/story.jhtml (accessed July 18, 2011).

Disney Stars and Teen Sensations

For many young people, the Disney Channel became *the* go-to entertainment zone during the first decade of the twenty-first century. With movies such as ***High School Musical*** (see entry under 2000s—TV and Radio in volume 6) and *Camp Rock,* and TV series such as *Hannah*

Montana, **Disney** (see entry under 1920s—Film and Theater in volume 2) managed to maintain its relevance and popularity among young people while launching a new parade of teen music idols.

Ever since ***The Mickey Mouse Club*** (see entry under 1950s—TV and Radio in volume 3) debuted on ABC in 1955, the Walt Disney Company has jumpstarted the careers of young celebrities. Six years after the Disney Channel was launched in 1983, the company continued to serve that purpose with a revamped version of *The Mickey Mouse Club.* In 2002, the channel underwent one of its most dramatic changes, pursuing a hipper image and focusing on new situation comedies, such as *Hannah Montana.* On the show, the title character is a teenager living a double life as a high school student by day and a famous pop star by night. Much like the title character she portrayed in the series, Miley Cyrus (1992–) enjoyed a successful pop music career, having hit records both as Hannah and Miley. *Hannah Montana* was a number one hit album in 2006, although none of the singles pulled from the record made much impression on the pop charts. Cyrus, daughter of pop country star Billy Ray Cyrus (1961–), sold more singles when releasing them under her own name, scoring a top ten hit with her debut "See You Again" in 2008, and additional ones with "7 Things," "The Climb," and "Party in the U.S.A."

Miley Cyrus's break-out success paved the way for more Disney idols to follow. In 2006, the Disney Channel aired *High School Musical.* The made-for-TV movie about teens competing for roles in a school play boosted the music and acting careers of several new stars, including Zac Efron (1987–), Vanessa Hudgens (1988–), and Ashley Tisdale (1985–). Hudgens released *V,* her debut album, in 2006. The album went gold. In 2008, she released a second album, *Identified.* Efron moved from the small screen to the big one in 2007 when he landed a role in an adaptation of the **Broadway** (see entry under 1900s—Film and Theater in volume 1) musical *Hairspray.* He followed up this musical success with several well-regarded nonmusical films, including *Me and Orson Welles* (2009) and *Charlie St. Cloud* (2010). In 2007, Tisdale released her hit debut album *Headstrong,* followed in 2009 by *Guilty Pleasures.*

While the stars of *High School Musical* carved out successful musical and acting careers, there was room for still more music by Disney stars on the public's playlist. The year 2008 saw the debut of Disney's *Camp Rock,* which introduced a young pop band called the Jonas Brothers to a new audience. Three Jonas brothers—Kevin (1987–), Joe (1989–), and

Nick (1992–)—released two albums before the Disney Channel movie first aired. They had two top ten hits, "Burnin' Up" and "Tonight," in the wake of *Camp Rock,* proving that Disney still has its fingers on the young generation's pulse after some ninety years in business.

Disney did not have a total lock on teen music sensations in the 2000s. Rival TV network Nickelodeon had successful programs that featured new teen stars, such as Drake Bell (1986–) from *Drake & Josh* (2004–2007) and Miranda Cosgrove (1993–) from *iCarly* (2007–). According to an April 2010 *People* magazine cover, the title "world's biggest pop star" belonged to Canadian teen pop sensation Justin Bieber (1994–), who said his musical success is partly due to the fact that he "didn't go through the Disney route." Instead, Bieber posted videos of himself on **YouTube** (see entry under 2000s—The Way We Lived in volume 6), where he was discovered in 2008 by a talent manager. Bieber's debut 2009 album, *My World,* went platinum. His follow-up 2010 album, *My World 2.0,* also reached platinum status. Bieber carried home armloads of awards in 2010, including artist of the year from the American Music Awards, and his 2010 hit song "Baby" topped charts around the world. What marked Bieber's true pop idol status was the teen world's reaction to his hair. Teen idols from the past—from the **Beatles** (see entry under 1960s—Music in volume 4) to David Cassidy (1950–) to Leif Garrett (1961–)—caused nearly as much sensation with their hairstyles as with their singing, and Bieber followed in this teen idol tradition. Bieber's soft, shimmery hair, swirled down in a mop across his forehead and cheeks, drove young girls wild, and inspired many teen boys to imitate him.

Michael Segretto

For More Information

Deming, Mark. "Miley Cyrus: Biography." *AllMusic.* http://www.allmusic.com/artist/miley-cyrus-p823418/biography (accessed July 12, 2011).

Fixmer, Andy, and Katie Hoffmann. "Disney Parlays *High School Musical* Phenomenon into Franchise." *Bloomberg* (August 16, 2007). http://www.bloomberg.com/apps/news?pid=newsarchive&sid=aWAWq4DtVtb8&refer=us (accessed July 12, 2011).

"Justin Bieber Glad He's Not a 'Corny' Disney Star." *Starpulse.com* (April 13, 2010). http://www.starpulse.com/news/index.php/2010/04/13/justin_bieber_glad_hes_not_a_corny_dis (accessed July 27, 2011).

Monger, James Christopher. "Jonas Brothers: Biography." *AllMusic.* http://www.allmusic.com/artist/jonas-brothers-p778430/biography (accessed July 12, 2011).

Shapiro, Marc. *Justin Bieber: The Fever!* New York: St. Martin's Griffin, 2010.

Eminem (1972–)

Eminem, the stage name of the rapper born Marshall Mathers III (1972–), was one of the best-selling recording artists of the 2000s. He has sold almost forty million albums in the United States. The popularity of his music was a central factor in the growth of **rap and hip-hop** (see entry under 1980s—Music in volume 5). His slashing and self-mocking style was hugely influential on other rappers in the early twenty-first century, though the content of his music also led to widespread criticism.

The rapper was raised by his mother, Deborah Mathers, after his father abandoned the family. Dealing with his anger at both his absent father and his struggling mother is a central theme in Eminem's music. In his preteen years, Eminem and his mother lived in the Detroit suburb of Warren, before moving to Detroit itself. It was here that his interest

Rapper Eminem performs at the 2009 Voodoo Experience at City Park in New Orleans, Louisiana, on October 30, 2009. © C. FLANIGAN/ FILMMAGIC/GETTY IMAGES.

in rap music grew. His mother estimated that between 1978 and 1999, Eminem attended over a dozen schools before dropping out of high school at age seventeen. Despite the poverty and violence of his neighborhood, Eminem focused intently on developing his rap style, both as a writer and as a "freestyle" (improvisational) performer. As he struggled to earn a living and work on his rap career, Eminem created an alter-ego, Slim Shady, through which he was able to find his distinctive voice as a rapper. A demo recording caught the notice of influential rapper and producer Dr. Dre, who oversaw his 1999 release, *The Slim Shady LP.* Eminem's distinctive style and his mixture of humor and graphically violent language led to rave reviews and the album sold millions of copies.

Eminem's second major label release, *The Marshall Mathers LP* (2000), was a global hit, selling over nineteen million copies. But it also attracted a great deal of negative attention. Many reviewers found its depictions of violence against women and its numerous slurs against homosexuals disturbing, especially since the audience for the album was primarily made up of teenagers and young people. Eminem's fame grew wider with the release of the semi-autobiographical film *8 Mile* in 2002. Eminem received strong reviews for his acting and a song from the film, "Lose Yourself," won an Academy Award. He also authored a best-selling memoir, *The Way I Am,* published in 2008.

Eminem's personal life has been as tumultuous as his music. He has struggled with addiction and mental health issues. His mother has criticized him in the media and written a tell-all memoir. His ex-wife, Kimberley Scott Mathers (1975–), also made allegations about Eminem's abusive behavior, and the two warred publically over custody of their daughter. In 2010, Eminem released *Recovery,* a Grammy Award–winning best-seller. Eminem's influence on the course and popularity of rap and hip-hop in the early twenty-first century is undeniable.

Patrick J. Walsh

For More Information

Doggett, Peter. *Eminem: The Complete Guide to His Music.* New York: Omnibus Press, 2005.

Eminem: Official Site. http://www.eminem.com/default.aspx (accessed July 12, 2011).

Eminem and Sacha Jenkins. *The Way I Am.* New York: Dutton, 2008.

"Eminem Biography." *Biography.com.* http://www.biography.com/articles/Eminem-9542093 (accessed July 12, 2011).

Emo

Emo is a style of music that proved popular in the 1990s and early 2000s. It is characterized by personal, introspective lyrics combined with intensely emotional vocals. The term "emo" is a shortened form of "emotional." Emo music developed as an evolution of—and a reaction to—American **punk** (see entry under 1970s—Music in volume 4) rock, which was characterized by loud, heavily distorted guitar sounds and angry vocals. While the lyrics in punk rock songs often focused on the state of the world (usually in a negative way), emo relied more upon individual feelings and experiences. Emo music that retains moments of especially loud or intense vocals similar to punk rock shouting or **heavy metal** (see entry under 1980s—Music in volume 5) screaming has been dubbed "screamo." The deeply emotional nature of emo has led some critics to link it to teen depression and suicide, even though overall teen suicide declined steadily during the years in which emo music became popular.

As with many subgenres of music, emo can represent a variety of different things to listeners, critics, and even the artists themselves. One popular band closely associated with the emo movement is Dashboard Confessional. Its 2001 song "Screaming Infidelities" was one of the first breakthrough emo hit singles. Its album *A Mark, a Mission, a Brand, a Scar* (2003) reached number two on the *Billboard* charts, and the band contributed the song "Vindicated" to the soundtrack for the hit film ***Spider-Man 2*** (see entry under 1960s—Print Culture in volume 4) in 2004. Another popular band that has been classified as emo is My Chemical Romance, though lead vocalist Gerard Way (1977–) has publicly rejected the label. The term emo has also been applied to bands such as Jimmy Eat World, Sunny Day Real Estate, and Fall Out Boy, while the band the Used is one of many that have been described as screamo. The emo movement has also become associated with other cultural trends such as **hipster** (see entry under 2000s—The Way We Lived in volume 6) fashion.

Greg Wilson

For More Information

Greenwald, Andy. *Nothing Feels Good: Punk Rock, Teenagers, and Emo.* New York: St. Martin's Griffin, 2003.

La Gorce, Tammy. "Finding Emo." *New York Times* (August 14, 2005). http://www.nytimes.com/2005/08/14/nyregion/nyregionspecial2/14njCOVER.html (accessed September 20, 2011).

Simon, Leslie, and Trevor Kelley. *Everybody Hurts: An Essential Guide to Emo Culture.* New York: HarperEntertainment, 2007.

Indie Music

Indie music, an extremely loose genre categorization encompassing musical acts that embrace an independent approach to recording and marketing their music, came into its own as a commercial force during the first decade of the 2000s. Beginning with the garage rock revival of the early 2000s, indie acts earned great success and notoriety throughout the decade, so much so that by the end of the first decade of the 2000s some music critics were questioning the relevance of the label "indie."

Since the very beginning of the music industry, there have been artists and record labels that have bucked the trend of chasing after

From Detroit, musicians Meg White and Jack White of the White Stripes bring their "garage rock" sound to Madison Square Garden on July 24, 2007, in New York City. © STEPHEN LOVEKIN/WIREIMAGE/GETTY IMAGES.

mainstream success, choosing instead to focus on the supposed purity of their musical vision unaffected by commercial considerations. **Punk** (see entry under 1970s—Music in volume 4) rock, particularly hardcore punk in the 1980s, took this philosophy to new levels. The indie subculture that took root in the 1980s duplicated in do-it-yourself miniature the infrastructure of the corporate music industry. There were indie record labels, distributors, even tour circuits. The primary difference lay in the indie artists' freedom to pursue their own creative direction rather than abide by the restrictions imposed by major record labels.

This freedom necessarily led to an incredible variety of musical styles and sounds, all equally fresh and engaging. The indie rock scene led to the mainstream explosion in popularity during the 1990s of **grunge** (see entry under 1990s—Music in volume 5) rock and the punk rock revival. By the first decade of the 2000s, as those scenes were dying out, new indie acts rose to national prominence. The White Stripes, the Strokes, and the Vines led the garage rock revival of 2001. Playing stripped-down, straight-ahead **rock and roll** (see entry under 1950s—Music in volume 3) in the vein of 1960s garage bands, these bands enjoyed a brief period of tremendous success, even being hailed as "saviors of rock" by some critics.

However, by the middle of the first decade of the 2000s, indie music was taking several unexpected turns. The indie scene that had produced the punk revival of the 1990s now brought about sudden mainstream interest in **emo** (see entry under 2000s—Music in volume 6) music, a style that had been around under various categorizations since the 1980s. Other indie acts explored electronic sounds reminiscent of 1980s-era synthpop. The bulk of indie acts tended to take on a softer, multi-instrumental approach, incorporating sounds from American **folk music** (see entry under 1960s—Music in volume 4) and instruments like the fiddle, banjo, or accordion. Acts like Modest Mouse, Death Cab for Cutie, and the Arctic Monkeys topped the charts, bringing in a new era of indie acts that were, some critics said, not so indie any more. One music critic derisively referred to the proliferation of sound-alike indie bands as the "indie landfill."

As the first decade of the 2000s came to a close, the future of indie music as a viable underground scene was called into question. With indie bands like Arcade Fire still topping the charts, indie's mainstream success seemed to be in good health, but many critics and fans were left waiting to see what the "new sound" of indie would be like in the 2010s.

"I don't know what, precisely, to expect," wrote Nitsuh Abebe of the leading indie music online magazine *Pitchfork*, "but I can't think of another time in my life this 'indie' world has looked quite so ripe for shaking itself up."

David Larkins

For More Information

Abebe, Nitsuh. "The Decade in Indie." *Pitchfork* (February 25, 2010). http://pitchfork.com/features/articles/7704-the-decade-in-indie/ (accessed August 16, 2011).

Korducki, Kelli. "Is Indie Rock Dead?" *Varsity* (July 17, 2007). http://thevarsity.ca/articles/99 (accessed August 16, 2011).

Simon, Leslie. *Wish You Were Here: An Essential Guide to Your Favorite Music Scenes—From Punk to Indie and Everything In Between.* New York: Harper, 2009.

Skancke, Jennifer. *The History of Indie Rock.* Detroit: Lucent, 2007.

Spitz, Marc. "The 'New Rock Revolution' Fizzles." *Spin* (May 2010): 95.

iPods

The first portable audio players appeared in the 1960s, but did not become a widespread phenomenon until the release of the **Walkman** (see entry under 1970s—Music in volume 4) in 1979. Unlike earlier systems, which played music on small, tinny speakers, the Walkman allowed its user to listen to music on a pair of headphones. The Walkman was an analog device that played cassettes. Later, the Discman allowed users to play **compact discs** (CDs; see entry under 1980s—Music in volume 5) on the go. In the late 1990s, the first digital audio players—such as the Rio PMP300 and the Eiger Labs MPMan F10—began to appear on shelves.

These early players could only hold a few dozen songs and suffered from poor design and even worse interfaces. Steve Jobs (1955–2011), the chief executive officer (CEO) of **Apple Inc.** (see entry under 1970s—The Way We Lived in volume 4), saw an opening in the market at a time when his company was expanding into the market of personal digital devices. Designed in less than a year, the iPod made its premiere on October 23, 2001. Sales were initially slow. The market for digital audio players was a new one, and the first generation iPods could only interact with Apple computers, which held a small share of the **personal**

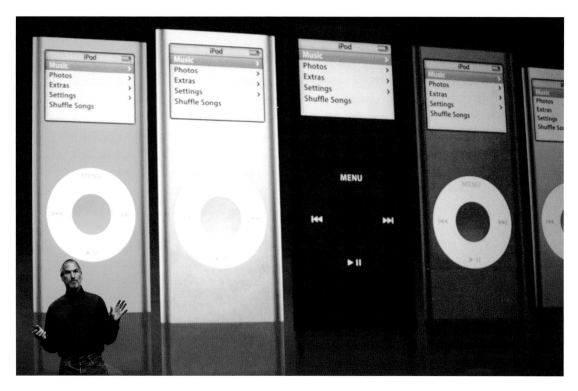

Apple CEO Steve Jobs introduces new iPod nanos in San Francisco on September 12, 2006. © DINO VOURNAS/REUTERS.

computer (see entry under 1970s—The Way We Lived in volume 4) market.

By 2004, with the market well established and PC-friendly iPods available, the iPod's popularity had exploded, constituting 70 percent of all personal audio players, digital or otherwise. The device's success was due to a variety of factors. Chief among these was Apple's commitment to consumer-friendly design and functionality. The iPod was relatively durable, had an easy-to-use "click wheel" interface, and sported a snazzy, modern design. The distinctive white earbud headphones that came with the iPod became a status symbol and fashion accessory, and Apple began to offer the iPod in a variety of colorful cases.

As the iPod grew in popularity, so did Apple's media player program, iTunes. Through the iTunes Store, customers could purchase and download music (and later videos) to play on their computers through iTunes or load onto their iPods. Successive generations of iPods offered larger storage capacities and longer battery lives, enabling consumers to amass huge portable digital music collections. The iTunes Store also allowed customers to purchase their music on an individual song-by-song basis, a radical change to music marketing conventions that had prevailed since the late 1960s. Previously, with the exception of commercial singles, consumers had been forced to buy a whole album even if they were only interested in one or two songs from the collection.

The iPod and iTunes were spearheads in the digital entertainment revolution that swept the industry from 2001 onwards. In 1998, as the first digital media players began to hit the market, the Recording Industry Association of America (RIAA) attempted to shut down the burgeoning technology, claiming digital music players encouraged piracy. The RIAA lost its suit, opening up the market to later dominance by Apple and the creation of a new model of music and movie marketing, the long-term implications of which still remained unclear a decade after the appearance of the first iPod.

David Larkins

For More Information

Kahney, Leander. *The Cult of iPod.* San Francisco: No Starch Press, 2005.

Knopper, Steve. *Appetite for Self-Destruction: The Spectacular Crash of the Record Industry in the Digital Age.* Berkeley, CA: Soft Skull Press, 2009.

Levy, Steven. *The Perfect Thing: How the iPod Shuffles Commerce, Culture, and Coolness.* New York: Simon & Schuster, 2007.

Beyoncé Knowles (1981–)

Beyoncé Knowles (often known as simply Beyoncé) has distinguished herself in a variety of areas in the entertainment world. She first gained popular attention as the lead singer for the 1990s **rhythm and blues (R&B)** (see entry under 1940s—Music in volume 3) trio Destiny's Child. In the 2000s, Beyoncé branched out as a solo pop artist, model, and actress. Her solo hits, such as "Crazy in Love" (2003) and "Single Ladies (Put a Ring on It)" (2008), were inescapable in the first decade of the 2000s.

Born on September 4, 1981, Beyoncé Giselle Knowles was already a multitalented performer by the age of seven. Singing and dancing in talent shows in her hometown of Houston, Texas, she developed the skills that would serve her well in the future. In high school, Beyoncé started singing with her cousin Kelly Rowland (1981–) and friends LaTavia Roberson (1981–) and LeToya Luckett (1981–). With Beyoncé's dad Matthew

Knowles (1951–) managing, the teens' group Girl's Tyme appeared on the popular talent-search TV program *Star Search* in 1992. Five years later, Columbia Records signed the group with its new name, Destiny's Child.

Destiny's Child was an instant success, scoring a top-five hit titled "No, No, No" from its self-titled debut album in 1998. The following year's album, *The Writing's on the Wall,* was even bigger, yielding three top-five hits, including the Grammy-winning "Say My Name."

Destiny's Child continued to be a presence on the R&B and pop charts with hits such as "Independent Women Pt. 1" and "Bootylicious," but there was trouble in the group as media and fan attention increasingly focused on Beyoncé. In 2001, she starred in a musical for **MTV** (see entry under 1980s—Music in volume 5) based on the opera *Carmen.* The next year she co-starred with comedian Mike Myers (1963–) in the feature film ***Austin Powers** in Goldmember* (see entry under 1990s—Film and Theater in volume 5).

Beyoncé released her first solo album, *Dangerously in Love,* in 2003. Her single "Crazy in Love" stayed at the top of the pop charts for two months. After Destiny's Child released its final album, *Destiny Fulfilled,* in late 2004, Beyoncé focused on distinguishing herself as a multifaceted solo performer. She received two Golden Globe awards for her lead role in the 2006 musical motion picture *Dreamgirls.* Her album *I Am … Sasha Fierce* (2008) sold more than seven million copies worldwide, largely due to the incredible popularity of the song "Single Ladies (Put a Ring on It)." In January 2009, Beyoncé performed Etta James's (1938–) classic ballad "At Last" at the Neighborhood Inaugural Ball, where the newly inaugurated **Barack Obama** (see entry under 2000s—The Way We Lived in volume 6) (1961–) and his wife Michelle (1964–) enjoyed their first dance together as president and first lady of the United States.

Michael Segretto

For More Information

Arenofsky, Janice. *Beyoncé Knowles: A Biography.* Westport, CT: Greenwood Press, 2009.

"Beyoncé." *RollingStone.com.* http://www.rollingstone.com/music/artists/beyonce/biography (accessed July 18, 2011).

"Beyoncé Knowles." *Internet Movie Database.* http://www.imdb.com/name/nm0461498/(accessed July 11, 2011).

Easlea, Daryl. *Beyoncé: Crazy in Love.* London: Omnibus, 2011.

Knowles, Beyoncé, Kelly Rowland, and Michelle Williams. *Soul Survivors: The Official Autobiography of Destiny's Child.* New York: Regan, 2002.

Lady Gaga (1986–)

Lady Gaga is the stage name of Stefani Joanne Angelina Germanotta (1986–). Raised in New York, she attended a private high school and later New York University's Tisch School of the Arts. Lady Gaga left college after her sophomore year to pursue a career in music. Ambitious and hardworking, she settled on dance music and adopted a new name in order to find success. Lady Gaga takes her name from the song "Radio Ga Ga," by the British rock band Queen. This is significant because Queen, especially lead singer Freddy Mercury (1946–1991), was famous for lavish and outrageous stage shows and Lady Gaga cites the group, along with David Bowie (1947–) and artist Andy Warhol (1928–1987), as key inspirations for her flamboyant public persona. By 2007, she was performing regularly in clubs and writing songs for acts including New Kids on the Block, Fergie (the stage name of Stacy Ferguson, 1975–), and **Britney Spears** (1981–; see entry under 1990s—Music in volume 5).

Lady Gaga's first album, *The Fame,* was released in 2008. Singles from the album topped the charts in the United States and all over the world. At the 2009 **MTV** (see entry under 1980s—Music in volume 5) Video Music Awards, Lady Gaga was named the best new artist; *Billboard* magazine gave her the Rising Star award that same year. Subsequent albums followed quickly—*The Fame Monster* in 2009 and *Born This Way* in 2011. These albums also received widespread critical acclaim while shooting to the top of the charts. The title song to *Born This Way* debuted at number one on the pop charts in February 2011.

What separates Lady Gaga from other pop stars in the eyes of fans, critics, and even academic theorists, is her self-conscious blending of music, fashion, and performance art. Lady Gaga has carefully crafted an image as a star, not unlike Bowie during the 1970s. She writes her songs, designs many of her outfits, and directs her stage show all with an eye on making a spectacle for the audience. As a celebrity, she seeks to entertain while trying to shock her audience into thought. For example, when she wore

Lady Gaga performs at Nokia Theatre L.A. Live on December 23, 2009, in Los Angeles.
© JEFF KRAVITZ/FILMMAGIC/ GETTY IMAGES.

a dress made entirely of raw meat to the MTV Video Music Awards in 2010, she spurred discussion in the media about issues from animal rights and women being treated "like pieces of meat" in American society. In 2010 and 2011, Lady Gaga began speaking out more on social issues, including raising money for relief after the earthquake in Haiti and the earthquake and tsunami in Japan. She is also a vocal supporter of equal rights for gay, lesbian, bisexual, and transgender people.

Patrick J. Walsh

For More Information

Callahan, Maureen. *Poker Face: The Rise and Rise of Lady Gaga.* New York: Hyperion, 2010.

Goodman, Lizzie. *Lady Gaga: Critical Mass Fashion.* New York: St. Martin's Press, 2010.

Herbert, Emily. *Lady Gaga: Behind the Fame.* New York: Overlook Press, 2010.

Lady Gaga Official Site. http://www.ladygaga.com/default.aspx#!tweets-official (accessed July 14, 2011).

Morgan, Johnny. *Gaga.* New York: Sterling, 2010.

Napster

Napster is a file-sharing program invented by Shawn Fanning (1980–) in 1999. The name of the program was taken from a nickname given to Fanning due to his **hairstyle** (see entry under 1900s—The Way We Lived in volume 1) at the time. Fanning wrote the original program while spending time at an **Internet** (see entry under 1990s—The Way We Lived in volume 5) company owned by his uncle, John Fanning (1963–), who later became the chief executive officer (CEO) of Napster. The program is widely regarded as the first successful peer-to-peer file-sharing software ever created; it allowed users with computers running the software (known as "peers") to exchange data files directly with other users. Napster was designed specifically for the exchange of digital music files, commonly known as MP3s. The program essentially allowed users to search through each other's digital music libraries and download their own copies of songs they wanted.

The file-sharing program was wildly successful, boasting more than twenty-six million users by 2001. However, Napster's success was short-lived. First, because college students were the main users of the program, many universities suffered major Internet traffic problems due to music-swapping and blocked use of the program through campus servers. Second, the exchange of copyrighted material—particularly unreleased songs from major artists like Metallica and **Madonna** (1958–; see entry under 1980s—Music in volume 5)—led to several lawsuits being filed against Napster. The music industry waged an all-out war against the downloading of songs, or music piracy, and aggressively pursued individuals involved in file-sharing activities. Some bands became vocal supporters of Napster and file-sharing. The band Radiohead's album *Kid A* (2000) was leaked onto Napster months before its release and became the band's first album to debut at number one in the United States, disproving the industry's claims that file-sharing substantially detracted from the success of musicians.

The original Napster service stopped operation in July 2001, and the company went bankrupt the following year. However, several other file-sharing programs like Gnutella and Kazaa sprang up in its place, all of which were targeted by anti-piracy groups. Napster later resurfaced as an online music subscription service which, other than the name and logo, bore little resemblance to the original file-sharing program.

Greg Wilson

For More Information

Ambrosek, Renee. *Shawn Fanning: The Founder of Napster.* New York: Rosen, 2007.

Knopper, Steve. "Napster Wounds the Giant." *Rocky Mountain News* (January 2, 2009). http://www.rockymountainnews.com/news/2009/jan/02/napster-wounds-the-giant/ (accessed August 22, 2011).

Menn, Joseph. *All the Rave: The Rise and Fall of Shawn Fanning's Napster.* New York: Crown, 2003.

Nickelback

Nickelback was one of the most popular rock bands of the first decade of the twenty-first century. The band's unusual name stems from the days when bassist Mike Kroeger (1972–) worked at the counter of a **Starbucks** (see entry under 1980s—Commerce in volume 5) **coffee** (see entry under 1990s—The Way We Lived in volume 5) shop, often finding himself handing customers their change while saying "Here's your nickel back." Along with his brother Chad Kroeger (1974–; vocals and guitar) and cousin Brandon Kroeger (drums), Mike formed the band that would have a significant influence on the contemporary rock scene.

Nickelback was founded in Hanna, a little town in Alberta, Canada. Guitarist Ryan Peake (1973–) rounded out the original lineup. The group recorded two albums for its own label before signing to Roadrunner and releasing *The State* in 1999. By that point Brandon Kroeger had left the band, leaving the drummer's spot to Ryan Vikedal (later drummers were Mitch Guindon [1970–] and Daniel Patrick Adair [1975–]. Although *The State* was not the breakout hit Roadrunner hoped it would be, the label's faith in Nickelback was justified by the band's next album. *Silver Side Up* was a tremendous hit in 2001, reaching number two on the album charts. The single "How You Remind Me," which drew on the heavy **grunge** (see entry under 1990s—Music in volume 5) sound popular in the early 1990s, went to number one.

From then on, Nickelback was a major force in the music industry, scoring additional hits with "Hero" from the ***Spider-Man*** (see entry under 1960s—Print Culture in volume 4) soundtrack in 2002, and "Someday," which hit the top ten in 2003 by recreating the "How You Remind Me" formula. Nickelback stayed true to its signature sound on *The Long Road* in 2003, *All the Right Reasons* in 2006, and *Dark Horse* in 2008. Each of the albums produced hit singles and zoomed into the top ten on album charts throughout the world. Nickelback ended the first decade of the twenty-first century having sold so much music that *Billboard* ranked the band as the top "Adult Pop Artist" of the decade.

Michael Segretto

For More Information

"Best of the 2000s: Adult Pop Artists." *Billboard.com.* http://www.billboard .com/#/charts-decade-end/adult-pop-artists?year=2009 (accessed July 18, 2011).

Leahey, Andrew. "Nickelback: Biography." *AllMusic.* http://www.allmusic.com/ artist/nickelback-p410589/biography (accessed July 11, 2011).

"Nickelback." *Rolling Stone.* http://www.rollingstone.com/music/artists/ nickelback/biography (accessed July 18, 2011).

Pandora

Pandora is an **Internet**-based service (see entry under 1990s—The Way We Lived in volume 5) that offers streaming music and a highly sophisticated recommendation service to introduce listeners to bands and artists they might enjoy. The service was launched in 2008 and offers both free subscription (which includes advertisements and limited use) and paid subscription options. The service is available on home computers as well as many mobile devices, including the iPad and most **smart phones** (see entry under 2000s—The Way We Lived in volume 6).

The core feature of Pandora is its application of the Music Genome Project, which was developed in 2000. The Music Genome Project attempts to define pieces of music based on hundreds of different traits or "genes," including rhythm, instrumentation, and chord patterns. In this way, the Music Genome Project creates a "genetic blueprint" of each piece of music in its database. Pandora can compare a song highly rated by a listener to all the other music in its database, and attempt to find songs similar in characteristics. The service relies upon input from the listener to continually improve its recommendation abilities; when a listener hears a new song, he or she can respond by giving it a "thumbs up" or "thumbs down." This helps determine how often a particular song or artist appears on the listener's playlist, and allows the recommendation algorithm to determine which musical qualities are most important to a listener.

In 2011, Pandora boasted approximately eighty million users. Like other Internet radio broadcasters, the company is required to pay higher song royalties than traditional or satellite radio stations. Despite this, Pandora became a publicly traded company in June 2011 with an estimated value of more than $2 billion.

Greg Wilson

For More Information
Cain Miller, Claire. "How Pandora Slipped Past the Junkyard." *New York Times* (March 7, 2010). http://www.nytimes.com/2010/03/08/technology/08pandora.html (accessed August 23, 2011).
Pandora Radio. www.pandora.com (accessed August 23, 2011).

Pop Country

Though born from the European **folk music** (see entry under 1960s—Music in volume 4) traditions of its originators, **country music** (see entry under 1940s—Music in volume 3)—in all its forms—is a truly original American musical tradition. Once considered the music of rural America, country music has since morphed into a phenomenon to rival the biggest hits on the pop charts. This new style of country, which blends old traditions and modern glamour, is known as pop country.

Rising from the American South during the earliest days of the twentieth century, country music evolved from European folk music. Acoustic instruments such as the guitar, banjo, violin, and mandolin were featured prominently in music meant to convey the hardships and heartaches of ordinary folks. In the heyday of **radio** (see entry under 1920s—TV and Radio in volume 2) in the 1930s and 1940s, country and **pop music** (see entry under 1940s—Music in volume 3) first blended in genres such as Western swing and honky tonk. Country songwriters and performers of this era, including Hank Williams (1923–1953), enjoyed widespread popularity and noticeable influence on the **rock and roll** (see entry under 1950s—Music in volume 3) musicians that followed them.

Through the years, country music started spreading its influence north of the Mason-Dixon line and beyond. Top hit makers such as **Elvis Presley (1935–1977)** (see entry under 1950s—Music in volume 3), the **Beatles** (see entry under 1960s—Music in volume 4), the **Rolling Stones** (see entry under 1960s—Music in volume 4), and **Bob Dylan (1941–)** (see entry under 1960s—Music in volume 4) dabbled in country, bringing it to a wider audience than ever. Pure country musicians such as Johnny Cash (1932–2003) and Willie Nelson (1933–) scored huge hits outside of the country charts. During the 1970s, country mingled with pop music with tremendous success, as Kenny Rogers (1938–), John Denver (1943–1997), Dolly Parton (1946–), and Crystal Gayle (1951–) toned down the style's rougher qualities to create a radio-friendly, polished sound pleasing to a large number of music listeners. Pop country continued to enjoy great popularity through the 1980s with such stars as Juice Newton (1952–) and Eddie Rabbit (1941–1998) and through the 1990s with Garth Brooks (1962–) and Shania Twain (1965–).

During the first decade of the 2000s, a new crop of stars kept the genre alive. In 2005, *American Idol* (see entry under 2000s—TV and Radio in volume 6) winner Carrie Underwood (1983–) scored a huge crossover hit with her debut single, "Inside Your Heaven." Two years later, she took home the first Grammy Award for best new artist given to a country artist since Shelby Lynne (1968–) in 2001. In 2008, Taylor

Swift (1989–) swept in as a fresh new talent on the pop country scene. Her singles "Love Story" (2008) and "You Belong with Me" (2009) broke records as the two best-selling country singles in history.

The contemporary pop country scene largely belonged to female artists following in the footsteps of earlier stars such as Parton, Twain, and the Dixie Chicks. However, male stars continued to make waves, such as when former Hootie and the Blowfish frontman Darius Rucker (1966–) released his first pop country record in 2008. *Learn to Live* was the first solo record to yield three number one country hits in a decade. With "Don't Think I Don't Think About It," he became the first African American to top the country charts since Charley Pride (1938–) scored with "Night Games" way back in 1983.

Michael Segretto

For More Information

Bonaguro, Alison. "Darius Rucker Is Breaking More Records." *CMT Blog* (August 5, 2009). http://blog.cmt.com/2009-08-05/darius-rucker-record-is-breaking-more-records/ (accessed July 11, 2011).

Marconette, Jaime. "Top 40 Singles of 2008: Darius Rucker—'Don't Think I Don't Think About It.'" *Roughstock* (December 16, 2008). http://www.roughstock.com/blog/top-40-singles-of-2008-darius-rucker-dont-think-i-dont-think-about-it- (accessed July 10, 2011).

Phares, Heather. "Carrie Underwood: Biography." *Billboard.com.* http://www.billboard.com/artist/carrie-underwood/bio/657654#/artist/carrie-underwood/bio/657654 (accessed July 10, 2011).

Sisario, Ben. "Record-Breaking Week for Taylor Swift." *New York Times* (February 25, 2009). http://artsbeat.blogs.nytimes.com/2009/02/25/record-breaking-week-for-taylor-swift/ (accessed July 10, 2011).

Pop Punk

The genre of pop punk combines the energy, fast tempos, and buzzsaw guitars of **punk** (see entry under 1970s—Music in volume 4) rock with the friendly melodies and more irreverent lyrical content of **pop music** (see entry under 1940s—Music in volume 3). In some ways, the Ramones, widely credited as the first pure punk group, also laid the groundwork for pop punk in later decades. Certainly many pop punk bands in the 1980s and 1990s proudly displayed their Ramones influences. Throughout the 1980s, bands like the Buzzcocks, the Undertones, and Bad Religion blurred the line between pop and punk, but it took the influence of hardcore punk bands like the Descendents and the Vandals to launch the true pop punk sound, pioneered by groups like Screeching Weasel and Social Distortion.

Pop punk went mainstream in the 1990s, spearheaded by the 1994 release of Green Day's *Dookie,* which spawned the hit songs "Longview," "Basket Case," and "When I Come Around." Hot on the heels of Green Day's success, the Offspring released *Smash* and enjoyed similar mainstream success, selling fourteen million albums by year's end. Like most punk bands, pop punk acts had been confined to the world of independent record labels and do-it-yourself production, but mainstream record labels soon came calling. By the decade's end, Green Day, the Offspring, Blink-182, and Lit all had major-label hit albums.

The first decade of the 2000s brought a new wave of pop punk bands like Sum 41, American Hi-Fi, New Found Glory, and Good Charlotte. Longtime fans of pop punk accused these new bands of simply chasing the latest trend and dismissed them as "bubblegum punk" (a play on the "bubblegum pop" label of the 1970s), yet the genre continued to enjoy massive popularity.

In 2004, Green Day released *American Idiot,* their seventh album. *American Idiot* was an ambitious rock opera and proved an immediate hit with fans and critics alike. It hit number one on the *Billboard* 200 chart and was named "Greatest Album of the Decade" in a **Rolling Stone** (see entry under 1960s—Print Culture in volume 4) magazine readers' poll.

David Larkins

For More Information

Diehl, Matt. *My So-Called Punk: Green Day, Fall Out Boy, the Distillers, Bad Religion—How Neo-Punk Stage-Dived into the Mainstream.* New York: St. Martin's Griffin, 2007.

Myers, Ben. *Green Day: American Idiots & the New Punk Explosion.* San Francisco: Disinformation Company, 2006.

Sanchez, George B. "White Punks on Warner Bros.: The Not-So-Covert Mainstreaming of Rancid." *East Bay Express* (November 5, 2003). http://www.eastbayexpress.com/gyrobase/white-punks-on-warner-bros/ Content?oid=1072038&storyPage=1 (accessed August 15, 2011).

2000s

Print Culture

As Americans turned from the paper and ink of printed material to the flicker and glow of computer screens, some questioned whether newspapers and books would become outdated media forms. Americans began to catch up on news on their smart phones instead of the morning edition of the paper. Rather than buying paperbacks at their local bookstores, readers downloaded novels to their e-readers from Amazon.com. In a decade where the value of information depended upon its speed, print seemed, to some, slow and outdated. Newspapers and magazines took heavy financial losses, and many moved to releasing online-only editions.

Still, books remained important to Americans seeking imaginative entertainment, whether they read by turning pages or scrolling down a screen. Following on the success of the *Harry Potter* books, series fiction for young readers, such as the *Percy Jackson* series and the *Twilight* series, drew in a new generation of readers. Adults seeking the thrill of suspense turned to the publishing sensations of *The Da Vinci Code* and, imported from Sweden, *The Girl with the Dragon Tattoo.* Perhaps the surest sign of success for these series is that all of them were adapted for film.

Not all best-selling books of the decade needed Hollywood to prove their appeal. Readers sought books for reasons other than cinema-style thrills. Memoirs, for example, became a popular genre, drawing readers enchanted by the lives of ordinary people, as well as the rich and famous. Sometimes readers flocked to books because of the questions they raised as well as the stories they told. Book groups remained a popular way for Americans to get together with friends to discuss a common reading, and increasingly such conversations also took place online. In this way and others, print culture did not disappear with the opening of the twenty-first century, but took on new forms. Americans were reading as much—perhaps more—than ever, but in new, technologically driven ways.

The Da Vinci Code

The Da Vinci Code (2003) is a mystery/thriller novel written by Dan Brown (1964–). It is the second in a series of books featuring intrepid Harvard professor Robert Langdon, whose study of ancient symbols leads to his involvement in uncovering various historical mysteries.

In *The Da Vinci Code,* Langdon is drawn into a murder investigation after the victim—curator of the Louvre Museum in Paris—leaves behind a message containing Langdon's name. As the prime suspect, Langdon breaks free from police surveillance with the help of cryptologist Sophie Neveu, granddaughter of the murdered curator, and sets out to discover the true murderer. His search leads to the discovery of a grand plot to discredit the Catholic Church by revealing a shocking truth about Jesus Christ: that he was married and had children with Mary Magdalene, a Christian disciple popularly viewed by many as a woman of low character or even a prostitute. In the novel, the Holy Grail—long considered to be the cup from which Jesus drank at the Last Supper—is actually the remains of Mary Magdalene, who was the vessel that carried the blood of Jesus (his children) within her.

Upon publication, *The Da Vinci Code* earned overwhelmingly negative reviews, with the author criticized equally for the novel's historical inaccuracies—many of which Brown has maintained are factual—and for its graceless writing style. But the book's criticisms were dwarfed by the attention paid to its controversial theory about Jesus. Catholic groups around the world condemned the book for its negative portrayal of their church as well as its fanciful theories. *The Da Vinci Code* was officially banned in Iran and Lebanon, and the 2006 film adaptation starring Tom Hanks (1956–) was banned in Pakistan, Sri Lanka, and other countries. Despite—or perhaps because of—the controversy, *The Da Vinci Code* became an international

best-seller (see entry under 1940s—Commerce in volume 3), with approximately forty million copies sold in its first two years in print.

Greg Wilson

For More Information

Miller, Laura. "The Last Word; The Da Vinci Con." *New York Times* (February 22, 2004). http://www.nytimes.com/2004/02/22/books/the-last-word-the-da-vinci-con.html (accessed September 16, 2011).

Newman, Sharan. *The Real History Behind the Da Vinci Code.* New York: Berkley Books, 2005.

Strobel, Lee, and Garry Poole. *Exploring the Da Vinci Code.* Grand Rapids, MI: Zondervan, 2006.

E-readers

E-readers, short for electronic readers, are handheld digital devices designed to function much like traditional books, but with several improved features. The first handheld devices with e-reader capabilities emerged in the 1990s, but the technology was cumbersome and the book selection severely limited. In addition, most early devices relied upon LCD screens that were difficult for users to stare at for extended periods due to glare. In 2006, Sony revolutionized the market with its first e-reader device. The Sony Reader utilized a display technology known as E Ink, which very closely resembled traditional ink and paper in appearance and ease of reading.

In 2007, online retail giant **Amazon.com** (see entry under 2000s—Commerce in volume 6) launched its own e-reader, the Kindle. The Kindle also sported an E Ink screen, but it provided another feature as well: wireless **Internet** (see entry under 1990s—The Way We Lived in volume 5) connectivity, which allowed readers to buy and download books directly to the Kindle instead of requiring the user to connect the e-reader to a computer for file transfers. Amazon supported the Kindle with a huge library of e-books available from its own online store, and the device quickly became the number one e-reader on the market.

The success of the Kindle inspired other companies to introduce their own e-readers, and has prompted some publishers to plan development of an e-book online store to compete against Amazon. One of the few retailers to rival Amazon and its Kindle successfully was **Apple** (see entry under 1970s—The Way We Lived in volume 4), whose tablet PC the iPad, can function as a large e-reader. In 2010, Apple's iBookstore

A Barnes & Noble Nook e-reader, a competitor to Amazon's Kindle. © NEWSCOM.

sold half a million e-books in its first month of operation. Still, Amazon remained the e-book leader. In May 2011, the company announced that its sales of e-books had surpassed sales of traditional paper books.

Greg Wilson

For More Information

Pogue, David. "New Kindle Leaves Rivals Farther Back." *New York Times* (August 25, 2010). http://www.nytimes.com/2010/08/26/technology/personaltech/26pogue.html (accessed August 30, 2011).

The Girl with the Dragon Tattoo

The Girl with the Dragon Tattoo is the first in a trilogy of mystery novels written by Swedish author Stieg Larsson (1954–2004) and published posthumously in Sweden in 2005. Along with its two sequels—*The Girl* who Played with Fire (2006) and *The Girl who Kicked the Hornet's Nest* (2007)—the novel was part of the "Millennium series," originally slated to include ten volumes. Larsson passed away of a heart attack in 2004 with just three books completed, though he reportedly left a nearly finished fourth novel as well as detailed outlines for some of the other installments.

The Girl with the Dragon Tattoo focuses on two main characters: Lisbeth Salander, a young female computer hacker with a traumatic past who uses her skills to earn a living as a private investigator; and Mikael Blomkvist, a publisher and investigative journalist (much like Larsson himself) who becomes involved, along with Salander, in a decades-old murder investigation. The character of Salander became a particular point of interest to many readers because she exacts violent revenge against men who abuse her.

Upon its original publication in Swedish, *The Girl with the Dragon Tattoo* became a **best-seller** (see entry under 1940s—Commerce in volume 3), and was chosen as the best novel of the year by the Crime Writers of Scandinavia. Translated versions of the book and its sequels soon became an international phenomenon, selling tens of millions of copies. The series was made into a trilogy of successful films in Sweden, and acclaimed director David Fincher (1962–) directed an English-language adaptation of *The Girl with the Dragon Tattoo* released in 2011.

Greg Wilson

For More Information

Baksi, Kurdo. *Stieg Larsson: The Man Behind "The Girl with the Dragon Tattoo."* New York: Gallery Books, 2011.

McGrath, Charles. "The Afterlife of Stieg Larsson." *New York Times* (May 20, 2010). http://www.nytimes.com/2010/05/23/magazine/23Larsson-t.html (accessed August 21, 2011).

Memoirs

In recent years, Americans have been fascinated by the memoir, a genre of literature in which writers share the true stories of their lives. **Best-seller** (see entry under 1940s—Commerce in volume 3) lists have been topped by firsthand accounts of celebrities rising to fame and ordinary people overcoming extraordinary obstacles. Some of the most successful books have included *The Liars' Club* (1996), an account by Mary Karr (1955–) of growing up in a troubled Texas family, and *Dreams from My*

Father: A Story of Race and Inheritance (1995), written by future president **Barack Obama** (1961–; see entry under 2000s—The Way We Lived in volume 6).

Autobiographical writing has always been an important part of American culture. In the first American best-seller, Puritan writer Mary Rowlandson (c.1637–1711) describes her ordeal as a prisoner of Native American captors. Benjamin Franklin's (1706–1790) account of his early years became a classic assigned to generations of American schoolchildren. Abolitionism (the movement to end slavery) was fueled by firsthand accounts of slavery's inhumanity, such as those written by escaped slave Frederick Douglass (1818–1895).

The recent memoir craze illustrates the fact that Americans continue to believe that all individuals can work hard and succeed. Celebrity memoirs allow American readers to see "rags-to-riches" stories in action. When they read accounts of more ordinary lives, readers empathize (feel

Former U.S. president Bill Clinton shakes hands with a woman at a book signing of his memoir My Life *at a Washington, D.C., bookstore on July 6, 2004.* © ALEX WONG/GETTY IMAGES.

compassion) and perhaps find strength to face their own hardships. One popular memoir type focuses on the quests of Americans to change their lives by taking on daily challenges. Popular novelist Barbara Kingsolver (1955–) wrote of her family's quest to eat only local foods for one year in *Animal, Vegetable, Miracle* (2007). In 2005, Julie Powell (1973–) published a memoir *Julie and Julia* about preparing all of the recipes in a cookbook by famous chef Julia Child (1912–2004) over the course of one year. Powell's book began as a **blog** (see entry under 2000s—The Way We Lived in volume 6), and in 2009, the book was adopted for film.

Since the appeal of memoirs lies in their truth, American readers have been outraged when a few popular memoirs were exposed as fabrications (made-up stories). James Frey's (1969–) memoir of overcoming drug addiction, *A Million Little Pieces,* became a bestseller after Oprah Winfrey (1954–) selected it for her **Oprah's Book Club** (see entry under 2000s—Print Culture in volume 6) in 2005. Journalists revealed that Frey had exaggerated the story of his confrontation with police officers and time in jail so that his book would be more dramatic. In other highly publicized cases of "fake" memoirs, controversy emerged when readers learned that writers had fabricated identities. Critics praised Margaret Jones's memoir of growing up as a mixed-race foster child among the gangs of inner-city Los Angeles, until investigators exposed that Jones was actually Margaret Seltzer (1975–), a white woman from a privileged background.

Some have criticized memoirs because they focus so extensively on extreme hardship and a writer's self-centered concerns. Nevertheless, the memoir remains a popular genre among Americans who want to learn about others' real-life stories, perhaps gaining new insights on their own.

Maureen Reed

For More Information

Barrington, Judith. *Writing the Memoir.* 2nd ed. Portland, OR: Eighth Mountain Press, 2002.

"James Frey and the *A Million Little Pieces* Controversy." *Oprah.com.* http://www.oprah.com/showinfo/James-Frey-and-the-A-Million-Little-Pieces-Controversy (accessed July 14, 2011).

Mendelsohn, Daniel. "But Enough About Me: What Does the Popularity of Memoir Tell Us About Ourselves?" *New Yorker* (January 25, 2010): 68.

Parini, Jay, ed. *The Norton Book of American Autobiography.* New York: Norton, 1999.

Yabroff, Jennie. "A Year of Selling Books." *Newsweek* (October 1, 2007): 84.

Yagoda, Ben. *Memoir: A History.* New York: Riverhead, 2009.

Zinsser, William, ed. *Inventing the Truth: The Art and Craft of Memoir.* Rev. ed. Boston: Houghton Mifflin, 1998.

Oprah's Book Club

In 1996, popular television **daytime talk show** (see entry under 1960s—TV and Radio in volume 4) host Oprah Winfrey (1954–) introduced a new component of her multimedia approach to entertainment: a book club. Winfrey selected books for her viewers to read and discuss, and episodes of the television show then focused on the book, sometimes featuring authors as guests. Motivated by her desire to inspire reading, as well as her own love of authors such as the Nobel Prize–winning Toni Morrison (1931–), Winfrey sought to create community through books.

Author Toni Morrison, seen here on November 12, 1996, promoting her new book Song of Solomon, *was one of the first authors to appear on Oprah Winfrey's Book Club segment.* © REUTERS/LANDOV.

New fiction and **memoir** (see entry under 2000s—Print Culture in volume 6), usually on subjects appealing to women readers, formed the bulk of the books that Winfrey selected: the first book chosen was Jacquelyn Mitchard's (1956–) novel *The Deep End of the Ocean* (1996), about the trauma faced by a mother whose young son is abducted, and the second was Toni Morrison's *Song of Solomon* (1977), the story of an African American family. Oprah's Book Club temporarily suspended recommendations in 2002, renewing itself a year later as a forum for "classics" that revived popular interest in books such as William Faulkner's (1897–1962) *Light in August* (1932) and Leo Tolstoy's (1828–1910) *Anna Karenina..* Eventually, contemporary authors became part of the book club again, much to the delight of publishers, who found that Winfrey's recommendations offered tremendous boosts in sales.

The spotlight offered by Oprah's Book Club occasionally created controversy. Jonathan Franzen (1959–), whose novels *The Corrections* (2001) and *Freedom* (2010) were both selected by Winfrey, spoke out in 2001 about fearing that Winfrey's endorsement would jeopardize the serious literary reputation of his work. When *The Corrections* was awarded the 2001 National Book Award, however, Franzen thanked Winfrey for her support. Winfrey also found herself at the center of a controversy about memoirs and truthfulness when she promoted *A Million Little Pieces* by James Frey (1969–). Frey's account of overcoming drug addiction ultimately proved to be exaggerated and, in some instances, falsified; Winfrey publicly confronted and chastised Frey for letting down his readers.

Oprah's Book Club also played a role in inspiring readers to form book clubs of their own. Whether readers came together to affirm friendships or discuss common interests, the 1990s and 2000s saw the rise of the book club phenomenon. Winfrey's Web site offered tips on how to form book groups, guiding readers through choosing members, books, meeting locations, and menus. Publishers began adding lists of discussion questions, aimed at book groups, to new releases. Book groups varied in how seriously they approached discussion—and, perhaps, not all members, not even in Oprah's Book Club, read all of the books. Yet book groups offered readers a way to come together to celebrate both community and reading in a world where online contact sometimes seemed to take precedence over in-person discussion, and where new media seemed to threaten books.

Maureen Reed

For More Information

Donahue, Deirdre. "Has Oprah Saved Books? But Some Wonder If People Are Really Reading." *USA Today* (December 12, 1996): 1D.

Farr, Cecilia Konchar. *Reading Oprah: How Oprah's Book Club Changed the Way America Reads.* New York: State University of New York Press, 2004.

"How to Start a Book Club." *Oprah.com* (June 22, 2008). http://www.oprah.com/oprahsbookclub/How-to-Start-Your-Own-Book-Club (accessed August 11, 2011).

"Oprah's Book Club Collection." *Oprah.com.* http://www.oprah.com/packages/oprahs-book-club-selections.html (accessed August 11, 2011).

Rooney, Kathleen. *Reading with Oprah: The Book Club That Changed America.* 2nd ed. Fayetteville: University of Arkansas Press, 2008.

Saslow, Linda. "Not in a Book Group Yet? Everybody Else Is." *New York Times* (December 5, 1999): 14LI.

Percy Jackson Series

The ***Harry Potter*** (see entry under 1990s—Print Culture in volume 5) book and film franchise heralded a massive shift in young adult and children's literature. Suddenly long books were fashionable, especially if they were published in a series. So too was "urban fantasy," a genre juxtaposing our own modern, urban world with elements of the fantastic. For Rick Riordan (1964–), an English and history teacher and great lover of Greek mythology, this shift proved timely. Based on bedtime stories he had read to his son in the early 1990s, his *Percy Jackson* novels fit in perfectly with the market created by *Harry Potter* and were eagerly sought out by young readers looking for the next series to sink their teeth into once the final installment in the *Potter* series came out.

Like Harry Potter, the eponymous hero of the *Percy Jackson* series is an ordinary kid, a bit of an underdog. He is not physically strong, he is a poor student due to his attention deficit hyperactivity disorder and dyslexia, and he has an abusive stepfather. In the course of the first novel, *The Lightning Thief* (2005), Percy discovers that he is actually the son of the Greek god Poseidon and that he may be destined to fulfill a great prophecy. He goes off to train at Camp Half-Blood, where he becomes friends with fellow demigods and mythological creatures and together they fight against an array of monsters from Greek and Roman myth.

In the tradition of urban fantasy, Percy's adventures through the world of Greek mythology are cleverly interwoven with the modern world. The Greek gods still dwell on Olympus, for example, but rather than being on top of a tall mountain, it is now located on the six hundredth floor of the **Empire State Building** (see entry under 1930s—The Way We Lived in volume 2).

Due to Riordan's sharp and often sardonic writing and his action-packed plots, the *Percy Jackson* novels rose above the increasingly crowded field of juvenile fantasy novels that exploded onto the literary market in the first decade of the 2000s. Four years after *The Lightning Thief*'s publication, the book had sold over 1.2 million copies. A further four novels completed the critically acclaimed series by 2009. A film based on the first book was released in 2010.

David Larkins

For More Information

Italie, Hillel. "*Potter* Publisher Looks to Promote Next Big Thing." *Fox News* (September 1, 2008). http://www.foxnews.com/wires/2008Sep01/0,46 70,Books39Clues,00.html (accessed August 15, 2011).

Mabe, Chauncey. "Rick Riordan: Percy Jackson vs. Harry Potter." *Sun Sentinel* (May 14, 2009). http://weblogs.sun-sentinel.com/features/arts/offthepage/blog/2009/05/rick_riordan_percy_jackson_vs_1.html (accessed August 15, 2011).

Shulman, Polly. "Harry Who?" *New York Times* (November 13, 2005). http://www.nytimes.com/2005/11/13/books/review/13shulman.html (accessed August 15, 2011).

A movie poster for Percy Jackson's The Lightning Thief *in New York City on December 17, 2009.* © ROB KIM/LANDOV.

Twilight

In 2005, author Stephenie Meyer (1973–) published *Twilight,* a young adult novel about a teenage girl who falls in love with a vampire. The book immediately became a **best-seller** (see entry under 1940s—Commerce in volume 3). Three more books followed, completing one of the decade's most popular book series: *New Moon* (2006), *Eclipse* (2007), and *Breaking Dawn* (2008). The release of each sequel became a highly publicized event, with crowds dominated by young women filling

Both as Young Adult novels and a film franchise, Twilight *is a hit among readers and moviegoers.* © NEWSCOM.

bookstores for release parties. Meyer—who transformed herself from stay-at-home mother to publishing sensation after a dream inspired her to begin writing the first novel—ultimately sold over one hundred million copies of books in the series that became known as the *Twilight Saga*.

At the beginning of the series, seventeen-year-old Isabella Swan, known as Bella, moves from Phoenix, Arizona, to the small town of Forks, Washington. Edward Cullen, a boy at her new high school, intrigues Bella because he is different and mysterious. She soon learns that he is a vampire, part of a family of vampires that lives in Forks. Endangered by the lust that Edward and rival vampires have for her blood, Bella willingly enters into a dangerous quest to pursue her love for Edward. The series follows her as she endures Edward's absence (he flees to protect her), befriends a werewolf named Jacob Black (he falls in love with Bella), travels to Italy to save Edward, fights off rival vampires, marries Edward, bears a child, and becomes a vampire herself.

By the end of 2010, films based on the first three novels of the series had been released, with attendance records rivaling that of films based on the ***Harry Potter* series** (see entry under 1990s—Print Culture in volume 5). Comparisons between the two series became common, with some noting that while *Harry Potter* appealed to both male and female readers, *Twilight* fans were overwhelmingly female. The *Twilight* series, despite its elements of suspense and the supernatural, is ultimately driven by a love story. Many readers have noted that Meyer, a devout Mormon (a member of the Church of Jesus Christ of Latter-day Saints), created a moralistic tale in which resistance to vampires can be seen as an analogy for resistance to premarital sex. Bella is ultimately a fairly traditional heroine, one who remains chaste (pure) until marriage. Nevertheless, because Bella's desire, and her quest to fulfill it, is central to the story, many twenty-first-century young women have found her story extremely appealing.

Maureen Reed

For More Information

Acocella, Joan. "In the Blood: Why Do Vampires Still Thrill?" *New Yorker* (March 16, 2009): 101.

Beahm, George. *Bedazzled: A Book About Stephenie Meyer and the "Twilight" Phenomenon.* Nevada City, CA: Underwood Books, 2009.

Meyer, Stephenie. *The Twilight Saga: The Official Illustrated Guide.* New York: Little, Brown, 2011.

Shapiro, Marc. *Stephenie Meyer: The Unauthorized Biography of the Creator of the "Twilight Saga."* New York: St. Martin's Griffin, 2010.

"Stephenie Meyer." *Hachette Book Group.* http://www.hachettebookgroup.com/teens_authors_Stephenie-Meyer-%281070099%29.htm (accessed August 8, 2011).

StephenieMeyer.com. http://www.stepheniemeyer.com/ (accessed August 8, 2011).

The Twilight Saga. http://www.thetwilightsaga.com/ (accessed August 8, 2011).

Yao, Laura. "Bitten and Smitten." *Washington Post* (August 1, 2008): C01.

2000s

Sports and Games

The sports scene of the first decade of the 2000s was dominated by a diverse roster of athletes excelling in a wide range of sports. Barry Bonds (1964–) distinguished himself as one of baseball's greatest stars by breaking numerous records. He took home seven Most Valuable Player awards, knocked out seventy-three home runs in a single season (2001), and hit a career total of 762 home runs—the all-time Major League record—before retiring. LeBron James (1984–) towered above his peers on the basketball court as he led the Cleveland Cavaliers to the NBA Finals for the first time in team history and scooped up bronze and gold medals as a member of the USA national team in the 2004 and 2008 Olympics. Over on the tennis court, sisters Venus Williams (1980–) and Serena Williams (1981–) racked up twenty wins in the Grand Slam tournament between them (seven for Venus; thirteen for Serena). Watchers of the 2008 Olympics cheered as swimmer Michael Phelps (1985–) brought home eight gold medals, matching Soviet gymnast Alexander Dityatin's (1957–) previous record as the most decorated Olympic athlete in history. Bicyclist Lance Armstrong (1971–) dazzled fans with his staggering speed, stamina, and personal courage. Despite being diagnosed with brain and testicular cancer in 1996, Armstrong won the grueling Tour de France a record seven consecutive times between 1999 and 2005.

While achievements such as these by "superathletes" were certainly inspiring, average sports fans found ways to get in the game from the privacy of their own living rooms. In 2006, Nintendo released a new game console called the Wii. Instead of the hand-operated joysticks and controllers common to video games of the past, the Wii functioned with a wireless controller detecting a variety of movements. Numerous Wii games required players to physically copy the movements a player would make if they were bowling in an actual alley or hitting fly balls on an actual baseball diamond. For the first time, playing video games actually became a form of physical exercise.

Sports fans interested in the more intricate aspects of professional athletics took up fantasy sports, in which players pretend to be team owners building and managing their own baseball, basketball, hockey, soccer, or football teams. They then competed against each other based on the actual statistics of the individual members of the teams they assembled. Though fantasy sports leagues had long been a popular hobby for sports fans, the Internet made the technical aspects of running a fantasy league much easier. According to the Fantasy Sports Trade Association, thirty-two million people over the age of twelve in the United States and Canada participated in fantasy sports in 2010, up 60 percent from 2006.

Whether in fantasy or reality, American remained devoted to the standard roster of major sports in the first decade of the twenty-first century. However, they also made room for a newer sport that offered an exotic form of competition: mixed martial arts (MMA), promoted through the Ultimate Fighting Championship (UFC) company. UFC bouts pitted fighters from different martial arts and fighting traditions against each other. Televised bouts regularly drew more than one million viewers, leading broadcasters, network executives, advertisers, athletes, and fans alike to declare MMA the "sport of the future."

Lance Armstrong (1971–)

Lance Armstrong is the most successful and famous American cyclist in history. His greatest achievement was winning the Tour de France—the world's most prestigious cycling race—a record seven times. That Armstrong accomplished this feat after surviving a bout with cancer only makes his string of victories more remarkable. He was born in Plano, Texas, in 1971. A highly active and athletic child, Armstrong took an early interest in running, swimming, and cycling. At thirteen, he won the Iron Kids triathlon and turned professional in that sport at sixteen. After being courted by the U.S. Cycling Federation, however, Armstrong decided to focus his intense rigor and discipline on bicycle racing. His success came quickly. In 1990, he took eleventh place at the World

Lance Armstrong wins his seventh Tour de France race on July 24, 2005. © AP IMAGES/ PETER DEJONG.

Amateur Cycling Championships and the following year, he won the American amateur crown.

Armstrong then turned professional as a cyclist and began to win major international races. By 1996, he had risen to the number one ranking in the world, but winning the sport's most prestigious race, that of the month-long Tour de France, still eluded him. In 1996, he fell ill during the race and was forced to withdraw. His performance in the **Olympic Games** (see entry under 1900s—Sports and Games in volume 1) that year also proved disappointing. In October 1996, Armstrong was diagnosed with testicular cancer and his career appeared to be over.

Armstrong suffered through brain surgery—which became necessary after his cancer spread—and chemotherapy, but he made a full recovery. Still, cycling fans were surprised when he announced that he was returning to the sport in 1998, only a year after beating cancer. In 1999, Armstrong competed in the Tour de France and fans delighted as he won four stages and easily took the overall competition. This victory lifted Armstrong into the top tier of American sports figures and gave new prominence to cycling in the United States.

If this triumph had been the peak of Armstrong's career, it would have been an inspiring story. Incredibly, he won the next six consecutive Tours. Four cyclists had won the Tour de France five times over their careers but none had dominated the sport as Armstrong did. In 2005, after completing his seventh consecutive victory, Armstrong announced his retirement from bicycle racing.

Outside of cycling, Armstrong founded the Lance Armstrong Foundation in 1997. The organization supported people battling cancer and worked to improve the quality of life for cancer survivors. Each October 2, the day Armstrong himself was diagnosed, the foundation hosts numerous "LIVESTRONG Day" events to raise money to fight cancer and to increase public awareness about the issue. In 2007, over two hundred fifty LIVESTRONG Day events were held nationally. In just two years, seven million LIVESTRONG wristbands were sold at a price of $1 each, raising millions of dollars.

After Armstrong's string of victories, the sport of cycling was riddled with scandals involving the use of performance-enhancing drugs. Numerous champions were stripped of their titles, including the winner of the 2006 Tour de France, Floyd Landis (1975–). Armstrong was accused of doping many times, but never failed a drug test.

After briefly considering a career as a marathon runner, Armstrong returned to cycling again in the late 2000s. Seeking his eighth Tour de France victory, he finished third in 2009. Officially retiring from professional cycling again in February 2011, Armstrong has earned his place as the most famous cyclist in history and is among the greatest of all sports champions.

Patrick J. Walsh

For More Information

Armstrong, Lance, and Sally Jenkins. *Every Second Counts.* New York: Random House, 2003.

Armstrong, Lance, and Sally Jenkins. *It's Not About the Bike: My Journey Back to Life.* New York: Berkley Trade, 2000.

Coyle, Daniel. *Lance Armstrong's War.* New York: HarperCollins, 2005.

Lance Armstrong Official Site. http://www.lancearmstrong.com/ (accessed August 8, 2011).

LIVESTRONG.COM. http://www.livestrong.com/ (accessed August 9, 2011).

Wilcockson, John. *Lance: The Making of the World's Greatest Champion.* New York: Da Capo Press, 2009.

Barry Bonds (1964–)

Barry Bonds has hit more home runs than any other player in the history of Major League Baseball, both in a single season and over the course of an entire career. Bonds, who left **baseball** (see entry under 1900s—Sports and Games in volume 1) after the 2007 season, was also a talented base stealer and outfielder. Statistically, Bonds is one of the top players in baseball history. Sadly, his career and legacy have been tarnished by allegations that he broke the rules of the game by using performance-enhancing drugs in order to increase his strength. Because of these allegations, Bonds became entangled in court cases. In 2011, he was convicted of obstruction of justice, though this decision did not prove whether or not he had cheated in his quest to be the greatest slugger of all time.

Bonds is the son of three-time all-star Bobby Bonds (1946–2003), who played fourteen seasons in the majors between 1968 and 1981. In the younger Bonds's twenty-two-year career with the Pittsburgh Pirates and the San Francisco Giants, he hit 762 homers, surpassing Hank Aaron's (1934–) 755 and the 714 hit by **Babe Ruth** (1895–1948; see entry under 1910s—Sports and Games in volume 1). In 2001, Bonds

Barry Bonds of the San Francisco Giants hits against the Florida Marlins on May 29, 2006. © AP IMAGES/TOM DIPACE.

also broke the record for most home runs in a single season. He hit seventy-three, breaking Mark McGwire's (1963–) short-lived record of seventy, set just three years before. Such amazing slugging numbers had not always been Bonds's claim to fame, however. In fact, he hit over forty home runs only once in his first ten years in the majors. At Pittsburgh, where he played his first seven seasons, Bonds established himself as a great all-around player, hitting for average, stealing bases, and playing in the outfield. As a fielder, Bonds won an impressive eight Gold Gloves, the award given to the top defensive player at each position.

After the 1992 season, Bonds signed what was then the most lucrative contract in baseball history, $43 million over six years, with the San Francisco Giants. The Giants were special to Bonds. It was for the Giants that his father and his godfather, the great Willie Mays (1931–), played most of their careers. In San Francisco, Bonds's offensive statistics ballooned. After his thirtieth birthday, when most hitters' numbers fall, Bonds began hitting for more power and higher average. Even as he slugged his seventy-three homers in 2001, rumors began about the use of banned steroids. In testimony before a grand jury, Bonds stated that he believed that injections given to him, which were apparently steroids, had been flaxseed oil and arthritis medicine, substances not banned by Major League Baseball. Although many associates alleged that Bonds knowingly took steroids, not enough evidence was presented in court to prove this claim. By the end of his career, fans were split regarding whether or not they thought Bonds was "clean."

Bonds was named Most Valuable Player in the National League seven times, more than any other player in history. He is the greatest home run hitter ever. Yet his place in the Hall of Fame remains unclear, a sad ending to an amazing career.

Patrick J. Walsh

For More Information

Fainaru-Wada, Mark, and Lance Williams. *Game of Shadows: Barry Bonds, BALCO, and the Steroids Scandal That Rocked Professional Sports.* New York: Gotham, 2007.

Official BarryBonds.com Site. http://www.barrybonds.com/ (accessed on July 12, 2011).

Pearlman, Jeff. *Love Me, Hate Me: Barry Bonds and the Making of an Antihero.* New York: HarperCollins, 2006.

Boston Red Sox and the "Curse of the Bambino"

The "Curse of the Bambino" was one of the great superstitions in American sports. It referred to the inability of **baseball**'s see entry under 1900s–Sports and Games in volume 1) Boston Red Sox to win the World Series after the team sold Babe Ruth (1985–1948; see entry under 1910s–Sports and Games in volume 1) to the New York Yankees in 1920. The origin of the term itself is not completely clear, but most sources state that it was adopted by fans from the title of Dan Shaughnessy's (1953–) book on the Red Sox, *The Curse of the Bambino* (1990). "Bambino," Italian for "baby," refers to Ruth himself.

Early in the twentieth century, the Boston Red Sox were a highly successful team. They won the World Series five times between 1903 and 1918. The final three of these victories were won in large part because of the Sox's young star, Ruth. Ruth was a pitching and hitting phenomenon. In 1918, for example, he won thirteen games as a pitcher and led the league in home runs. In 1919, Ruth set the record for home runs in a season. The following year, Red Sox owner Harry Frazee (1986–1929) sold Ruth to the New York Yankees in order to finance a **Broadway** (see entry under 1900s—Film and Theater in volume 1) show.

After Ruth left the Red Sox, the team could not win a championship. In fact, the Sox finished last every year but two between 1923 and 1932. Between 1946 and 1986, the Red Sox appeared in the World Series four times. Each time they won three games but lost a deciding game seven. In game six of the 1986 series, the Red Sox were one strike away from beating the New York Mets for the series win. On a 2-2 count, relief pitcher Bob Stanley (1954–) threw a wild pitch, letting in the tying run. After batter

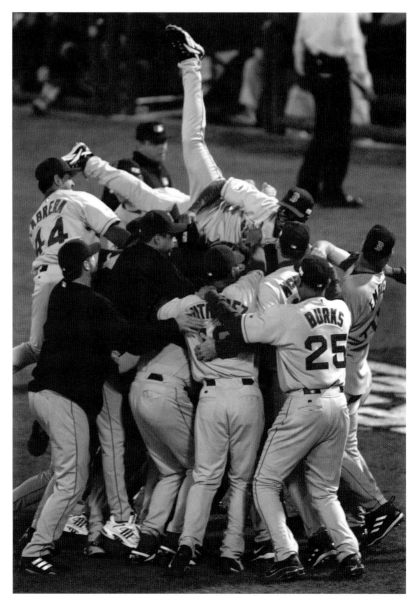

Pokey Reese jumps on his teammates after the Boston Red Sox defeated the St. Louis Cardinals in Game 4 of the 2004 World Series, their first Series win since 1920. © AP IMAGES/MARK HUMPHREY.

Mookie Wilson (1956–) fouled off two pitches, he hit a slow ground ball that rolled through the legs of first baseman Bill Buckner (1949–), allowing the Mets to win the game. The next day, the Mets took the title.

In 2004, the so-called curse came to an end when the Red Sox beat the St. Louis Cardinals, the team they had lost to in 1946 and 1967, to win the World Series. Some very superstitious fans have noted that the Cardinal who made the final out, Edgar Renteria (1976–), wore number three, also Ruth's number. Even if no real curse existed, the eighty-six-year drought made for an excruciating wait for Red Sox fans, many of whom wondered what would have happened if only Ruth had never left their team.

Patrick J. Walsh

For More Information

"The Curse of the Bambino." *Sports Illustrated.com.* http://sportsillustrated.cnn.com/baseball/mlb/news/2000/03/22/the_curse_timeline/#top (accessed July 14, 2011).

"History of 'the Curse of the Bambino.'" *NBC Sports* (October 28, 2004). http://nbcsports.msnbc.com/id/6323070/ (accessed July 14, 2011).

The Curse of the Bambino (video). Home Box Office, 2003.

Shaughnessy, Dan. *The Curse of the Bambino.* New York: Dutton, 1990.

Shaughnessy, Dan. *Reversing the Curse: Inside the 2004 Boston Red Sox.* Boston: Houghton Mifflin, 2005.

Computer Games

Computer gaming in the twenty-first century has experienced a dramatic shift toward more casual and social gaming experiences. Prior to 2000, computer gaming was largely a solitary activity that required sophisticated hardware and a relatively advanced skill level from players. In addition to mouse and keyboard controls, many games required users to memorize and utilize keyboard commands. The wide variety of computer hardware available also meant that gamers would often have to tweak different settings, both within the game and within their computer's operating system, in order to get a game to function properly.

One of the most fundamental changes in computer gaming occurred not because games became more sophisticated, but rather because less sophisticated, casual games allowed inexperienced gamers an entry point into the gaming world. Titles like *Bejeweled*—released in 2001 by casual gaming giant PopCap Games—relied upon simple controls and easily understandable game mechanics to attract players intimidated by higher-profile games. These casual games could be played in any web browser and usually only required a few minutes to complete.

At the other end of the gaming spectrum, complex single-player game experiences gave way to multiplayer games such as *Battlefield 1942* (2002), which utilized **Internet** (see entry under 1990s—The Way We Lived in volume 5) connectivity to allow as many as sixty-four players to compete against each other or as teams in mock combat. At around the same time, developers began experimenting with the creation of persistent virtual worlds in which users could interact with each other and where the virtual world did not cease to exist just because users turned off their computers. *Second Life* (2003) was a major milestone in the creation of persistent virtual worlds. In the game, users could buy property, interact with other players, and engage in other activities much like those in the real world.

The concepts of large-scale multiplayer games and persistent virtual worlds came together in massively multiplayer online role-playing games (MMORPGs). The most successful example of a MMORPG is *World of Warcraft* (2004), a fantasy-themed adventure game in which players can create an alter ego from a variety of available races and character classes. The game's fantasy world is populated by other players, also participating in real-time, as well as other characters and creatures. Many players choose to join a group, or guild, and work together to complete quests and improve their characters' abilities. In 2011, *World of Warcraft* boasted more than eleven million subscribers, making it the most successful massively multiplayer online game in the world.

The trends of casual gaming and social gaming came together with the rise of social networking sites such as **Facebook** (see entry under 2000s—The Way We Lived in volume 6). Games such as *FarmVille* and *Mafia Wars* are linked directly into social networking accounts and encourage players to interact with other users to achieve goals. With more than two hundred million active players each month in 2011, social network games grew into a multibillion-dollar business and confirmed that computer gaming was, at last, recognized as mainstream entertainment.

Greg Wilson

For More Information

Hof, Robert D. "My Virtual Life." *Bloomberg Businessweek* (May 1, 2006). http://www.businessweek.com/magazine/content/06_18/b3982001.htm (accessed September 28, 2011).

Ward, Mark. "Casual Games Make a Serious Impact." *BBC News* (March 18, 2008). http://news.bbc.co.uk/2/hi/technology/7301374.stm (accessed September 28, 2011).

Fantasy Sports

Fantasy sports is a term used to describe a type of statistics game that revolves around the real-world performance of athletes in different professional sports. In a fantasy sports league, each participant, known as a "manager," chooses a team of players from the current players within a professional sports league, such as the **National Football League** (NFL; see entry under 1920s—Sports and Games in volume 2). Generally this is done through a mock "draft," where each manager selects a single player each round according to predetermined order, much like an actual sports league draft. In the end, managers have their own fictional team created from real players across the league.

Fantasy sports are played concurrently with the actual sport season. As games are played, real-world player statistics—for example, the number of successful base hits in **baseball** (see entry under 1900s—Sports and Games in volume 1) or the number of yards run in football—are tallied for each player and converted into a score. This yields a point score for each player. Each week, the manager of a fantasy sports team adds up the point scores for all the players on his fictional team. This score is generally compared against another fantasy team in the same league, and the team with the higher score is the winner for the week. Ultimately, the fantasy teams with the best winning record face off to determine the overall league winner.

Although fantasy sports were conceived decades ago, their popularity exploded with the spread of the **Internet** (see entry under 1990s—The Way We Lived in volume 5), which allowed fantasy team managers quick and easy access to detailed player statistics. It is estimated that one in five American males age twelve and over participates in fantasy sports each year. Some sports writers have criticized the growing popularity of fantasy sports, suggesting that they overshadow the actual sports upon which they are based. Another common criticism of fantasy sports is that it emphasizes the importance of individual performance over real-world team accomplishments, since each fantasy sports team consists of players from different teams in a league.

Greg Wilson

For More Information

ESPN Fantasy Games. http://search.espn.go.com/espn-fantasy-games/ (accessed August 12, 2011).

Harmon, Michael. *The Savvy Guide to Fantasy Sports.* Indianapolis, IN: Indy-Tech, 2005.

Klayman, Ben. "Technology Spurs Growth of Fantasy Sports." Reuters. September 25, 2008. http://www.reuters.com/article/2008/09/25/us-fantasysportsnews-idUSTRE48O1VE20080925. (accessed August 12, 2011).

Tozzi, Lisa. "The Great Pretenders." *Austin Chronicle* (July 1, 1999). http://www.austinchronicle.com/issues/vol18/issue44/xtra.fantasy.html (accessed September 17, 2011).

LeBron James (1984–)

LeBron James is one of the most famous living figures in professional sports. As a star forward for the Miami Heat in the **National Basketball Association** (NBA; see entry under 1940s—Sports and Games in volume 3), James commands constant media attention off the court. On the court, his six-foot-eight-inch, 240-pound frame, coupled with quickness and tremendous strength, lead to comparisons with all-time great **Michael Jordan** (1963–; see entry under 1990s—Sports and Games in volume 5). Although James can be a dominant player and has been named an NBA All-Star seven times and league Most Valuable Player twice, he is also a genuinely selfless player, passing the ball to teammates and working hard to support them during games.

Born in Akron, Ohio, James was already a nationally recognized star in his teens. In fact, he appeared on the cover of ***Sports Illustrated*** (see entry under 1950s—Sports and Games in volume 3) before he finished high school. Like only a handful of other players, James skipped college and went directly into the NBA from high school. His story as a player was even more compelling because he joined the Cleveland Cavaliers, his "hometown" team. James was rookie of the year in the 2003–2004 season and quickly made the Cavaliers into a contender for the NBA championship. James came close, reaching the NBA Finals in 2007 and the Eastern Conference Finals in 2010.

In July 2010, the sports world held its breath as James, a free agent, decided whether to remain in Cleveland or move to another team in search of a championship. In an announcement carried live on television, James declared his decision to leave the Cavaliers for the Miami Heat, where he was joined by two more major stars, Chris Bosh (1984–) and Dwyane Wade (1982–). James did little to dampen expectations, promising fans

*The Cleveland Cavaliers'
LeBron James shoots for two
against the Denver Nuggets
on November 5, 2003.*
© NATHANIEL S. BUTLER/NBAE/
GETTY IMAGES.

that the Heat would win upwards of seven titles. The Heat immediately became the favorite to win the NBA championship and the central focus of media attention. James himself became less popular with fans, many of whom felt he had betrayed his home state by seeking to create a dominant team elsewhere. In his first season with Miami, however, James was no more successful than he had been in Cleveland. The Heat struggled early in the season though the team easily made the playoffs. They advanced to the NBA Finals where they were defeated by the Dallas Mavericks. James's quest for a title remained unfulfilled at the end of the 2010–2011 season, but his stature as a basketball legend in the making was unquestioned.

Patrick J. Walsh

For More Information

Freedman, Lew. *LeBron James: A Biography.* Westport, CT: Greenwood Press, 2007.

LeBron James. http://lebronjames.com/ (accessed July 11, 2011).

Pluto, Terry, and Brian Windhorst. *LeBron James: The Making of an MVP.* Cleveland, OH: Grey & Company, 2009.

Michael Phelps (1985–)

Former University of Michigan swimmer Michael Phelps shows off his gold medal during the 2009 FINA World Championships in Rome.
© QUINN ROONEY/GETTY IMAGES.

Michael Phelps is an American swimmer who dominated the sport for most of the first decade of the twenty-first century. Some argue that he is among the greatest athletes in history. By 2011, Phelps was the world record holder in seven different events. He has also won fourteen gold medals and two bronze medals at the summer **Olympic** (see entry under 1900s—Sports and Games in volume 1).

Phelps was raised in a suburb of Baltimore, Maryland, the son of a state trooper and a middle school teacher. Phelps began swimming when his two older sisters joined a local swim team. His long arms made him a natural in the pool and when he watched the swimming at the 1996 Olympic Games in Atlanta, Georgia, Phelps began dreaming of one day competing at that level himself. Central to Phelps's success was meeting his coach, Bob Bowman, who coached him at the University of Michigan and during the 2004 and 2008 Olympics. Under Bowman, Phelps qualified for the 2000 Olympics at the age of fifteen. The following year, before turning sixteen, Phelps broke the world record in the 200-meter butterfly.

Phelps soon rose to become a dominant swimmer in a number of events. At the 2003 World Championships, Phelps broke three world records. The following year, Phelps won eight medals—six of them gold—at the Olympic Games in Athens, Greece. In the process, he set two more world records. Over the next four years, Phelps dominated the world of swimming, winning countless championships and setting more world records. The apex of Phelps's career came with the 2008 Olympic Games in Beijing, China. Going into the competition, Phelps was a favorite in all eight races that he entered. In front of a global audience, he won every race (three of them as part of a relay team) and set seven world records. By doing so, he surpassed the record seven gold medals won by Mark Spitz (1950–) at the 1972 Olympics, a seemingly unsurpassable mark.

Phelps is perhaps the most dominant athlete in the history of swimming. He has set world records an astounding thirty-nine times. He will long be the measure by which other great athletes are measured.

Patrick J. Walsh

For More Information

Phelps, Michael. *Beneath the Surface.* Champaign, IL: Sports Publishing, 2008.

Phelps, Michael, and Alan Abrahamson. *No Limits: The Will to Succeed.* New York: Free Press, 2009.

Schaller, Bob. *Michael Phelps: The Untold Story of a Champion.* New York: St. Martin's Griffin, 2008.

UFC and Mixed Martial Arts

Debuting in 1993, the Ultimate Fighting Championship (UFC) showcased a new type of sport fighting known as mixed martial arts (MMA). Initially decried as barbaric and even called "human cockfighting" by U.S. senator John McCain (1936–) of Arizona, the UFC gradually gained mainstream acceptance through the 1990s by instituting rules and regulations that reduced the chance of injury to fighters. By the middle of the first decade of the 2000s, the popularity of UFC-style competitions was skyrocketing, positioning MMA as a rival to boxing and wrestling in cultural relevance and profitability.

The history of "no holds barred" fighting matches goes back to ancient Greece and Rome, but by modern times sanctioned sport fighting tended to be rigidly controlled. For example, boxers were only allowed to punch above the waistline, were not allowed to grapple their opponents or attempt takedowns, and had to wear padded gloves. East Asian martial arts like karate, kickboxing, and judo all operated under similar restrictions specific to their individual styles. Through the twentieth century,

Georges St-Pierre (kicking) defeats Matt Hughes in UFC mixed martial arts on December 29, 2007, in Las Vegas, Nevada.
© JOSH HEDGES/ZUFFA LLC/GETTY IMAGES.

however, there arose proponents of mixing different **martial arts** (see entry under 1960s—The Way We Lived in volume 4) styles from East and West. Bruce Lee (1940–1973), called "the father of mixed martial arts," was a vocal proponent of borrowing effective techniques from a variety of styles. In Brazil, the Gracie family developed their own unique form of judo, called Gracie Jiu-Jitsu, and established a standing challenge that they could beat any other martial artist of any style.

In 1993, the Brazilian no-holds-barred fighting style pioneered by the Gracies came to the United States in the form of the UFC. Initially, the UFC resembled the Gracie Challenge: any fighter of any style could enter, with the idea being to find "the most effective style" through tournament elimination bouts. There were practically no rules. Head butts and other potentially dangerous moves were legal, and the match lasted until knockout or submission with no rounds or weight classes. Over the course of the 1990s, the UFC gradually instituted more rules in order to find broader mainstream appeal. Furthermore, as the Gracie-style emphasis on takedowns and holds dominated competition, MMA evolved into a style all its own, one that largely supplanted the traditional martial arts styles that had dominated sport fighting for over a century.

Ten years after its first bout, however, the UFC was still facing millions of dollars in losses and potential bankruptcy. The turning point came in 2005, when the UFC launched a reality competition show called *The Ultimate Fighter* on the cable network Spike TV. With the sport's visibility significantly raised, revenues from ticket and pay-per-view sales began to soar. The 2006 *UFC 66* special was the first in UFC history to exceed one million purchases.

UFC matches also moved beyond pay-per-view, with cover stories on UFC fighters appearing in **Sports Illustrated** (see entry under 1950s—Sports and Games in volume 3) magazine in 2007 and extensive coverage on sports network **ESPN** (see entry under 1970s—TV and Radio in volume 4) beginning in 2009. The UFC signed endorsement deals with major advertisers and began buying up or merging with other MMA organizations like World Extreme Cagefighting and Japan's Pride Fighting Championships. Despite two fatalities after MMA bouts between 2007 and 2010, states that had previously banned the sport in the 1990s began to allow matches during the first decade of the 2000s. The UFC and MMA showed every sign of increasing their popularity still further through the 2010s.

David Larkins

For More Information

Fontanez, Erik. "UFC Mirrors NBA and NFL Rise to Mainstream with Strikeforce Purchase." *MMAWeekly.com* (March 13, 2011). http://mmaweekly.com/ufc-mirrors-nba-and-nfl-rise-to-mainstream-with-strikeforce-purchase (accessed August 15, 2011).

Gentry, Clyde. *No Holds Barred: Ultimate Fighting and the Martial Arts Revolution.* Preston, England: Milo Books, 2003.

Gerbasi, Thomas. *UFC Encyclopedia.* Indianapolis, IN: DK/Brady Games, 2011.

Miller, Matthew. "Ultimate Cash Machine." *Forbes* (May 5, 2008).

Snowden, Jonathan, and Kendall Shields. *The MMA Encyclopedia.* Toronto: ECW Press, 2010.

Telander, Rick. "Sweet Science Morphing into Brutality TV." *Chicago Sun-Times* (October 11, 2006). http://web.archive.org/web/20071012154640/http://findarticles.com/p/articles/mi_qn4155/is_20061011/ai_n16768457 (accessed August 15, 2011).

Shaun White (1986–)

The sport of snowboarding grew rapidly in popularity during the first decade of the 2000s, and a major reason for this trend is Shaun White, whose genial personality and long red hair (which earned him the nickname "Flying Tomato") made him a popular symbol of the sport. White was born with a heart condition, called Tetralogy of Fallot, and as an infant he endured multiple surgeries to correct it. By the age of six, he was well enough to play actively, including taking up snowboarding. His talent was immediately obvious, earning him a sponsorship with Burton snowboards while he was still in elementary school. Skateboarding legend Tony Hawk (1968–) also took notice of the nine-year-old White, amazed at the skills of someone so young. As a teenager, White won five amateur titles before competing in his first X Games in 2002. White has been a fixture of the X Games ever since, winning over a dozen medals, more than anyone else.

White's career was given a boost when the International Olympic Committee decided to add snowboarding to the competition, beginning with the 1998 Winter **Olympics** (see entry under 1900s–Sports and Games in volume 1). In 2006, White competed at the Olympics in Torino, Italy. He won the gold medal in the halfpipe competition and emerged as a global celebrity. In the intervening years before the next Olympics, White won scores of other competitions including three more golds at the annual Winter X Games. At the 2010 Olympics in Vancouver, British Columbia, Canada, all eyes were on White, the favorite and best-known competitor. If he was nervous he did not show it, unveiling a spectacular new move, the "Double McTwist 1260," on his way to a dominant, gold-medal performance.

White's informal demeanor and happy-go-lucky personality contribute greatly to his popularity, especially with young people. He is a star who appears to be a normal person and who does not seem to take himself too seriously. In this way he reflects the informality of

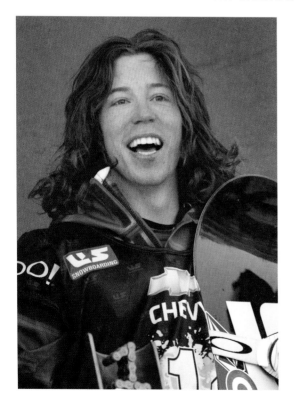

Shaun White after winning the Chevrolet U.S. Snowboard Grand Prix Freeway Half Pipe on December 15, 2007, in Breckenridge, Colorado. © DOUG PENSINGER/ AFP/GETTY IMAGES.

snowboarding culture. Yet White is also a businessman. He has signed endorsement deals with many companies including Target, Red Bull, Hewlett-Packard, and American Express. These contracts earn him millions of dollars each year.

Patrick J. Walsh

For More Information

"Shaun White." *New York Times.* http://2010games.nytimes.com/athletes/shaun-white-usa.html (accessed August 17, 2011).

Shaun White Official Website. http://www.shaunwhite.com/ (accessed August 9, 2011).

Young, Jeff C. *Extreme Athletes: Shaun White.* Greensboro, NC: Morgan Reynolds, 2008.

Wii

The Wii is a **video game** (see entry under 1970s–Sports and Games in volume 4) console created by Nintendo that features a motion-activated control system. The Wii was released during the Christmas 2006 shopping season, and its limited availability led to crowds of frenzied shoppers camping out at stores in an attempt to purchase one. The Wii quickly became the top-selling non-portable game system in the world, easily beating out both Microsoft's Xbox 360 and Sony's PlayStation 3. More than eighty million Wiis have been sold worldwide, and the minigame collection *Wii Sports*—usually included with each new system purchased—has earned the title of best-selling video game of all time.

The Wii's motion control system requires special accessories included with the console. A motion sensor bar must be placed on or near the television screen, and each player must hold a special remote that contains accelerometers and optical sensors. The remote can be pointed at the television to select items on the screen, similar to a laser pointer or light gun. It can also sense movements, such as the simulated swing of a golf club or rapid shaking back and forth. Games that have enjoyed the greatest success on the Wii tend to focus on generating physical activity, such as *Wii Sports,* in which players participate in simulated athletic contests such as tennis and boxing. The exercise game *Wii Fit,* which requires the use of a special balance board, also proved wildly successful, selling more than twenty million units.

Teens play tennis with the Nintendo Wii. © ROBYN BECK/NEWSCOM.

Some gamers have dismissed the Wii as a "kiddie" console, noting that the motion controls are mainly utilized for simple, casual gaming experiences. The console also failed to deliver high-definition graphics in an era where consumers were rapidly making the transition to **high definition TVs** (see entry under 2000s—The Way We Live in volume 6). However, the Wii also earned praise for opening up the gaming market to a whole new group of potential customers that traditionally avoided video games.

Greg Wilson

For More Information

Orland, Kyle. *Wii for Dummies.* Hoboken, NJ: Wiley, 2008.
Smith, Tracy. "The Big Ideas Behind Nintendo's Wii." *Bloomberg Businessweek* (November 16, 2006). http://www.businessweek.com/technology/content/nov2006/tc20061116_750580.htm (accessed August 22, 2011).

Venus Williams (1980–) and Serena Williams (1981–)

Venus and Serena Williams, sisters born just a year apart, dominated women's tennis in the first decade of the 2000s. Each attained the top ranking in the world during the decade and both won more than twenty Grand Slam titles. Coached and managed from a very early age by their father, Richard Williams (1942–), and their mother, Oracene Price (1952–), Venus and Serena combine power with finesse on the court.

Now glamorous global celebrities, the Williams sisters began learning tennis on public courts in Compton, California, a low-income, high-crime section of Los Angeles. Both girls excelled in youth tournaments, and the family moved to West Palm Beach, Florida, in 1990 so the sisters could train at a well-known tennis academy there. Despite the focus on tennis, Venus and Serena's parents tried hard to let them grow up as normally as possible, even stepping away from the tournament circuit for a few years. Also significant in their experience as excellent young players was the fact that as African Americans playing in a sports almost completely dominated by whites, they faced increased scrutiny and even discrimination on and off the court.

Venus is the elder of the two sisters and she was first to make her mark in professional tennis. She turned pro at fourteen, and while still a teenager, she made the final of the U.S. Open on her first try. She played a powerful, hard-hitting style of tennis and is reported to have hit the fastest recorded serve in a tournament of any woman player ever. After first winning championships in doubles, Venus won her first Grand Slam singles title at Wimbledon in 2000. She has won there four times since. After a dominant period in the early years of the first decade of the 2000s, Venus's career faltered in the middle of the decade, in part due to injury. After 2007 she made a comeback, including a victory at Wimbledon in 2009 when few expected her to advance far into the tournament. Venus has a total of at least nine Grand Slam titles and forty-three singles titles overall.

Despite battling numerous injuries, Serena has had a long career near the top of the rankings as well. Her first Grand Slam singles title came at the 1999 U.S. Open, where she beat the defending champion, Lindsay Davenport (1976–) and then the number one player in the world, Martina Hingis (1980–). In July 2002, she rose to the number one ranking in the world, a position she has held several times since.

Serena played a power game, mostly from the baseline, but was also known to take risky shots, a habit that made her exciting to watch. Perhaps her greatest victory came in 2007 after she returned from a knee injury. Despite being ranked eighty-first in the world and widely regarded as out of shape, she prevailed in the Australian Open. Overall, Serena has won thirteen Grand Slam singles titles and is the most recent woman to complete the slam by winning the Australian Open, Wimbledon, the French Open, and U.S. Open in a row. By 2009, she had won more prize money than any other woman athlete in history.

Venus and Serena have played each other in a number of Grand Slam title matches. Because of their strong support of one another, it is difficult to call it a rivalry, but their confrontations on the court have often led to exciting matches. They have met twenty-three times in competition, with Serena winning thirteen times. In Grand Slam finals, however, Serena's edge is greater, at six to two. In addition to their success as singles players, the Williams sisters have won many titles together as a doubles team. Between 1999 and 2010, the sisters won twelve Grand Slam doubles titles and an **Olympic** (see entry under 1900s–Sports and Games in volume 1) gold medal.

Both sisters have made names for themselves off the court as well. Venus is the chief executive officer of an interior design firm, V Starr Interiors. She is also a fashion designer with her own line of clothing. Serena is interested in fashion as well and has done some modeling. She is engaged in charitable work, notably helping to fund the construction of a school in Kenya. She has also been active in campaigns against breast cancer. Together, Venus and Serena are partial owners of the Miami Dolphins in the **National Football League** (NFL; see entry under 1920s–Sports and Games in volume 2).

Patrick J. Walsh

For More Information

Edmondson, Jacqueline. *Venus and Serena Williams: A Biography.* Westport, CT: Greenwood Press, 2005.

Serena Williams. http://www.serenawilliams.com/ (accessed August 10, 2011).

Venus Williams. http://www.venuswilliams.com/ (accessed August 10, 2011).

Williams, Serena. *Queen of the Court.* New York: Simon & Schuster, 2009.

Williams, Serena, and Daniel Paisner. *On the Line.* New York: Grand Central, 2009.

Williams, Venus, and Kelly E. Carter. *Come to Win: Business Leaders, Artists, Doctors and Other Visionaries on How Sports Can Help You to the Top of Your Profession.* New York: Amistad, 2010.

2000s

TV and Radio

Television in the first decade of the 2000s could largely be summed up by two words: reality television. The genre of unscripted footage of real people interacting in "real" situations had been a minor one until the summer of 2000, when the American version of *Big Brother* and a new show called *Survivor* premiered. The shows were a sort of long-form game show in which various everyday people competed in a nominally real environment, such as a house or an exotic locale, in a variety of physical and mental challenges over a period of weeks. The contestants had to work together to a point, and then turn on each other in pursuit of the final large cash prize.

The format proved immediately arresting, and *Survivor* clones such as *The Amazing Race, Temptation Island, The Mole, The Bachelor, The Bachelorette,* and many others made their debuts. Although some, including *Survivor* and *Big Brother,* were still airing by the end of the decade, most were quickly forgotten by both a fickle viewing public and increasingly irritated critics who decried the lack of intelligent, scripted programming on broadcast television.

As it turned out, there was room for those sorts of shows, but they were no longer airing on the major networks. Shows like *The Sopranos, Deadwood,* and *Mad Men* aired on cable networks like HBO and AMC and proved wildly popular with critics and viewers alike. Almost an antidote to the perceived emptiness of reality television, these series featured complex characters, intricate story lines spanning multiple seasons, unexpected twists, and sophisticated psychological portraits of the human experience. The popularity of these shows—as well as the proliferation of original series on basic cable and Conan O'Brien's (1963–) eventual move in 2010 from NBC to TBS—reflected the rising popularity and increased access to cable television in American homes. By 2009, scripted television was making a comeback against reality shows. A second generation of reality shows, such as *American Idol* and *Dancing with the Stars,* tended to be of a more "talent show" variety reminiscent of 1980s shows like *Star Search* and *Circus of the Stars.*

The state of radio in the 2000s perhaps best reflected the chaotic, uncertain state of the entertainment industry in the face of evolving digital technology. MP3 players like the iPod rapidly eclipsed the radio, once the only way to access music and broadcast entertainment while on the go. Broadcast radio stations were threatened by the appearance of satellite and Internet radio that allowed listeners to customize their listening preferences. In response, many radio stations began streaming their broadcast feeds over the Internet. Others, like Los Angeles' legendary KNAC, switched over to an Internet-only format entirely.

At the end of the decade, both television and radio looked towards the Internet and digital streaming as the probable future of mass entertainment. Web sites like Hulu, operating in concert with networks, offered on-demand access to shows from current and past seasons. Digital subscription services like TiVo gave viewers the option to record their favorite shows automatically and watch them at their leisure, skipping over commercials in the process. It was clear the old business models were changing rapidly. Heading into the 2010s, the only question that remained was how the new model would shape up.

American Idol

On June 11, 2002, a pop culture phenomenon debuted that would hold America in its thrall for the rest of the 2000s decade. Every week, a parade of people with dreams of pop stardom—plus a select few with the right stuff—auditioned for a panel of sometimes encouraging, sometimes downright cruel, judges. Television viewers tuned in to *American Idol* as much to cheer on the winners as they did to jeer at the often

Comments from American Idol *judges (L to R) Randy Jackson, Paula Abdul, and Simon Cowell can help make or break a contestant.* © RAY MICKSHAW/AMERICAN IDOL PROD./19 TELEVISION/FOX TV NETWORK/FREMANTLE MEDIA NORTH AMERICA/THE KOBAL COLLECTION/ART RESOURCE, NY.

off-key, unintentionally (and occasionally intentionally) humorous folks who did not make the cut. The show went on to become the most-watched American series of the decade.

American Idol was conceived after British producer Simon Fuller (1960–) saw an Australian program titled *Popstars*. In 2001, that show inspired Fuller's own *Pop Idol,* a British **reality TV** (see entry under 1990s–TV and Radio in volume 5) series in which contestants compete for a shot at a career as a pop singer. A quartet of judges and home viewers voting via phone and text messaging decided each week who would progress to the next level of the game after watching contestant auditions. Although there were some genuinely good singers, many hopefuls gave somewhat embarrassing performances. The sharply worded assessments judge Simon Cowell (1959–), a British record company executive, offered to these unfortunate contestants became one of the most famous, and infamous, aspects of the program.

Less than a year after its first airing in the United Kingdom, *Pop Idol* came to the Fox network in America as *American Idol*, with Cowell in tow. Grammy-winning producer Randy Jackson (1956–) and former pop idol Paula Abdul (1962–) rounded out the original judges' panel. Just as it had been in Britain, *American Idol* was an instant sensation in America. That first season concluded with the victory of twenty-year-old Kelly Clarkson (1982–), who went on to have numerous smash hits beginning with her debut single "A Moment Like This."

Clarkson was not the only Idol to achieve a successful pop career in their own right. Stars such as Carrie Underwood (1983–), Katharine McPhee (1984–), Adam Lambert (1982–), and Jennifer Hudson (1981–, who later won an Academy Award) got their starts on the show. Although Abdul and the controversial Cowell would eventually leave the program to make way for a new revolving selection of celebrity judges, *American Idol* was still at the top of the entertainment heap as the next decade dawned.

Michael Segretto

For More Information

Fuller, Simon. "Simon Fuller on How *Idol* Began." *Variety* (May 20, 2011). http://www.variety.com/article/VR1118037190?refcatid=14 (accessed July 14, 2011).

Halperin, Shirley. *"American Idol": Celebrating 10 Years.* New York: Abrams Image, 2011.

Mock, Janet, and Julia Wang. "Kelly Clarkson Biography." *People.com.* http://www.people.com/people/kelly_clarkson/biography (accessed July 14, 2011).

Rushfield, Richard. *"American Idol": The Untold Story.* New York: Hyperion, 2011.

CSI: Crime Scene Investigation

CSI: Crime Scene Investigation is a dramatic television series centered on a team of criminalists in Las Vegas. The team was originally led by Gil Grissom (played by William Petersen, 1953–), but ex-showgirl Catherine Willows (played by Marg Helgenberger, 1958–) became the supervisor of the crime lab after Grissom's retirement. Other regular cast members include George Eads (1967–) as criminalist Nick Stokes and

Paul Guilfoyle (1949–) as homicide detective Jim Brass. In the show's ninth season, acclaimed actor Laurence Fishburne (1961–) became a regular member of the cast.

Since its debut in 2000, *CSI* has become known for its flashy and often gruesome visualizations of trauma inflicted on victims in each episode. Typically, the cases are solved thanks to forensic evidence—everything from fibers and blood spatters to DNA and fingerprints—gathered by the criminalists. The show often focuses on the seedier side of Vegas life; for example, criminal investigator Warrick Brown (played by Gary Dourdan, 1966–) is a recovering gambling addict. The show also famously uses the song "Who Are You" by the band the Who as its theme.

CSI has been criticized for what some see as an unrealistic portrayal of the role criminalists play in homicide investigations. Typically, crime scene analysts collect and interpret evidence, but homicide detectives perform the bulk of the investigating. Regardless of criticism, the formula has proven successful: *CSI* is the most popular television drama in the world. The series has also spawned two successful spinoffs: *CSI: Miami,* starring David Caruso (1956–), and *CSI: NY,* starring Gary Sinise (1955–).

Greg Wilson

For More Information

"CSI Show 'Most Popular in World.'" *BBC News* (July 31, 2006). http://news.bbc.co.uk/2/hi/entertainment/5231334.stm (accessed July 14, 2011).

Fletcher, Connie. *Crime Scene: Inside the World of the Real CSIs.* New York: St. Martin's Paperbacks, 2006.

Ramsland, Katherine M. *True Stories of "C.S.I.": The Real Crimes Behind the Best Episodes of the Popular TV Show.* New York: Berkley Boulevard, 2008.

Smith, Tracy. "Why TV Crime Shows Are to Die For." *Sunday Morning* (May 16, 2010). http://www.cbsnews.com/stories/2010/05/16/sunday/main6488704.shtml (accessed August 21, 2011).

The Daily Show

The Daily Show with Jon Stewart, a news parody television show airing on **cable TV** (see entry under 1970s–TV and Radio in volume 4) network Comedy Central, premiered in 1996 but did not begin to make a lasting cultural impact until the year 2000. The show's original host,

Craig Kilborn (1962–), was replaced by comedian Jon Stewart (1962–) in 1999, and the show's focus, which had been an equal mix of entertainment news and human interest stories, began to shift in a more explicitly political direction. The contentious 2000 election, covered by *The Daily Show* under the parodist name "Indecision 2000," gave the show its focus and identity that it would retain for the remainder of the decade.

That identity could be broadly categorized as intelligent satire of American politics. As the show's popularity took off, it came to occupy a curious and distinctly post-modern position in American politics and popular culture, functioning simultaneously as "both the smartest, funniest show on television and a provocative and substantive source of news," as the **New York Times** (see entry under 1900s–Print Culture in volume 1) put it in a 2008 article. A 2007 study conducted by the Pew Research Center found Stewart tied for fourth alongside "serious" news anchors Brian Williams (1959–), Tom Brokaw (1940–), Dan Rather (1931–), and Anderson Cooper (1967–) as "most admired journalist." A 2009 online poll posted by **Time** (see entry under 1920s—Print Culture in volume 2) magazine named Stewart as the most trusted newscaster on television, comfortably ahead of the broadcast news anchors.

These were truly remarkable accolades for a show that had never billed itself as a legitimate source of news, one that featured reporters with titles like "Senior Child Molestation Correspondent." Yet Stewart's catchphrase of "Are you insane!?"—often shouted rhetorically at footage of a politician or public figure acting in a particularly hypocritical manner—struck a chord with Americans in the post-2000 election, post-**9/11** (see entry under 2000s—The Way We Lived in volume 6) world. Repeated polls and studies found that the show's millions of viewers skewed towards the better-educated and younger end of the spectrum. Some media analysts even expressed concern that *The Daily Show* was actually encouraging increased cynicism and apathy among younger viewers.

The Daily Show was also widely criticized as having a liberal bias. The show's creators offered the defense that the show came into its own during a time in which the Republican Party dominated all three branches of the federal government, virtually guaranteeing that most of its satire for much of the decade would be directed at that party. Regardless of perceived biases, the show's popularity ensured it a place as a venue for public figures to be seen. The show's interview segment hosted world leaders, politicians, military officers, and entertainers from the full range of political ideologies.

The Daily Show came into its own during the financial crisis of 2008–2009 and the concurrent election and inauguration of **Barack Obama** (1961–; see entry under 2000s—The Way We Lived in volume 6). Obama appeared on the show shortly before the 2008 election, drawing over three million viewers. *The Daily Show*'s coverage of Obama's subsequent inauguration drew a similar level of viewership. In March 2009, Stewart initiated a feud with financial news network CNBC, particularly singling out its reporters Rick Santelli (1953–) and Jim Cramer (1955–), that drew national media attention. The keys to the show's ongoing success could be seen in Stewart's week-long attack on CNBC, which he accused of abandoning its journalistic integrity in favor of shilling Wall Street interests right up to the 2008 financial crisis. Stewart's culminating interview with Cramer, airing on March 12, 2009, reflected public frustration with both Wall Street's perceived greed and American journalism's declining standards.

Throughout *The Daily Show*'s remarkable rise to cultural relevance over the course of the first decade of the 2000s, Stewart and his team continued to insist they were just a bunch of comedians. Yet it was perhaps the show's sardonic, half-smirking, half-cringing approach to serious stories over the course of a dark and troubled decade that brought it such a large audience of viewers looking for a little sugar to help them swallow what were often bitter pills of reality.

David Larkins

For More Information

Cave, Damien. "If You Interview Kissinger, Are You Still a Comedian?" *New York Times* (October 24, 2004). http://www.nytimes.com/2004/10/24/weekinreview/24cave.html (accessed September 22, 2011.)

Goodnow, Trischa, ed. *"The Daily Show" and Rhetoric.* Lanham, MD: Lexington Books, 2011.

Kakutani, Michiko. "Is Jon Stewart the Most Trusted Man in America?" *New York Times* (August 15, 2008). http://www.nytimes.com/2008/08/17/arts/television/17kaku.html (accessed September 22, 2011).

Levin, Gary. "Fans Like Their Dose of *Daily* News." *USA Today* (October 6, 2003). http://www.usatoday.com/life/television/news/2003-10-06-daily_x.htm (accessed September 22, 2011).

Morin, Richard. "Jon Stewart, Enemy of Democracy?" *Washington Post* (June 23, 2006). http://www.washingtonpost.com/wp-dyn/content/article/2006/06/22/AR2006062201474.html (accessed September 22, 2011).

Stewart, Jon. *The Daily Show with Jon Stewart Presents America (The Book) Teacher's Edition: A Citizen's Guide to Democracy Inaction.* New York: Grand Central Publishing, 2006.

Dancing with the Stars

Reality TV (see entry under 1990s—TV and Radio in volume 5) shows were *the* television sensation of the early 2000s. Following the smash success of ***American Idol*** (see entry under 2000s—TV and Radio in volume 6), other competition-based reality game shows began appearing on American television. One of the most popular was *Dancing with the Stars.* Professional dancers and celebrities from the worlds of acting, music, sports, modeling, and elsewhere team up to win the championship. Viewers assisted a panel of judges in deciding which team possessed the most dazzling dance skills.

Like *American Idol, Dancing with the Stars* started on British television. *Strictly Come Dancing* debuted in 2004, a year before crossing the Atlantic Ocean and landing in America as *Dancing with the Stars.* The program initially aired on ABC in a series of month-long mini-seasons. In its first season, host Tom Bergeron (1955–) presented performances by an eclectic array of once-popular stars hoping to revive their careers, including model Rachel Hunter (1969–), singer Joey McIntyre (1972–) of the 1980s pop group New Kids on the Block, and boxer Evander Holyfield (1962–). Kelly Monaco (1976–) of the **soap opera** (see entry under 1930s—TV and Radio in volume 2) *General Hospital* was the first star to dance her way to victory.

Dancing with the Stars expanded to two, two-month-long seasons per year in its third season. The show's basic concept has since spread across the globe. By 2008, variations had popped up in thirty-eight countries, including Russia, Israel, China, Brazil, Poland, Sweden, Pakistan, Estonia, and Turkey. Colin Jarvis (1972–), director of BBC TV in the United Kingdom, attributed the series' popularity to its niceness, telling BBC News that television viewers had become tired of the confrontation and tension that have long been ingredients of *American*

Former pop group *N Sync member Joey Fatone and Kym Johnson take to the floor in 2007 on Dancing with the Stars. © CAROL KAELSON/BBC AMERICA/ABC-TV/THE KOBAL COLLECTION/ART RESOURCE, NY.

Idol. He suggested that *Dancing with the Stars* drew in viewers by offering "a bit of glamour and dressing up." Meanwhile in America, appearances by stars such as Joey Lawrence (1976–), Mel B (1975–), Marie Osmond (1959–), Brooke Burke (1971–), and Kelly Osbourne (1984–) kept viewers tuning in throughout the early 2000s.

Michael Segretto

For More Information

"Strictly 'World's Most Watched.'"*BBC News* (November 10, 2008). http://
news.bbc.co.uk/2/hi/entertainment/7719968.stm (accessed July 14, 2011).
Washington, Julia E. "*Dancing with the Stars* Steps Its Way Toward Its 100th
Episode." *Cleveland Plain Dealer* (April 30, 2008). http://www.cleveland
.com/entertainment/index.ssf/2008/04/_abcjulianne_hough_kicks_up.html
(accessed July 14, 2011).

Desperate Housewives

Desperate Housewives is an hour-long, prime time dark comedy/**soap opera** (see entry under 1930s–TV and Radio in volume 2) about a quartet of women struggling with their families and friendships in a seemingly peaceful suburban setting. The pretty lawns and white picket fences of Wisteria Lane conceal an assortment of sins. Murder, adultery, child abuse, suicide, and arson are just a sample of what occurs every week on the most popular prime time dramatic comedy of the early twenty-first century.

Desperate Housewives was conceived after writer/producer Marc Cherry (1962–) and his mother discussed Andrea Yates (1959–), a Texas woman who made headlines after killing her five children in 2001. The conversation inspired Cherry to create a series centering on the crumbling lives of four women living on a seemingly ideal, upscale suburban street. Numerous networks passed on *Desperate Housewives* before it landed on ABC. On October 3, 2004, viewers first met clumsy Susan Meyer (Teri Hatcher, 1964–), prim Bree Van de Kamp (Marcia Cross, 1962–), exasperated Lynette Scavo (Felicity Huffman, 1962–), and sultry Gabrielle Solis (Eva Longoria, 1975–). Narrating their adventures was Mary Alice Young (Brenda Strong, 1960–), a fellow housewife whose suicide sparks the central mystery of season one. Each season that followed featured a new mystery and a series of new characters and guest stars, including Alfre Woodard (1952–), Dana Delany (1956–), Dixie Carter (1939–2010), and Kyle MacLachlan (1959–), that showed up to further complicate the heroines' already complicated lives. Nicollette Sheridan (1963–), James Denton (1963–), Doug Savant (1964–), Ricardo Antonio Chavira (1971–), and Kathryn Joosten (1939–) rounded out the core cast as husbands, boyfriends, and neighbors residing on Wisteria Lane.

The cast of residents on
Desperate Housewives: (L to
R) Nicolette Sheridan, Felicity
Huffman, Marcia Cross, Eva
Longoria, and Teri Hatcher.
© MOSHE BRAKHA/ABC-TV/
THE KOBAL COLLECTION/ART
RESOURCE, NY.

Desperate Housewives was a hit with critics, who enjoyed its eccentric characters and cleverly meandering storylines. The cast and crew collected several Emmy, Golden Globe, People's Choice, Screen Actors Guild, and Television Critics awards for their work on the show. Viewers were equally enamored with *Desperate Housewives*. Some 21.6 million people watched the series premiere. By the end of that debut season, thirty million were tuning in to find out why Mary Alice Young took her own life. By 2007, the show had attracted an international audience of

120 million viewers and ended the first decade of the 2000s as the most-watched dramatic comedy series in the world.

Michael Segretto

For More Information

Bauder, David. "ABC's *Housewives* Starts Strong." *Boston Globe* (October 6, 2004). http://www.boston.com/news/globe/living/articles/2004/10/06/abcs_housewives_starts_strong/ (accessed July 14, 2011).

"Desperate Housewives": Behind Closed Doors. New York: Hyperion, 2005.

"*Desperate Housewives* on SABC3 Confirmed." *TVSA* (April 3, 2007). http://www.tvsa.co.za/default.asp?blogname=news&articleID=4566 (accessed July 14, 2011).

McDougall, Charles. "Desperately Seeking a Ratings Hit." *The Telegraph* (January 5, 2005). http://www.telegraph.co.uk/culture/tvandradio/3634415/Desperately-seeking-a-ratings-hit.html (accessed July 14, 2011).

"Suburbia Sizzles in *Housewives.*" *Today Television* (September 30, 2004). http://today.msnbc.msn.com/id/6133690/ns/today-entertainment/t/suburbia-sizzles-housewives/ (accessed July 14, 2011).

Dora the Explorer

Dora the Explorer is the title character of a popular children's TV show of the same name. It was created by Chris Gifford, Valerie Walsh Valdes, and Eric Weiner. Parents and children alike appreciate Dora's interest in and energy for outdoor adventure. Children wear **T-shirts** (see entry under 1910s–Fashion in volume 1) and carry backpacks decorated with Dora's smiling face. Because she is a bright seven-year-old Latina girl, her character has broken new ground in the depiction of both girls and ethnic minorities on American television.

Dora the Explorer premiered in 2000 on the **cable TV** (see entry under 1970s–TV and Radio in volume 4) network Nick, Jr., Nickelodeon's preschool channel. Each episode begins with Dora inviting viewers to step into a **computer game** (see entry under 2000s—Sports and Games in volume 6)-like adventure with her. Dora, always shown wearing a backpack, carries a map that allows her to navigate obstacles and find her way to her destination. Accompanied by her pet monkey, Boots, or her cousin, Diego, Dora demonstrates kindness, curiosity, and bravery, and always manages to fend off Swiper, a fox who tries to take things from her. Action often pauses while Dora asks viewers to give input on

Dora the Explorer and her friend Boots the Monkey. © PHOTOFEST, INC.

questions, so that kids watching can try to figure out, alongside Dora, the best way to climb a mountain or cross a river. The cartoon mimics a computer screen, and when viewers are asked to make a choice, a mouse pointer clicks on the correct answer. Because Dora often uses Spanish words, the television show also introduces English-language viewers to a new language. Each show ends with Dora's mission accomplished, and a song and dance that declares "We Did It!"

Within a year of its debut, *Dora the Explorer* became the most popular show for preschoolers on commercial television. While some pointed to Dora's popularity as a victory for Latinos in America, others stressed that what ensured the show's success was its "crossover" appeal (its appeal to more than one type of audience). Dora speaks primarily English, and non-Latino audiences account for most of her success. Still, because of the growing Latino population in the United States, Dora's popularity in television and popular culture is considered a breakthrough for a group that had previously been barely represented, or poorly represented, on television. In 2010, the U.S. Census Bureau, with the cooperation of Nickelodeon, used Dora's image in publicity aimed at creating more awareness of the census and the benefits of participation, especially for children and underrepresented groups.

Maureen Reed

For More Information

"About *Dora the Explorer*." *Nick Jr.* http://www.nickjr.com/dora-the-explorer/about-dora-the-explorer/about-dora-the-explorer-tv-show.html (accessed July 14, 2011).

Levin, Gary. "Hispanics Finally Break the TV Barrier." *USA Today* (September 10, 2003): 1A.

Navarro, Mireya. "Nickelodeon's Bilingual Cartoon *Dora* Is a Hit." *New York Times* (July 2, 2001): C1.

"A 2010 Census Message from Nickelodeon's Dora the Explorer." *2010 Census Media Center*. http://2010.census.gov/mediacenter/awareness/dora-explorer.php (accessed July 14, 2011).

Family Guy

The premiere of **The Simpsons** (see entry under 1980s—TV and Radio in volume 5) as a prime-time, half-hour television series in 1989 ushered in a new era for television animation. Long confined to Saturday mornings and weekday afternoons and widely dismissed as "kid's stuff" by critics and viewers, animation took on new audiences and new possibilities during the 1990s and the first decade of the 2000s. *Family Guy*, created by Seth MacFarlane (1973–), was one of the animated shows that found success in the wake of *The Simpsons*. *Family Guy* took the irreverence, family dysfunction, and pop culture references that first made *The Simpsons* a cultural phenomenon and cranked them up to an absurd degree.

Family Guy premiered on the Fox network immediately after the **Super Bowl** (see entry under 1960s—Sports and Games in volume 4) on January 31, 1999. Beginning its regular run in April of that year, the show struggled to find an audience despite initially promising ratings. Fox canceled the show in February 2002. The story might have ended there had it not been for the cable network Cartoon Network's Adult Swim programming block including syndicated reruns of *Family Guy* simultaneous to the series being released on DVD, an emerging

The Griffin family from the FOX Network's Family Guy: *Meg, Peter, Lois, Chris, baby Stewie, and Brian the dog.*
© 20TH-CENTURY FOX LICENSING/MERCHANDISING/EVERETT COLLECTION.

phenomenon in TV entertainment. Both the reruns and DVDs proved enormously popular, and Fox ordered the series back starting in 2004. *Family Guy* remained tremendously popular for the remainder of the decade and into the 2010s.

Like *The Simpsons, Family Guy* centers around a dysfunctional middle-class American family consisting of a crude father, a long-suffering mother, and three children: an older brother, a middle sister, and a baby. Where *Family Guy* departs from the model of *The Simpsons* is in its absurdist and often crude humor. The baby, Stewie, talks in a British accent and acts like a megalomaniacal genius/arch villain. The family also owns a dog, Brian, who can walk and talk like his owners and enjoys the finer things in life. Much of the humor of the show is derived from cutaway gags that do nothing to advance the overall plot but instead make a humorous observation or reference, often to some bit of pop culture or other television shows.

Family Guy is perhaps the greatest comeback story in recent television history. Canceled and consigned to the scrapheap of failed TV shows, the series not only was renewed but went on to experience wild success. It spawned a series of direct-to-DVD feature movies and a spin-off series, *The Cleveland Show* (2009–). Although often the target of criticism from moral watchdogs offended by the show's lowest-common-denominator humor and from television critics who feel the show is too derivative of *The Simpsons* and not as clever as shows like **South Park** (see entry under 1990s—TV and Radio in volume 5), *Family Guy* remained as popular as ever among its loyal fan base as it entered its second decade of production.

David Larkins

For More Information

Bartlett, James. "Seth MacFarlane—He's the 'Family Guy.'" *The Great Reporter* (March 12, 2007). http://greatreporter.com/content/seth-macfarlane-he-s-family-guy (accessed August 14, 2011).

Dean, Josh. "Seth MacFarlane's $2 Billion *Family Guy* Empire." *Fast Company* (November 1, 2008). http://www.fastcompany.com/magazine/130/family-values.html (accessed August 14, 2011.)

Oldenburg, Ann. "Younger Viewers Tune in to 'Toons Aimed at Adults." *USA Today* (July 11, 2005).

Fox News Channel

Fox News Channel is a **cable TV** (see entry under 1970s–TV and Radio in volume 4) news and commentary channel created in 1996 by billionaire and News Corporation head Rupert Murdoch (1931–). The channel is available in over forty countries, and routinely boasts an audience twice the size of its closest cable news channel competitors in the United States. Although it is often referred to as a twenty-four-hour news channel, the network broadcasts original live programming about sixteen to eighteen hours each day. Approximately half of its schedule is devoted to editorial programming and features popular commentators such as Bill O'Reilly (1949–) and Geraldo Rivera (1943–).

Fox News Channel is frequently accused of displaying a politically conservative bias, and the vast majority of its editorial shows are hosted by conservative-leaning figures. Because of this perceived bias, the network simultaneously holds the distinction of being one of the most trusted and one of the most distrusted news sources among American respondents. Some studies have suggested that the network was responsible for a noticeable conservative shift in the voting habits of Americans during the early twenty-first century; this has been dubbed the "Fox News effect." Representatives of Fox News Channel maintain that their news coverage is "fair and balanced"—which is also one of the network's promotional slogans—and have argued that there is a clear distinction between the network's news coverage and the opinions of its editorial commentators.

What is unquestionable is Fox News's success in the first decade of the twenty-first century. Fox News started the decade trailing cable news network **CNN** (see entry under 1980s—TV and Radio in volume 5) both in daytime and primetime viewership. By 2010, Fox was the leader in all time slots, and CNN had fallen to third, behind MSNBC, in prime time.

Greg Wilson

For More Information

Collins, Scott. *Crazy Like a Fox: The Inside Story of How Fox News Beat CNN.* New York: Portfolio, 2004.

Holcomb, Jesse, Amy Mitchell, and Tom Rosenstiel. "Cable: By the Numbers." *State of the News Media 2011: An Annual Report on American Journalism.* http://stateofthemedia.org/2011/cable-essay/data-page-2/ (accessed August 9, 2011).

Morin, Richard. "The Fox News Effect." *Washington Post* (May 4, 2006). http://www.washingtonpost.com/wp-dyn/content/article/2006/05/03/AR2006050302299.html (accessed July 30, 2011).

Grey's Anatomy

Grey's Anatomy is a television medical drama created by Shonda Rhimes (1970–) that debuted in 2005 on ABC. The show's title is a play on the popular medical reference book *Gray's Anatomy,* but it also refers to the show's main character and frequent narrator, Meredith Grey (played by Ellen Pompeo, 1969–). The show takes place at fictional Seattle Grace Hospital, where Grey and four other characters begin as interns and eventually become resident doctors. Much of the show centers on

Grey's volatile romantic relationship with neurosurgeon Derek Shepherd (played by Patrick Dempsey, 1966–), popularly known as "McDreamy." One of the show's defining characteristics is the involvement of patients in the personal lives of the medical staff, and vice versa.

Grey's Anatomy relied upon lesser-known actors to round out its cast, and the show's popularity launched several of them to greater success. Most notably, actress Katherine Heigl (1978–), who played Izzie Stevens during the show's first six seasons, went on to star in a string of major Hollywood films. One of the most prominent cast members during its first three seasons, Isaiah Washington (1963–), was dropped from the show after he allegedly made disparaging remarks on set regarding the sexual orientation of co-star T. R. Knight (1973–), who played George O'Malley. Despite a handful of major cast changes, *Grey's Anatomy* remained popular with audiences years into its run, and spawned a spinoff series, *Private Practice,* in 2007.

Greg Wilson

For More Information

Johnson, Pamela K. "The Cutting Edge: Shonda Rhimes Dissects *Grey's Anatomy*." *Written By* (September 2005). http://www.wga.org/writtenby/ writtenbysub.aspx?id=883 (accessed August 2, 2011).

High School Musical

High School Musical is a an original feature-length musical produced for the **Disney Channel** (see Disney Stars and Teen Sensations entry under 2000s—Music in volume 6) in 2006. Loosely based on *Romeo and Juliet* by William Shakespeare (1564–1616) and influenced by the perky **Broadway** (see entry under 1900s—Film and Theater in volume 1) hit *Grease* (1971), the television movie generated a best-selling soundtrack album and a pair of popular sequels.

High School Musical is the tale of Troy Bolton (Zac Efron, 1987–) and Gabriella Montez (Vanessa Hudgens, 1988–), two high school juniors from different social spheres who strike up a friendship when they both audition for their school musical. In little over a month after its premier on January 20, 2006, *High School Musical* broke records by becoming the Disney Channel's most-watched movie. Its ratings success was a victory for producer Bill Borden, who had been trying to sell his idea for over a year without success before finding a home at the Disney Channel. Borden's persistence paid off when his film became

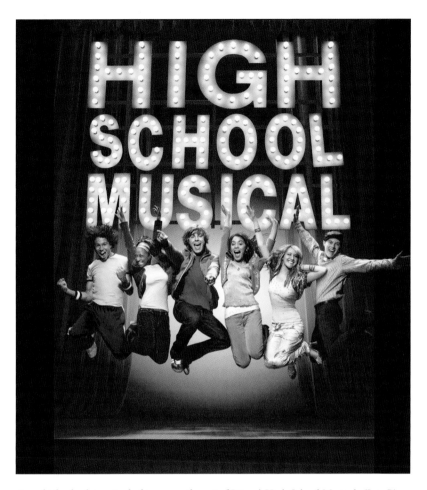

From high school stage to the big screen, the cast of Disney's High School Musical: *(L to R) Corbin Bleu, Monique Coleman, Zac Efron, Vanessa Hudgens, Ashley Tisdale, and Lucas Grabeel.* © THE DISNEY CHANNEL/THE KOBAL COLLECTION/ART RESOURCE, NY.

a rage among "tween" viewers—pre-teen kids between the ages of ten and twelve. Disney capitalized on that success with a line of *High School Musical* merchandise, including a soundtrack that was the best-selling album of 2006.

High School Musical 2 followed in 2007 and proved to be another big hit with viewers. The Disney Channel movie attracted a record-breaking 18 million viewers. The franchise became such a hit that *High School Musical 3: Senior Year* skipped television altogether in favor of a theatrical release in 2008. The film made more money during its opening weekend than any other musical in history. Troy, Gabriella, and their friends headed toward graduation, but were not soon forgotten by the legions of tweens that made them and the *High School Musical* series pop-culture landmarks of the first decade of the 2000s.

Michael Segretto

For More Information

Garrity, Brian. "Making the Magic Happen." *Billboard* (January 13, 2007). http://www.billboard.com/features/making-the-magic-happen-1003528294.story#/features/making-the-magic-happen-1003528294.story (accessed August 27, 2011).

Gold, Matea. "Disney Scores Kid Points with *High School Musical*." *AZCentral.com* (March 1, 2006). http://www.azcentral.com/ent/tv/articles/0302highschool.html (accessed July 16, 2011).

Goodman, Dean. "*High School Musical* Tops Box Office." *Reuters* (October 26, 2006). http://www.reuters.com/article/2008/10/27/us-boxoffice-idUSTRE49M98K20081026 (accessed July 16, 2011).

Hetrick, Adam. "Bet on It: Disney Plans Fourth *High School Musical*." *Playbill.com* (April 9, 2009). http://www.playbill.com/news/article/116643-Bet-On-It-Disney-Plans-Fourth-High-School-Musical- (accessed July 16, 2011).

Lost

Lost is an American drama series that aired on ABC from 2004 until 2010. The two main creative forces behind the show were writers/producers J. J. Abrams (1966–) and Damon Lindelof (1973–), who were approached by ABC executives to create a dramatic show in the same vein as the classic novel *Lord of the Flies* (1954) and the successful reality game show *Survivor* (2000–; see entry under 2000s—TV and Radio in volume 6).

The central story of the show begins when Oceanic Airlines Flight 815, traveling from Sydney, Australia to Los Angeles, California, crashes somewhere in the Pacific Ocean. The survivors of the flight, led by Dr. Jack Shephard (played by Matthew Fox, 1966–), find themselves on a mysterious island filled with dangers, both mundane and supernatural. In addition to the main story of the survivors' time on the island, the series relied heavily upon various narrative techniques—including flashbacks and, later, flashforwards—to provide a deeper glimpse into the lives of the main characters. The show was an immediate critical and popular success, winning awards from the Writers Guild, Producers Guild, Director's Guild, and Screen Actors Guild—as well as two Emmy

The cast of Lost: *(clockwise from upper left) Terry O'Quinn, Jorge Garcia, Ian Somerhalder, Maggie Grace, Naveen Andrews, Emilie De Ravin, Harold Perrineau, Malcolm David Kelley, Daniel Dae Kim, Kim Yunjin, Josh Holloway, Evangeline Lilly, Matthew Fox, and Dominic Monaghan.*
© TOUCHSTONE/ABC/THE KOBAL COLLECTION/ART RESOURCE, NY.

Awards—for its first season. Several cast members, including Josh Holloway (1969–), Evangeline Lilly (1979–), Jorge Garcia (1973–), and Daniel Dae Kim (1968–), became stars through their work on the show.

As *Lost* progressed, the storylines became increasingly complex and relied more heavily upon science fiction elements such as time travel. The show's ratings steadily declined, though it was widely recognized as the most-recorded show on television, and maintained a dedicated fan following. The series finale, which aired May 23, 2010, sharply divided audiences. Some felt that it provided a satisfying conclusion to the series, while others complained that many fundamental questions related to the nature of the mysterious island were left unanswered.

Greg Wilson

For More Information

Jensen, Jeff, and Dan Snierson. "*Lost* and Found." *Entertainment Weekly* (February 11, 2007). http://www.ew.com/ew/article/0,,20011203,00.html (accessed August 2, 2011).

Terry, Paul, and Tara Bennett. *"Lost" Encyclopedia.* Indianapolis, IN: DK/ BradyGames, 2010.

Mad Men

Mad Men, a television drama, chronicles the personal and professional lives of the employees of a New York advertising agency in the 1960s. When it premiered in 2007, on the **cable TV** (see entry under 1970s—TV and Radio in volume 4) network AMC (American Movie Classics), it won immediate critical praise. The opening episode explains that men who worked in New York advertising agencies, such as **J. Walter Thompson** (see entry under 1900s—Commerce in volume 1), called themselves "mad men" because many ad agencies were located on New York's Madison Avenue. The title takes on further meaning through the show's depiction of the 1960s, including the "madness" of working to sell products to increasingly cynical Americans, and the sexist ideas of "manliness" that dominated society in this era.

The show's main character is the elusive, attractive, and successful Don Draper, played by Jon Hamm (1971–). When the series opens, Draper has it all. He leads the creative department of an advertising agency, and he has a beautiful wife and two children. Viewers soon learn that Draper is actually Dick Whitman, who assumed the identity of Draper after he died next to Whitman during the Korean War (1950–1953). Whitman hoped to escape his humble origins by becoming someone else. The story of Draper's identity brings out a theme echoed in the show's depiction of advertising: how much Americans desire and value the appearance of success, even when it involves deceit.

Another main character of the show, Peggy Olson (played by Elisabeth Moss, 1982–), illustrates how women fared in the 1960s. Peggy begins the series as Draper's secretary and eventually works her way up to a copywriter position. She is paid less than her male co-workers, shut out of their after-work outings, and forced to endure their sexist jokes.

Though many critics and viewers appreciated the extent to which *Mad Men* sets and costumes recreate a glamorous look for the 1960s, the show's depiction of gender relations and its occasional references to the **civil rights movement** (see entry under 1960s—The Way We Lived in volume 4) also illustrate the deep injustices of the era.

In 2011, the fans of *Mad Men* were disappointed when protracted contract negotiations between AMC and producer Matthew Weiner (1965–) resulted in the delay of the show's fifth season until early 2012. Some hoped for the return of *Mad Men* because of its attention to visual detail; some wanted to know where Draper's path would lead next. Regardless of their motivations for watching this period drama, devoted fans clamored for more, intrigued by the ways it both glamorized and criticized 1960s America.

Maureen Reed

For More Information

Carveth, Rod, and James B. South, eds. *Mad Men and Philosophy: Nothing Is as It Seems.* Hoboken, NJ: John Wiley and Sons, 2010.

"*Mad Men.*" *AMC.* http://www.amctv.com/shows/mad-men (accessed August 17, 2011).

Stelter, Brian. "Season 5 of *Mad Men* Is Delayed until 2012." *New York Times* (March 30, 2011): C1.

Vargas-Cooper, Natasha. *Mad Men Unbuttoned: A Romp through 1960s America.* Detroit: Wayne State University Press, 2009.

Yabroff, Jennie. "A Word from Our Sponsor." *Newsweek* (August 4, 2008): 58.

Conan O'Brien (1963–)

Tall, gangly Conan O'Brien seemed an odd choice when first tapped to host NBC's *Late Night* in 1993. Yet with his self-deprecating and often bizarre sense of humor, he went on to host the show for sixteen years, earning a massive fan base in the process. O'Brien seemed the obvious

From the writers' room to the host's desk: Conan O'Brien.
© NBC-TV/THE KOBAL COLLECTION/ART RESOURCE, NY.

choice to step up behind the helm of late-night television leader *Tonight Show* as its longtime host, Jay Leno (1950–), prepared to retire, but the transition did not go smoothly, sparking one of the most controversial and galvanizing showdowns in the history of late-night talk shows.

O'Brien was born in Brookline, Massachusetts, to an Irish American family and went on to attend Harvard University. There, in what would prove to be the start of his career as comedy writer, he wrote for the university's famous *Harvard Lampoon* humor magazine. After graduating from Harvard, O'Brien soon landed a position on the writing team at **Saturday Night Live** (see entry under 1970s—TV and Radio in volume 4) in 1988. O'Brien wrote for *SNL* for three years, then moved over to the writing staff of **The Simpsons** (see entry under 1980s—TV and Radio in volume 5). Although he was only with the show for two years, O'Brien's unique comedic vision had a lasting effect on the show's direction and style.

Through his connection with *SNL* producer Lorne Michaels (1944–), O'Brien was able to audition as host of *Late Night,* the long-running follow-up to *The Tonight Show. Late Night's* previous host, **David Letterman** (1947–; see entry under 1980s—TV and Radio in volume 5), was leaving NBC to start his own show on CBS. Letterman had built up a tremendous cult following during his tenure at *Late Night* from 1982 to 1992, and NBC was seen as taking a tremendous risk in bringing in a relatively unknown writer as his replacement. The fate of *Late Night with Conan O'Brien* was in doubt for the first three years of the show's run, with NBC keeping O'Brien on an almost week-to-week renewal basis. By its fourth season, however, O'Brien and his writers found their stride and the show began to garner critical praise for its surrealistic sketches and O'Brien's distinct persona.

When O'Brien renewed his contract with NBC in 2004, the contract stipulated that he would take over hosting *The Tonight Show* when Leno retired in five years. Yet when it came time to hand over the reins, things went wrong quickly, resulting in a public relations disaster for NBC. The source of the conflict came from the fact that Leno did not actually retire but rather started up a new program, *The Jay Leno Show,* that aired at 10 PM Monday through Friday. The show fared poorly in the ratings, and NBC's president, Jeff Zucker (1965–), decided to shorten the show to a half-hour and move it to the 11:35 PM time slot previously held by *The Tonight Show,* which would be bumped back to a 12:05 AM start time. O'Brien bristled at this change, particularly as he had only been hosting *Tonight* for seven months.

A public battle erupted between NBC, Leno, and O'Brien, with O'Brien's fans and supporters going so far as to march in protest and start online petitions against the change. "I'm with Coco" (a humorous nickname O'Brien had picked up from frequent guest Tom Hanks, 1956–) became a catchphrase to show support for O'Brien, but Zucker and Leno would not back off their decision. Finally, in January 2010, O'Brien and his staff were paid $45 million to walk away from *Tonight*.

In an unprecedented move, O'Brien took his show to basic **cable TV** (see entry under 1970s—TV and Radio in volume 4). The hour-long late-night talk show format had long been firmly in the domain of the old broadcast networks. O'Brien's new show, entitled simply *Conan*, premiered on November 8, 2010. The premiere bested *The Tonight Show*, hosted again by Leno, leading many to pronounce O'Brien the winner of the latest round of "talk show wars." The ratings victory, however, was brief; viewership for O'Brien's show has lagged far behind both Leno and Letterman's shows.

David Larkins

For More Information

Aucoin, Don. "Understanding Conan." *Boston Globe Magazine* (August 31, 2003).

Carter, Bill. *The War for Late Night: When Leno Left Early and Television Went Crazy.* New York: Viking, 2010.

"Conan O Brien." *New York Times.* http://movies.nytimes.com/person/1548315/Conan-O-Brien/biography (accessed August 15, 2011).

Hibberd, James. "*Conan* Premiere Beats Leno, Letterman." *Hollywood Reporter* (November 9, 2010).

Ortved, John. "A Q&A with Conan O'Brien." *Vanity Fair* (July 5, 2007).

Schuker, Lauren A. E. "'Conan' Falls Flat in Season 1." *Wall Street Journal* (August 18, 2011). http://online.wsj.com/article/SB1000142405311190363940457651469127341148.html (accessed January 9, 2012).

Satellite Radio

Satellite **radio** (see entry under 1920s—TV and Radio in volume 2) is a technology that allows radio stations to broadcast virtually anywhere in the world—a marked improvement over traditional radio station broadcasts, which are limited by the strength of their radio signal. Rather than relying upon radio transmission towers positioned throughout a broadcast area, satellite radio stations transmit their signal through satellites in space. To receive satellite radio transmissions, a listener must have a special receiver capable of finding and decoding the signal. While such receivers were once large and required a fixed position, receivers eventually became portable and could be installed easily in an automobile. Several carmakers include satellite radio receivers as a feature in new vehicles.

For those who drive long distances and those who live in remote areas, satellite radio offers a service unmatched by local providers. For example, a truck driver traveling across the country can listen to the same satellite radio station for the entire journey. Satellite radio providers also generally offer a wide variety of music and **talk radio** (see entry under 1980s—TV and Radio in volume 5) formats for listeners to enjoy, rather than the handful of stations typically found in a given broadcast area. The sound quality of satellite radio is often better than FM or AM radio broadcasts, though the satellite signal may be lost while in some urban or underground environments. In addition, most satellite radio programming is commercial-free. The main disadvantage of satellite radio is that—unlike AM or FM radio—it requires a paid subscription.

Since its inception in 2001, satellite radio has proven very popular across the United States. In 2006, popular **shock radio** (see entry under 1980s—TV and Radio in volume 5) personality Howard Stern (1954–) ended his nationally syndicated broadcast radio show and launched a new show exclusively for satellite radio subscribers. In 2008, the two main satellite programming providers, Sirius and XM, merged to form a single company that provides service to more than twenty million subscribers.

Greg Wilson

For More Information

Keith, Michael C. *The Radio Station: Broadcast, Satellite & and Internet.* 8th ed. Burlington, MA: Focal Press, 2010.

Osborne, Spencer. "A Month without Sirius XM—What I Learned." *Seeking Alpha* (September 1, 2011). http://seekingalpha.com/article/291038-a-month-without-sirius-xm-what-i-learned (accessed September 18, 2011).

Sex and the City

The popular television series *Sex and the City* premiered on the **cable TV** (see entry under 1970s—TV and Radio in volume 4) network HBO in 1998. Loosely based on a *New York Observer* newspaper column and book of the same name, written by Candace Bushnell (1958–), *Sex and the City* followed the lives of four single women in Manhattan as they sought romantic and professional fulfillment. The main character was Carrie Bradshaw, played by actress Sarah Jessica Parker (1965–), who also was one of the show's producers. Carrie worked as a newspaper columnist, and her musings narrated each episode, linking scenes from her three best friends's lives with her own experiences. Episodes often featured Carrie and her friends—Miranda Hobbes, a feminist corporate lawyer (played by Cynthia Nixon, 1966–); Samantha Jones, a sexually adventurous publicist (played by Kim Cattrall, 1956–); and Charlotte York Goldenblatt, an art dealer in search of the perfect husband (played by Kristin Davis, 1965–)—sitting together at a diner, enjoying brunch.

The show ran for six successful seasons, enjoying extreme popularity among women who identified with its themes of love, friendship, and fashion. One of the key questions explored by the show was what it meant to be a successful, mature woman in the 1990s and 2000s. Because the characters, ranging in age from their mid-thirties to mid-forties, juggled their love of independence with their desire for sexual and romantic companionship, many saw the series as breaking new ground. Others pointed out that few American women lived and dressed as these glamorous Manhattan characters did, and that most viewers enjoyed it more as a fantasy of single life rather than a realistic portrayal. The explicit language and sex scenes, hallmarks of the show when it debuted, were cut when it made its way to a wider audience through syndication in 2003.

By the time the series ended in 2004, it had earned the reputation of being the most fashion-conscious show in television. Episodes promoted the careers of shoe designers such as Jimmy Choo (1961–) and Manolo Blahnik (1942–), as well as fashion houses such as Hermès and Fendi, either by directly mentioning product names or simply because of what the characters wore. Many viewers and commentators acknowledged that they watched *Sex and the City* "for the clothes."

Sex and the City gained devoted fans for reasons beyond clothing, however. It featured strong female characters that approached their careers and their sex lives thoughtfully and boldly, thus offering many viewers an appealing look at what it meant to be a woman at the beginning of the twenty-first century. After the show ended its run, two feature films were released, titled *Sex in the City* (2008) and *Sex in the City 2* (2010).

Maureen Reed

For More Information

De Moraes, Lisa. "*Sex and the City,* Minus Some Naughty Bits." *Washington Post* (September 11, 2003): C07.

Givhan, Robin. "*Sex and the City* Gives High Style a Leg Up." *Washington Post* (January 9, 2004): C01.

James, Caryn. "In Pursuit of Love, Romantically or Not." *New York Times* (June 5, 1998): E1.

Jermyn, Deborah. *Sex and the City.* Detroit: Wayne State University Press, 2009.

"*Sex and the City.*" *HBO.* http://www.hbo.com/sex-and-the-city (accessed August 16, 2011).

Sohn, Amy. *"Sex and the City": Kiss and Tell.* London: Melcher Media, 2004.

Webley, Kayla. "*Sex and the City 2*: $10 Million Wardrobe? Worth Every Penny." *Time NewsFeed* (September 8, 2009). http://newsfeed.time.com/2010/05/19/sex-and-the-city-2-wardrobe-worth-10-million/ (accessed August 16, 2011).

The Sopranos

The Sopranos is a television series that centers on a **Mafia** (see entry under 1960s—The Way We Lived in volume 4) mob family in New Jersey. The show was created for HBO in 1999 by David Chase (1945–), who drew on his own Italian American background to bring the world of *The Sopranos* to life. The series ran for six seasons and became the most watched **cable TV** (see entry under 1970s—TV and Radio in volume 4) series of all time.

The main focus of the show is Tony Soprano (played by James Gandolfini, 1961–), a leader of the DiMeo crime family. In addition to depicting Tony's criminal enterprises—run from a back office inside a strip club named Bada Bing!—the show explores the tense relationships within his family, particularly with his wife Carmela (played by Edie Falco, 1963–) and his daughter Meadow (played by Jamie-Lynn Sigler, 1981–). Another important facet of the show is Tony's relationship with his psychiatrist, Dr. Jennifer Melfi (played by Lorraine Bracco, 1954–). Melfi is privy to many of Tony's darkest secrets, which makes her a potential mob target.

The Sopranos received an astounding 111 Emmy Award nominations and twenty-one Emmy wins during its broadcast run, including two for best drama. The show received an overwhelmingly positive response from critics, though the final moments of the last episode left viewers divided. The series ends with an abrupt cut to black, without any obvious climax or resolution. Chase declined to comment on the meaning of this unusual conclusion.

Greg Wilson

Stars of The Sopranos: *(L to R) Michael Imperioli, James Gandolfini, Tony Sirico, and Steven Van Zandt.* © HBO/THE KOBAL COLLECTION/ART RESOURCE, NY.

For More Information

Martin, Brett. *"The Sopranos": The Book.* New York: Time Inc. Home Entertainment, 2007.

Remnick, David. "Family Guy." *New Yorker* (June 4, 2007). http://www .newyorker.com/talk/comment/2007/06/04/070604taco_talk_remnick (accessed August 9, 2011).

Yacowar, Maurice. *"The Sopranos" on the Couch: Analyzing Television's Greatest Series.* 3rd ed. New York: Continuum, 2005.

Survivor

• •

Survivor is a **reality TV** (see entry under 2000s—TV and Radio in volume 5) **game show** (see entry under 1950s—TV and Radio in volume 3) that first aired in the United States on CBS in 2000. The show is based on *Expedition Robinson,* which was launched in Sweden in 1997. The premise of the show is simple. A number of contestants are

Host Jeff Probst extinguishes the torch of Survivor: Micronesia *contestant Jon "Jonny Fairplay" Dalton after he was voted off the island in 2008.* © CBS-TV/THE KOBAL COLLECTION/ART RESOURCE, NY.

divided into "tribes" and placed in a remote location with a small supply of food and survival gear. The groups must not only build shelter and find food but must also participate in competitions against opposing tribes and maintain relationships within their own tribe to keep from being "voted out," or eliminated from the competition. The final survivor left at the end of the competition is declared the winner and receives a $1 million prize. The show's tribal council ceremony, in which contestants are voted out of the game, is the source of the iconic pop-culture phrase, "The tribe has spoken." The phrase originated with the show's host, Jeff Probst (1962–), who won several Emmy Awards for his work on the show.

Survivor has been filmed in exotic locations around the world, including Borneo, Australia, Africa, China, and Thailand. The show debuted as summertime programming, but its runaway success quickly earned it a place on the regular primetime schedule. Each *Survivor* season, which covers thirty-nine days of competition, lasts half as long as a typical television season. For this reason, the show normally runs two separate seasons per programming year, one in the fall and one in the spring.

Survivor is widely credited with—or blamed for—launching the era of reality television. Numerous reality-based game shows have followed in its wake, with many taking elements directly from *Survivor*'s simple and compelling format. Some *Survivor* contestants have gone on to achieve modest success in the entertainment industry. Elisabeth Hasselbeck (1977–), who came in fourth place during the show's second season, later became a co-host of the daily talk show *The View*.

Greg Wilson

For More Information

Burnett, Mark, and Martin Dugard. *The Psychology of "Survivor."* Dallas, TX: BenBella Books, 2007.

Gerrig, Richard J. *"Survivor": The Ultimate Game.* New York: TV Books, 2000.

Hatch, Richard. *101 Survival Secrets: How to Win $1,000,000, Lose 100 Pounds, and Just Plain Live Happily.* New York: Lyons Press, 2000.

"Larry King Live: What's Driving the Popularity of 'Reality TV'?" *CNN* (August 27, 2000). http://transcripts.cnn.com/TRANSCRIPTS/0006/27/lkl.00.html (accessed on August 2, 2011).

24

● ●

24 is a television series that ran for eight seasons on the Fox network. The central concept of the show is that it takes place in real time, with each season devoted to a single "day" divided into twenty-four hour-long episodes. The series centered on counterterrorism agent Jack Bauer, played by Kiefer Sutherland (1966–). Over the course of each season, Bauer encounters a terrorist plot and must stop it before time runs out. At several points during each episode, a digital display would show the time of day as it related to the show's own timeline, and split-screen techniques were often employed to show how parallel storylines played out simultaneously. The first season was originally scheduled to air beginning in October 2001—about a month after the **9/11** (see entry under 2000s—The Way We Lived in volume 6) terrorist attacks—but was delayed until November 2001.

The series received twenty Emmy Awards during its run, including one for outstanding drama series. The "real time" concept has been hailed as a landmark in television history, and its anti-terrorist storylines proved popular with viewers in the wake of the 2001 attacks. However, the show was frequently criticized for its portrayal of torture as an effective interrogation technique and for its repeated use of certain ethnic groups or nationalities—such as Muslims and Russians—as the villains who Bauer must stop. Supporters point out that the show broke ground by putting African American actor Dennis Haysbert (1954–) in the role of U.S. president David Palmer in the series' second season. In the show, Palmer is the first African American president. Haysbert has been quoted as saying that he believed the popularity of his character—a smart, tough, terrorism-fighting president—helped pave the way for the presidential election victory of **Barack Obama** (1961–; see entry under 2000s—The Way We Lived in volume 6) in 2008.

The series ended its run on May 24, 2010, but it was announced in January 2012 that filming for a movie would begin later in the year.

Greg Wilson

For More Information

Claustro, Lisa. "Haysbert Says *24* Role Paved the Way for Presidential Hopeful Barack Obama." *Los Angeles Times* (January 22, 2008).

Goldman, Michael. *"24": The Ultimate Guide.* New York: Dorling Kindersley, 2007.

Poniewozik, James. "The Evolution of Jack Bauer." *Time* (January 14, 2007). http://www.time.com/time/magazine/article/0,9171,1576853,00.html (accessed July 31, 2011).

Weed, Jennifer Hart, Richard Brian Davis, and Ronald L. Weed, eds. *"24" and Philosophy: The World According to Jack.* Malden, MA: Blackwell, 2008.

The West Wing

The West Wing (1999–2006) is an hour-long television series created by acclaimed screenwriter Aaron Sorkin (1961–) that ran for seven seasons on NBC. The show is a political drama set in the White House, and mainly focuses on fictional Democratic president Josiah Bartlet (played by Martin Sheen, 1940–) and his dedicated staff of advisors. Other major characters on the show include first lady Abbey Bartlet (played by Stockard Channing, 1944–), Deputy Chief of Staff Josh Lyman (played by Bradley Whitford, 1959–), and White House press secretary C. J. Cregg (played by Allison Janney, 1959–).

In addition to dealing with the various domestic and foreign crises faced daily by the president and his staff, the show also dealt with

Cast members of The West Wing *attend a presidential news conference: (L to R) Allison Janney, Richard Schiff, John Spencer, and Martin Sheen.* © PHOTOFEST, INC.

President Bartlet's reelection campaign during seasons three and four, and with the election of Bartlet's replacement in the sixth and seventh seasons. For these final two seasons, many of the show's storylines focused on Democratic nominee Matt Santos (played by Jimmy Smits, 1955–) and his opponent, Republican nominee Arnold Vinick (played by Alan Alda, 1936–).

Though the show was criticized by some as an attempt to legitimize liberal ideas, the show's writers, producers, and directors employed advisors from across the political spectrum in an attempt to capture the feel of working in the White House. For its first season, *The West Wing* won nine Emmy Awards, the most ever awarded to a single season of a television show. Over the course of its seven seasons, *The West Wing* won twenty-seven Emmys, including four awards for outstanding drama series—the most Emmys ever won by a drama.

Greg Wilson

For More Information

Crawley, Melissa. *Mr. Sorkin Goes to Washington: Shaping the President on Television's "The West Wing."* Jefferson, NC: McFarland, 2006.

Jackman, Ian, and Peter Ruditis. *"The West Wing" Companion.* London: Channel 4, 2002.

Rollins, Peter C. *"The West Wing": The American Presidency as Television Drama.* New York: Syracuse University Press, 2003.

Stelter, Brian. "Following the Script: Obama, McCain, and *The West Wing.*" *New York Times* (October 29, 2008). http://www.nytimes.com/2008/10/30/arts/television/30wing.html (accessed August 1, 2011).

Will & Grace

Airing for eight seasons on the NBC network, the hit **sitcom** (see entry under 1950s—TV and Radio in volume 3) *Will & Grace* (1998–2006) broke new ground in American television by featuring a gay main character in a mainstream program. Created by television veterans David Kohan (1964–) and Max Mutchnick (1964–), *Will & Grace* focused on anxious interior decorator Grace Adler (played by Debra Messing, 1968–) and stuffy lawyer Will Truman (played by Eric McCormack, 1963–). Living together in an apartment on Manhattan's Upper West Side, homosexual Will and heterosexual Grace shared a platonic friendship loving enough to be mistaken for a romantic relationship. Other regular characters were Grace's bawdy, bisexual assistant Karen Walker (played Megan Mulally, 1958–) and Will's friend Jack McFarland (played by Sean Hayes, 1970–). Stereotypically effeminate, Jack was the focus of criticism *Will & Grace* received during its early seasons. Gay advocates also took issue with Will's lack of a romantic partner, viewing the show as too cowardly to portray the aspects of a gay character that might make some heterosexual viewers uncomfortable.

Despite such criticisms, *Will & Grace* became a sizable mainstream hit, remaining among the top twenty most-watched shows for half its run and winning sixteen Emmy Awards. Even more vindicating were the seven Media Awards the sitcom won from the Gay & Lesbian

Title characters Will (Eric McCormack) and Grace (Debra Messing).
© PHOTOFEST, INC.

Alliance Against Defamation (GLAAD). The group praised *Will & Grace* for its "gay characters that audiences welcomed into their homes each week—along with one of network television's first gay kisses and discussions of gay parenting, marriage equality and more."

Michael Segretto

For More Information

Colucci, Jim. *"Will & Grace": Fabulously Uncensored.* New York: Time Home Entertainment, 2004.

Gairola, Rahul. *"Will & Grace." Pop Matters.* http://popmatters.com/tv/reviews/w/will-and-grace.html (accessed July 15, 2011).

Lauerman, Kerry. "Series Wrap-up: *Will & Grace." Salon.com* (May 19, 2006). http://www.salon.com/entertainment/tv/review/2006/05/19/will_grace/ (accessed July 15, 2011).

"Will & Grace Resource Guide." *GLAAD.* http://archive.glaad.org/eye/will_grace.php (accessed July 15, 2011).

2000s

The Way We Lived

A new millennium meant a new way of life for Americans. Technology moved at an ever-increasing pace. News and literature that once required a printing press could be read on phones. Even e-mail and chat rooms seemed outdated in an age in which Americans communicated by texting or tweeting. A new electronic age captivated Americans' imaginations, and took its toll on their pocketbooks, as they struggled to keep up with the latest technologies required for life in the digital age.

Of course, technology could not solve every problem. The greatest crisis of the decade—the terrorist attacks on September 11, 2001—left Americans feeling shocked and vulnerable, looking for answers that could not be found, even with the newest, smartest smart phone. Hurricane Katrina, in 2005, also exposed the limitations of technology. Racism and poverty, as well as natural disasters, still threatened Americans. Moreover, technology seemed to be creating some problems of its own. The sedentary, consumption-oriented lifestyle fashioned by Americans who poured time into the entertainment offered by high-definition television (HDTV), YouTube, and Facebook seemed to be contributing to an obesity epidemic, not to mention climate change.

Technology could, and did, however, bring Americans together in new ways. It allowed Americans who shared common concerns to unite into powerful, even if exclusively virtual, communities. Many cited the use of what became known as "social media" as a decisive factor in the 2008 election of President Barack Obama (1961–). Even countercultural communities, such as hipsters, achieved cohesion through the Internet. Furthermore, tools such as Google and Wikipedia made more information accessible to more people than ever before, and even those who lamented the shorter attention spans that seemed to accompany new technologies acknowledged the breathtaking ways in which they overcame the limitations of time and space. A "friend" on Facebook was not the same as a friend next door. But Americans, optimistic and forward-looking as ever, were more than willing to consider giving these new ways of living a try.

Blogging

In many ways, blogs represent what people mean when they talk about Web 2.0 technology: easily accessible and interactive Web sites that facilitate online community-building, socialization, and the free exchange of ideas. Blogs take many forms but usually feature some combination of text, image, and video devoted to a particular subject or the blogger's personal life. Since their explosion in popularity during the first decade of the 2000s, blogs have revolutionized news coverage, political discussion, and public relations.

Blogging comes from the term "Web log" (or "Weblog"), first coined in 1997 to describe a type of Web site that took the form of an online diary. In 1999, the term Web 2.0 was coined to describe the next generation of online technology. Initially, the World Wide Web consisted of static web pages that required a fairly sophisticated level of knowledge regarding computer coding and file management to create and maintain. These Web pages were individual entities that did not allow any level of public interaction from their readers. Community-based elements of the **Internet** (see entry under 1990s—The Way We Lived in volume 5), such as Usenet and message forums, were separate and distinct entities. Web 2.0 technology aimed to combine all these technologies into a single whole. Blogs were at the forefront of this movement.

Unlike traditional Web sites, the blogging sites that began appearing in 1999, such as Blogger.com and LiveJournal, made updating a Web site as easy as entering text; no knowledge of HTML coding or FTP software was required. Furthermore, these new blogs facilitated user comments, creating a level of interactivity not previously seen on static Web pages.

Blogs were at first primarily used as online diaries, but in the post-**9/11** (see entry under 2000s—The Way We Lived in volume 6) world they began to garner greater importance and attention as they became used as tools by political activists and amateur reporters. At first dismissed by the mainstream media, this new corps of online commentators was instrumental in breaking important news stories through 2002 and 2003. Unlike mainstream media outlets, political bloggers saw no compulsion to maintain a veneer of neutrality. Left-wing and right-wing blogs competed to outdo each other in political mudslinging and damaging scoops.

By 2004, the importance of blogs had become undeniable, and many political and media figures began using blogging technology to their own advantage. With the advent of "micro-blogging" sites like **Twitter** (see entry under 2000s—The Way We Lived in volume 6), blogs went truly mainstream. Politicians, entertainers, and other public figures began using their blogs to interact directly with their base, bypassing their public relations agents sometimes with disastrous results for their public image.

By the end of the first decade of the 2000s, over 150 million blogs had been set up on the Internet. With this increased ability to speak one's mind to the rest of the world came unforeseen consequences. People lost their jobs over opinions expressed on their personal blogs, and other bloggers have been sued for defamation over opinions posted on their sites. Critics have also noted that giving everyone a voice through blogs resulted in an unprecedented level of metaphorical noise in the democratic political process, with many bloggers increasingly polarized towards either end of the political spectrum, shouting to be heard over the din of millions of other voices.

David Larkins

For More Information

Blood, Rebecca. "Weblogs: A History and Perspective." *Rebecca's Pocket* (September 7, 2000). http://www.rebeccablood.net/essays/weblog_history.html (accessed August 15, 2011).

Gardner, Susannah, and Shane Birley. *Blogging for Dummies.* 4th ed. Hoboken, NJ: Wiley, 2011.

Sanderson, Catherine. "Blogger Beware!" *Guardian Unlimited* (April 2, 2007). http://www.guardian.co.uk/commentisfree/2007/apr/02/bloggerbeware (accessed August 15, 2011).

Wortham, Jenna. "After 10 Years of Blogs, the Future's Brighter Than Ever." *Wired.com* (December 17, 2007). http://www.wired.com/entertainment/theweb/news/2007/12/blog_anniversary (accessed August 15, 2011).

Craigslist

Craigslist is a Web site network devoted to ad listings similar to the classified ads section of a traditional newspaper. It was created by Craig Newmark (1952–) in 1996 as a way of sharing news of local events in and around San Francisco, focusing on events of interest to computer programmers and other technology industry professionals. As its popularity grew, the site expanded to include job listings, items for sale, and even unwanted items that could be picked up for free. Most ads can be placed free of charge by users of the site, and images can also be uploaded to accompany ad text. The success of the San Francisco–based site led to portals devoted to other major cities and, ultimately, to other countries as well. By 2011, Craigslist ranked as one of the ten most popular Web sites in the United States and among the top forty sites in the world.

The free, user-oriented nature of its ads has led to some controversy surrounding Craigslist. In 2010, Craigslist completely removed the "Adult Services" section on its pages in the United States after criticism that the site was promoting prostitution. In addition, the site's anonymous nature has allegedly been a key component in numerous crimes, including identity theft and murder. In 2009, Minnesota teen Michael John Anderson was convicted of luring a woman to his parents' house in 2007 and killing her; Anderson selected his victim through Craigslist, where she had posted an ad looking for a job as a nanny.

Greg Wilson

For More Information

"'Craigslist Killer' Michael John Anderson Gets Life in Murder of Katherine Olson." *New York Daily News* (April 3, 2009). http://www.nydailynews.com/news/national/2009/04/02/2009-04-02_craigslist_killer_michael_john_anderson_.html (accessed September 4, 2011).

"Fact Sheet." *Craigslist.org* (November 29, 2010). http://www.craigslist.org/about/factsheet (accessed September 4, 2011).

Press, Skip. *The Complete Idiot's Guide to Making Money with Craigslist.* Indianapolis, IN: Alpha Books, 2009.

Facebook

Facebook is a social networking Web site that allows users to keep in touch with friends and acquaintances through status updates, picture-sharing, messaging, and other features. Facebook was originally created by Mark Zuckerberg (1984–) in 2004 as a social directory and networking site for Harvard University students. The idea was based on university facebooks, directories of students and faculty members provided to help the students become familiar with each other and their instructors. While some other colleges had already developed online facebook directories for students, Harvard had not. Zuckerberg and a small group of fellow students and roommates, including Eduardo Saverin (1982–), Chris Hughes (1983–), and Dustin Moskovitz (1984–), expanded upon the idea of a simple student directory and included the ability for students to control their own pages, listing their interests and making connections to pages belonging to their friends. These features resembled existing social networking sites such as Myspace, but they offered a more streamlined, user-friendly experience that made it easy for new users to create an account and link up with friends.

Facebook has become the second most visited Web site in the United States. © IAIN MASTERTON/ALAMY.

The site was originally open only to Harvard students, but its immediate success led Zuckerberg and his cofounders to expand the site to include other major colleges. In 2005, the site was made available to high school students by invitation only; in 2006, Facebook finally became available to all users at least thirteen years of age. Although it was not the first social networking site, Facebook quickly became the leader of the field, overtaking Myspace in 2008. One of Facebook's simplest and most iconic features is the ability of users to "like" messages, photos, or pages devoted to a particular cause or interest; this "like" status is reflected by a thumbs-up icon. The site also popularized the use of the word "friend" as a verb; accepting a request to be linked to another user's page is known as "friending" that person.

By 2011, Facebook had become the second-most visited Web site in the United States and boasted more than 750 million users, with more than half being between eighteen and thirty-four years old. Because of its widespread popularity, the site has been instrumental in helping old friends and acquaintances reconnect after losing contact in the past. The site was estimated to have earned more than $4 billion in 2011, mainly through advertising revenue. Facebook's success has not been without controversy, however. Three former Harvard students accused Zuckerberg of stealing their idea for a social networking site after he was hired to create one for them. Another lawsuit was filed by cofounder Saverin after he had a falling-out with Zuckerberg and other financial experts brought in as the company expanded. Both lawsuits were settled for undisclosed amounts. The two lawsuits formed much of the narrative for the Academy Award–winning film *The Social Network* (2010), which was based on the creation of and subsequent legal battle over Facebook.

Facebook has also been criticized for its emphasis on superficial relationships and encouragement of what some see as time-wasting activities. The site keeps track of each user's number of "friends," and some users strive to increase their friend count by including other users that they may not know at all. Many users check their Facebook account several times each day, posting updates on mundane activities such as what they ate for lunch or what they are watching on television. Many companies have blocked Facebook on their employee computers since the site is believed to result in a loss of productivity, as employees check and update their statuses instead of performing their normal job duties. Some studies have even suggested that Facebook is responsible for a growing number of divorces, due to the ease with which former lovers and new acquaintances can link up online.

Despite these criticisms, Facebook has also been credited with helping to spread democracy around the world. In 2011, democratic movements in Tunisia and Egypt were aided greatly by the social networking site, which allowed protestors—many of whom were young and technologically savvy—to coordinate public demonstrations and share news when local media was under state control. For this reason, the 2011 Middle East democracy movement has been dubbed by some "the Facebook Revolution."

Greg Wilson

For More Information

Abram, Carolyn, and Leah Pearlman. *Facebook for Dummies.* 4th ed. Hoboken, MJ: Wiley, 2011.

Facebook Official Site. http://facebook.com (accessed September 27, 2011).

Hasday, Judy L. *Facebook and Mark Zuckerberg.* Greensboro, NC: Morgan Reynolds, 2012.

Kirkpatrick, David. *The Facebook Effect: The Inside Story of the Company That Is Connecting the World*. New York: Simon & Schuster, 2010.

McDonald, Soraya Nadia. "'Facebooking' the Rage on College Campuses." *Seattle Times* (July 4, 2005). http://community.seattletimes.nwsource.com/archive/?date=20050704&slug=btfacebook04 (accessed September 27, 2011).

Mezrich, Ben. *The Accidental Billionaires: The Founding of Facebook for Dummies*. New York: Anchor Books, 2010.

Vargas, José Antonio. "The Face of Facebook Opens Up." *New Yorker*. September 20, 2010. http://www.newyorker.com/reporting/2010/09/20/100920fa_fact_vargas (accessed September 27, 2011).

Global Warming

Global warming is a term first coined in 1975 to describe the overall pattern of climate change that has been observed by climate scientists for decades. It is a bit of a misnomer (untrue interpretation), as "global

Scientists tread carefully through a combination of ice, sea, and meltwater in the Canada Basin of the Arctic on July 22, 2005. Some scientists believe that the breakup of ice is a result of global warming. © JEREMY POTTER/NEWSCOM.

warming" can also lead to longer, colder winters in some parts of the planet. When discussing the phenomenon, scientists generally prefer the term "climate change." Global warming, as a term, has however stuck with the media and popular vocabulary since its popularization.

The public first became largely aware of global warming in the late 1980s, when reports that had been circulating in the scientific community for a decade began to receive greater attention from the media and government. These reports stated that carbon dioxide (CO_2) released by the burning of fossil fuels such as oil, gasoline, and coal, as well as man-made chemicals such as chlorofluorocarbons (CFCs), were building up in Earth's atmosphere at alarming rates and threatening to cause dramatic changes. CFCs, for example, were identified as the culprits behind a growing depletion of ozone levels in the atmosphere. CO_2, meanwhile, was threatening to raise the planet's temperature through the so-called "greenhouse effect."

Scientists had long observed that an excessive amount of CO_2 in the atmosphere has an effect similar to the glass panes of a greenhouse: it allows light in but prevents heat from escaping. Although fluctuations in the Earth's climate and temperature are natural, these usually occur over hundreds of thousands of years, allowing living species to adapt to the changes. Scientists warning of the greenhouse effect were concerned that the massive amount of CO_2 released into the atmosphere since the beginning of the Industrial Revolution and subsequent widespread burning of fossil fuels was dramatically accelerating climate change at a rate too fast for animals and plants to adapt to.

Although all available data pointed towards a general rise in temperatures and photographic evidence showed receding glaciers and icecaps, along with coastal islands inundated by the rising waters caused by the melting ice, there remained considerable debate both among scientists and the general public regarding the cause behind the warming trend. The first decade of the 2000s saw discussion and coverage of global warming reach an all-time high, with many calling the phenomenon a man-made environmental disaster. Former vice president Al Gore (1948–) significantly raised the profile of the debate with his book and movie documentary, *An Inconvenient Truth* (2006). By 2011, 97 percent of publishing scientists were in agreement that global warming was being significantly accelerated by man-made technology. During the tenure of President George W. Bush (1946–), the issue became increasingly politicized in the United States, resulting in an ongoing divide between those who agreed with the scientific community's consensus and those who argued otherwise.

Regardless of lingering public and political doubt as to global warming's cause, serious efforts were underway to limit "greenhouse gas" emissions in the hope of slowing or reversing the trend of global warming throughout the first decade of the 2000s. Various international protocols led by the United Nations were proposed and subscribed to by dozens of nations, although the United States, one of the greatest greenhouse gas emitters, notably bowed out of the landmark Kyoto Protocol of 2005. By 2011, efforts were still being made to limit greenhouse gas emissions and raise awareness of global warming among all countries, including the world's poor and developing nations.

David Larkins

For More Information

Anthony, Sharon, Thomas W. Brauch, and Elizabeth J. Longley. "What Should We Do about Global Warming?" *Chem Connections Workbook* (August 12, 2008). http://chemistry.beloit.edu/Warming/index.html (accessed August 1, 2011.)

Gore, Al. *An Inconvenient Truth: The Planetary Emergency of Global Warming and What We Can Do about It.* Emmaus, PA: Rodale Books, 2006.

National Oceanic and Atmospheric Administration. "Global Warming: Frequently Asked Questions." *National Climatic Data Center.* (August 20, 2008). http://www.ncdc.noaa.gov/oa/climate/globalwarming.html (accessed August 1, 2011).

Spencer, Roy W. *Climate Confusion.* New York: Encounter Books, 2008.

"What Is Global Warming?" *National Geographic* http://environment. nationalgeographic.com/environment/global-warming/gw-overview.html (accessed August 1, 2011).

Google

Google is a Web search engine that launched a multibillion-dollar technology business. The name "Google" comes from a play on "googol," a number defined as one followed by one hundred zeroes. The basic structure of the search engine was created in 1996 by two Stanford University computer science students, Sergey Brin (1973–) and Larry Page (1973–). The trait that set Google apart from other popular search engines at the time was the way it determined the relevance of a page to a user's search term. Many users preferred Google's search function to its many competitors, believing that Google yielded higher-quality results. As its popularity soared, Google became recognized as the premier search engine on the **Internet** (see entry under 1990s—TV and Radio in volume 5). By 2011, Google had earned its place as the most-visited Web site in the world, with around one billion unique visitors each month.

In addition to its domination in the field of Web searches, Google has expanded into various other fields. Most notably, in 2006 Google purchased **YouTube** (see entry under 2000s—The Way We Lived in volume 6), a video streaming site that allows users to upload and share their own creations. Google has also offered its own brand of email (Gmail), social networking (Google+), Web browsing (Google Chrome), and mapping site (Google Maps/Google Earth). The company was instrumental in the development of the Android operating system, specially created for mobile devices such as **smart phones** (see entry under 2000s—The Way We Lived in volume 6). Despite its massive growth, Google still operates according to ten basic principles, one of which has become a well-known critique of modern American corporate culture: "You can make money without doing evil."

This core tenet was tested when Google received permission to have its search engine accessible within China in 2005. Prior to that time, Google was not consistently available to mainland Chinese users. Because the Chinese government closely monitored the Web sites available to its citizens—blocking or shutting down sites that were critical of the government, or favorable toward democracy—Google agreed to allow the Chinese government to censor its search results. Some critics considered this a violation of Google's basic principles, but Google executives argued that offering limited search information to Chinese citizens was more beneficial than having the site banned completely. Human rights and free speech organizations such as Amnesty International and Reporters Without Borders condemned Google's actions.

In late 2009, the Gmail accounts of some Chinese political activists were hacked in an attempt to discover personal information. After this security breach, which many believe was carried out by agents of the Chinese government, Google announced that it would no longer censor its search results in China. Instead, it offered Google China users a link to access Google through Hong Kong, a special region of China not subject to censorship restrictions.

Greg Wilson

For More Information

Battelle, John. "The Birth of Google." *Wired* (August 2005). http://www.wired .com/wired/archive/13.08/battelle.html (accessed September 5, 2011).

Girard, Bernard. *The Google Way: How One Company Is Revolutionizing Management as We Know It.* San Francisco: No Starch Press, 2009.

Levy, Steven. *In the Plex: How Google Thinks, Works, and Shapes Our Lives.* New York: Simon & Schuster, 2011.

"Our Philosophy." *Google.com.* http://www.google.com/intl/en/about/ corporate/company/tenthings.html (accessed September 5, 2011).

Vise, David A., and Mark Malseed. *The Google Story.* Updated ed. New York: Delacorte Press, 2008.

High-definition TV

High-definition television (commonly known as HDTV) came into its own during the first decade of the 2000s, arriving hand in hand with the advent of digital TV broadcasting. **Television** (see entry under 1940s— TV and Radio in volume 3) creates images on the screen using horizontal lines; high-definition TV significantly increases the number of lines on the screen, resulting in a picture that is sharper and clearer than standard definition broadcasts. For years, the barriers to the introduction of high-definition televisions to the market were technological limitations and price factors.

In the 1980s, President Ronald Reagan (1911–2004) was shown a demonstration of HDTV and afterwards said that transitioning to the new technology should become a national priority. Yet it was in Japan that HDTV first became common. Japanese broadcasters sent out high-definition signals over traditional analog signals. This proved an impractical solution for American markets, as the high-definition signals took up too much bandwidth to be commercially viable to broadcasters. American researchers shifted their focus to digital signals, and by 1992, the first digital high-definition TV broadcasts were being demonstrated.

Six years later, high-definition televisions began hitting the market. Their prices, ranging from $6,000 to $9,000, made them prohibitively expensive for the average consumer. The lack of TV stations actually broadcasting anything in high definition further reduced their utility. It was not until the middle of the first decade of the 2000s that high-definition TV began to look like an attractive option. The new televisions hitting the market were more affordable and came with more

A Panasonic 103-inch high-definition TV in 2006. © RICHARD B. LEVINE/NEWSCOM.

features. Of note is the fact that the standard shape of the TV screen stretched horizontally. Since their invention, TV screens had been almost square-shaped. High-definition TVs came in a rectangular shape reminiscent of a movie theater screen, which made them more suitable for showing recorded films.

As the first decade of the 2000s came to a close, more and more stations across the country were broadcasting at least some of their local programming in high definition. The possibilities of merging TV and computer functionality were beginning to be explored with the appearance of Internet-ready TVs. Because high-definition TV sets were already set up to receive digital information, the next logical step was to merge **Internet** (see entry under 1990s—The Way We Lived in volume 5) access with TV reception.

As HDTV sets became increasingly common in American homes, many more programs across all the major networks were going out in high definition over digital signals. From 2007 onwards, all televisions, high-definition or not, were mandated to be sold with built-in digital receivers. On June 12, 2009, all analog broadcasting by major networks in the United States came to an end, replaced by digital transmissions. After years of development, the high-definition TV revolution was finally under way. By decade's end, nearly two-thirds of American homes had at least one high-definition TV set. In just a few short years, the way Americans watched television had changed forever.

David Larkins

For More Information

Briere, Daniel D., and Pat Hurley. *HDTV for Dummies.* 2nd ed. Hoboken, NJ: Wiley, 2007.

Cianci, Philip J. *High Definition: The Creation, Development and Implementation of the Technology.* Jefferson, NC: McFarland, 2011.

Elmer-Dewitt, Philip. "The Picture Suddenly Gets Clearer." *Time* (March 30, 1992). http://www.time.com/time/magazine/article/0,9171,975191-1,00.html (accessed August 16, 2011).

O'Malley, Chris. "HDTV Is Here! So What?" *Time* (October 5, 1998). http://www.time.com/time/magazine/article/0,9171,989234-1,00.html (accessed August 16, 2011).

Winslow, George. "Nielsen: Two Thirds of All TV Homes Now Have an HD Set." *Multichannel News* (June 15, 2011). http://www.multichannel.com/article/469806-Nielsen_Two_Thirds_of_All_TV_Homes_Now_Have_An_HD_Set.php (accessed August 16, 2011.)

Hipsters

Hipsters are part of a youth subculture that rose to prominence in the 1990s and early 2000s. Hipsters are defined largely by their relationship to popular culture. They tend to reject—even mock—anything deemed popular or mainstream in favor of the obscure or deliberately, ironically "bad." For example, a hipster may choose to wear a gaudy vintage scarf precisely because it would not normally be considered fashionable. By rejecting the accepted definition of "cool," hipsters attempt to achieve a level of cool beyond that of mainstream society. Hipsters often engage in competitive searches for obscure entertainment not because of the inherent value it contains, but because one who discovers and brings new cultural elements into the social group earns a status as a trendsetter. In this sense, hipsters may be viewed as scavengers on the fringe of culture.

Scavengers on the fringe of culture: hipsters. © SHUTTERSTOCK.COM.

For a subculture based on the rejection of what is normally viewed as popular, the hipster aesthetic can be surprisingly consistent. Hipsters are known for wearing vintage clothing items that are distinctively out of style; hipster males are credited with popularizing **skinny jeans** (see entry under 2000s—Fashion in volume 6) for men. Hipsters are often pictured wearing oversized or horn-rimmed glasses, and the movement is closely associated with alternative and **indie music** (see entry under 2000s—Music in volume 6). Perhaps most significantly, very few young people who fit the accepted definition of a hipster would classify themselves as one. As hipsterism has become defined and incorporated into mainstream culture, rejection of the label is arguably the most predictable thing a hipster would do.

Greg Wilson

For More Information

Décharné, Max. *Straight from the Fridge, Dad: A Dictionary of Hipster Slang.* 2nd ed. Harpenden, England: No Exit, 2009.

Fletcher, Dan. "Hipsters." *Time* (July 29, 2009). http://www.time.com/time/arts/article/0,8599,1913220,00.html (accessed September 20, 2011).

Lanham, Robert. *The Hipster Handbook.* New York: Anchor, 2003.

Hurricane Katrina

Hurricane Katrina was one of the most devastating hurricanes to ever strike the United States. It began as a tropical storm in the Caribbean Sea on August 24, 2005, and by the time it reached Florida the following day, Katrina had been upgraded to Category 1 hurricane status. The hurricane cut a path of destruction across southern Florida and continued west into the Gulf of Mexico. In the open waters of the Gulf, Katrina strengthened to a Category 5 hurricane—the most intense storm classification possible. As it grew, the hurricane also shifted course northward toward the coasts of Louisiana and Mississippi.

Because of the intensity of the storm, forecasters issued warnings to Gulf Coast residents days before Katrina made contact with land. On August 27, 2005, President George W. Bush (1946–) issued a state of emergency for parts of Mississippi, Alabama, and Louisiana. Oddly, the state of emergency did not include New Orleans and its surrounding areas. New Orleans was a special focus of concern, because most of the city was built below sea level and was flanked by bodies of water—the Mississippi River to the south and Lake Pontchartrain, a saltwater estuary connected to the Gulf of Mexico, to the north.

Well aware of the threat posed by a Category 5 hurricane, New Orleans mayor Ray Nagin (1956–) ordered a mandatory evacuation of the city for the first time in its history on August 28, 2005. With only twenty-four hours to clear the city, tens of thousands of residents—including many of the poorest residents and those with debilitating health problems—were left behind. Katrina made landfall in Louisiana and Mississippi on the morning of August 29 as a Category 3 hurricane, with winds in excess of one hundred miles per hour. As destructive as the hurricane winds were, the true devastation came from the sea itself.

Because New Orleans sat mostly below sea level, man-made barriers known as levees had been built around the city to prevent flooding during storms. The levees were part of a project undertaken by the U.S. Army Corps of Engineers in 1965. However, the levee project still remained incomplete forty years later due to political disagreements and funding problems. When Hurricane Katrina reached New Orleans, it brought with it a massive rise in water level known as a storm surge. The storm surge was large enough to flow over the tops of levees in some locations, while in other places the poorly designed levees gave way and allowed the flood waters to rush into the city. More than three-quarters of New Orleans was left underwater because of levee breaches. Some later investigations placed the responsibility for the failed levee system squarely on the Army Corps of Engineers.

In the eyes of many, the failure of the federal government did not end with the breached levees. As some residents were left stranded for days atop their roofs by the rising flood waters, the Federal Emergency Management Agency (FEMA)—the U.S. Department of Homeland Security organization in charge of coordinating disaster response—came under fire for failing to act swiftly and decisively in its rescue and relief efforts. The head of FEMA, Michael Brown (1954–), resigned from his position two weeks later. In all, more than eighteen hundred people died as a result of Hurricane Katrina, most of them in New Orleans, and more than eight hundred thousand people were displaced. Total damages from Katrina exceeded $100 billion, making it the costliest hurricane in the history of the United States. However, extensive media coverage of the disaster and its aftermath spurred individual donors across the globe to contribute more than $4 billion in aid. Reconstruction of New Orleans began almost immediately; by 2010, the city's population had returned to 75 percent of its pre-Katrina level. Federal disaster preparedness also became an important focus in the wake of the hurricane, as politicians strive to avoid being part of "another Katrina."

Greg Wilson

For More Information

Brinkley, Douglas. *The Great Deluge: Hurricane Katrina, New Orleans, and the Mississippi Gulf Coast.* New York: Morrow, 2006.

Cooper, Christopher, and Robert Block. *Disaster: Hurricane Katrina and the Failure of Homeland Security.* New York: Times Books, 2006.

Horne, Jed. *Breach of Faith: Hurricane Katrina and the Near Death of a Great American City.* New York: Random House, 2008.

"Hurricane Katrina." National Oceanic and Atmospheric Administration (NOAA). http://www.katrina.noaa.gov/ (accessed September 6, 2011).

Kirkpatrick, David D., and Scott Shane. "Ex-FEMA Chief Tells of Frustration and Chaos." *New York Times* (September 15, 2005). http://www.nytimes.com/2005/09/15/national/nationalspecial/15brown.html (accessed September 6, 2011).

Murphy, Verity. "Fixing New Orleans' Thin Grey Line." *BBC News* (October 4, 2005). http://news.bbc.co.uk/2/hi/americas/4307972.stm (accessed September 6, 2011).

Hybrid Cars

Hybrid cars utilize both gasoline and electric power to operate. In addition to a standard internal combustion engine, hybrid cars contain a large bank of batteries that supply power when the internal combustion engine is not needed, such as when the car is idling. This allows hybrid cars to maintain much higher fuel efficiency than that of conventional cars. Many hybrid vehicles also feature regenerative braking, in which

The 2012 plug-in Toyota Prius. © ROBYN BECK/NEWSCOM.

the friction energy created by applying the brakes—wasted in traditional cars—is used to charge the battery. Some hybrid cars can be plugged in to recharge and can operate solely on electric power for relatively short distances. The Chevrolet Volt, for example, can travel about thirty-five miles on a charge without using any gas at all.

Although hybrid cars have existed in various forms for over a century, the first successful modern hybrid car was the Toyota Prius, launched in Japan in 1997. The Honda Insight, released in 1999, was the first hybrid car available in the United States. In just over a decade, the number of hybrid cars sold in the United States reached nearly two million. Although hybrids initially cost more than comparable combustion engine cars, hybrid owners generally save more over a five-year period due to lower fuel costs. In addition, hybrid cars have much lower emissions than conventional cars since the combustion engine is smaller, operates more efficiently, and can be shut off while idling or stopped.

However, hybrid cars also have some disadvantages when compared to standard engine cars. For example, the rare earth metals required to create the battery packs used in hybrids are in short supply, meaning that large-scale adoption of current hybrid models would be impossible. Another feature that has proven to be a potential problem is the virtual absence of engine noise while hybrid cars are in operation. Because they are so quiet, pedestrians and bicyclists are less likely to notice them, and safety groups have reported an increase in car-on-pedestrian accidents involving hybrids. Newer models of hybrids are expected to include special sound indicators to warn pedestrians of their presence.

Greg Wilson

For More Information

Anderson, Curtis D., and Judy Anderson. *Electric and Hybrid Cars: A History.* 2nd ed. Jefferson, NC: McFarland, 2010.

Hantula, Richard. *How Do Hybrid Cars Work?* New York: Chelsea Clubhouse, 2010.

Motavalli, Jim. "Is This the End of the Hybrid Price Premium?" *New York Times* (July 22, 2010). http://wheels.blogs.nytimes.com/2010/07/22/is-this-the-end-of-the-hybrid-price-premium/ (accessed September 19, 2011).

Simpson, Sarah. "Are Hybrid Cars Too Quiet to Be Safe for Pedestrians?" *Scientific American* (August 2008). http://www.scientificamerican.com/article.cfm?id=are-hybrid-cars-too-quiet (accessed September 19, 2011).

9/11

On September 11, 2001, terrorists from the militant Sunni Islamist group al-Qaeda hijacked four commercial airliners, flying two into the Twin Towers of Manhattan's World Trade Center and one into the Pentagon. The fourth crashed in Pennsylvania after passengers overcame the hijackers. Some three thousand people were killed during the attacks now known collectively as 9/11. That fateful day sent numerous shockwaves through global politics. Shortly after the attacks, President George W. Bush (1946–) ordered the invasion of Afghanistan, where the hard-line Islamist government had harbored al-Qaeda operatives. The desperate need to hunt and capture other terrorists that might be plotting against the United States led to the passage of the USA Patriot Act in 2001, a law that granted broad powers to American intelligence and law enforcement

New York City's World Trade Center burns on September 11, 2001, after terrorists, in a suicide attack, flew hijacked airplanes into both towers. More than twenty-eight hundred people were killed. © NEWSCOM.

agencies but, critics said, dangerously infringed on the rights of private citizens. U.S. intelligence mounted a ten-year hunt for al-Qaeda leader Osama bin Laden (1957–2011), the world's most wanted mass murderer.

America seemed to be stunned into immobility on the days that followed September 11, 2001. Regular television programming ceased on most network and local stations in favor of around-the-clock coverage of the attacks, the collapse of the Twin Towers, the search for victims, and theories about the causes and results of the attacks. Many stations did not resume regular broadcasting for days. The writing staffs of topical comedy programs such as *The Daily Show* (see entry under 2000s—TV and Radio in volume 6) and *Saturday Night Live* (see entry under 1970s—TV and Radio in volume 4) struggled to figure out how to deal with a post-9/11 world. Little seemed funny amidst the violent, disastrous images bombarding news and channels programs at all hours.

Americans accustomed to the safety and feeling of invulnerability that come with being citizens of a superpower were shaken by the fact that a small group of zealots could organize and go through with an attack more deadly than the Japanese raid on Pearl Harbor in 1941. Also disturbing were scenes on the nightly news of citizens in many Muslim countries crowding into the streets and cheering the news of al-Qaeda's deadly strikes against the United States. Americans accustomed to believing that their country was an international force for peace, freedom, and democracy were forced to confront the fact that millions of people in the world had a deeply negative view of America's history and role in world politics.

Subsequent U.S. actions—including the invasion of Afghanistan, the 2003 invasion of Iraq, and the long-term detention and alleged torture of terrorism suspects—served to make anti-American sentiment in the world even more widespread. Even among U.S. allies, disapproval of American foreign policy and the American government was strong. A Pew Research Center poll of global attitudes showed that by 2007, as the wars in Afghanistan and Iraq continued, 60 percent of the world had an unfavorable view of the United States, and 80 percent had an unfavorable view of President Bush personally. The global reputation of the United States rebounded sharply after the election of President **Barack Obama** (1961–; see entry under 2000s—The Way We Lived in volume 6) in 2008 and the withdrawal of U.S. combat troops from Iraq in 2010. According to the annual Pew Global Attitudes Project poll, 60 percent of the world had a favorable view of the United States in 2010.

A deeply shaken society eventually returned to something resembling normalcy, even as the war in Afghanistan raged on and airline passengers were subjected to increasingly invasive security procedures, including full-body scans. Then, nearly ten years after 9/11, on the evening of May 1, 2011, President Obama took to the airwaves with an announcement that brought Americans some feeling of closure. After years of painstaking intelligence work, Osama bin Laden had been found and killed in a nighttime raid on his compound in Pakistan by a U.S. Navy special ops team. He was buried at sea.

Michael Segretto

For More Information

DiMarco, Damon. *Tower Stories: An oral History of 9/11.* 2nd ed. Santa Monica, CA: Santa Monica Press, 2007.

Dwyer, Jim, and Kevin Flynn. *102 Minutes: The Untold Story of the Fight to Survive Inside the Twin Towers.* New York: Times Books, 2005.

Pew Global Attitudes Project. http://pewglobal.org/ (accessed July 21, 2011).

"Post-9/11 Timeline." PBS.org. http://www.pbs.org/flashpointsusa/20040629/infocus/topic_01/timeline_sep2001.html (accessed July 16, 2011).

Smith, Sean, and Jac Chebatoris. "A Dark Day Revisited." *Newsweek* (April 10, 2006). http://www.newsweek.com/2006/04/09/a-dark-day-revisited.html (accessed July 16, 2011).

Summers, Anthony, and Robbyn Swan. *The Eleventh Day: The Full Story of 9/11 and Osama bin Laden.* New York: Ballantine, 2011.

Wolk, Josh. "*The Daily Show* & *SNL*: Post-9/11 Comic Relief." *Entertainment Weekly* (January 22, 2011). http://www.ew.com/ew/article/0,,254104,00.html (accessed July 16, 2011).

Barack Obama (1961–)

In 2008, Americans elected Barack Obama as the forty-fourth president of the United States. As the first African American president, he represented to many both a break with America's difficult racial past and the ongoing possibilities of the American dream.

Obama was born in Hawaii, where his parents had met as university students. His mother was from a white family with roots in the Midwest, and his African father had come from Kenya to study economics. His father left Hawaii a few years later to study at Harvard University, and then returned to Kenya. After his parents divorced, his

U.S. senator Barack Obama of Illinois campaigns at a rally in Rodney Square on February 3, 2008, in Wilmington, Delaware, during the presidential campaign. © MISTYDAWNPHOTO/SHUTTERSTOCK.COM.

mother's marriage to an Indonesian man took the family overseas. His mother, who would go on to earn a Ph.D. herself, sent Obama back to the United States for high school, stressing the importance of a good education. Eventually he would attend both Occidental College and Columbia University.

After graduating from college, Obama worked in finance in New York City, but he soon moved to Chicago and began work as a community organizer. This experience gave him deeper roots in the African American community and cemented his interest in politics. Obama left Chicago to attend Harvard Law School, gaining national attention because he served as the first African American editor of the prestigious *Harvard Law Review*. With his degree in hand, he returned to Chicago and began to practice civil rights law in 1991. Three years later, he published *Dreams from My Father*, a memoir about his search for heritage. He was elected to the Illinois state senate in 1996 as a

Democrat, and, in 2004, he gained national attention by winning a decisive victory in a race for U.S. Senate. That year, he also impressed national audiences with a rousing keynote speech at the Democratic National Convention.

Obama won his party's nomination for president in 2008, after an intense primary campaign that pitted him against, among others, U.S. senator Hillary Rodham Clinton (1947–) of New York, wife of the forty-second U.S. president, Bill Clinton (1946–). Obama's campaign stressed the theme of hope, and a well-known campaign poster featured his face above that word. Young voters, in particular, identified with Obama's optimism and his **Internet** (see entry under 1990s—The Way We Lived in volume 5)-savvy approach to reaching the public. Obama ultimately defeated the Republican candidate, U.S. senator John McCain (1936–) of Arizona, by a comfortable margin.

In his 2009 inaugural address, Obama challenged Americans to "re-affirm our enduring spirit; to choose our better history." Despite such faith in his constituents and their nation, Obama's presidency faced immediate challenges. Wars continued in Iraq and Afghanistan, and the economic crisis that had begun in the months leading up to his election deepened in its impact. While the Obama administration succeeded in its goal of overhauling the nation's health care system, political divisiveness intensified as the economy remained sluggish. Criticism of the president and his policies, especially in the form of an anti-federal government movement known as the Tea Party, gained a strong foothold. Nevertheless, Obama's life story continued to affirm many Americans' faith in the possibilities of both their culture and their government.

Maureen Reed

For More Information

Abramson, Jill, et al. *Obama: The Historic Journey.* New York: Callaway Adult, 2009.

Finnegan, William. "The Candidate: How the Son of a Kenyan Economist Became an Illinois Everyman." *New Yorker* (May 31, 2004): 32.

Obama, Barack. *The Audacity of Hope: Thoughts on Reclaiming the American Dream.* New York: Crown Publishers, 2006.

Obama, Barack. *Dreams from My Father: A Story of Race and Inheritance.* New York: Times Books, 1995.

"President Barack Obama." *WhiteHouse.gov.* http://www.whitehouse.gov/administration/president-obama (accessed August 21, 2011).

Remnick, David. *The Bridge: The Life and Rise of Barack Obama.* New York: Alfred A. Knopf, 2010.

Obesity Epidemic

Obesity is described as excessive body mass due to fat; it is considered a separate and more severe classification than simply being overweight. The problem of obesity has grown at an alarming rate in recent decades, with even some developing nations experiencing significant obesity rates. According to the World Health Organization, overall obesity around the world doubled between 1980 and 2011. In two out of every three countries, obesity is a health issue greater than malnutrition and starvation. The obesity epidemic reveals itself most dramatically in the United States, where nearly two out of three Americans are classified as overweight or obese.

The spread of obesity in the United States has been especially shocking over the past thirty years. In the early 1980s, only a handful of states suffered from obesity rates higher than 10 percent of the population. By 2010, every single state reported obesity rates greater than 20 percent, and twelve states had obesity rates higher than 30 percent. The highest rates were found in the South and Midwest. The cause of these epidemic levels of obesity are the source of debate, though in the simplest terms, people are consuming more calories than their bodies are using. This suggests that the main problem areas are poor **diet** (see entry under 1950s—The Way We Lived in volume 3) and lack of exercise.

The American diet has transformed dramatically in the late twentieth and early twenty-first century, as have American eating habits. The foods Americans consume tend to be highly processed rather than natural, with an emphasis on inexpensive substitute ingredients such as high-fructose corn syrup, which is used in place of sugar. In fact, while Americans in 2005 consumed 28 percent less sugar than in 1970, they consumed 500 percent more corn-based sweetener. However, the problem is not simply one of quality, but of quantity. Americans in 2005 consumed an average eight hundred calories per day more than Americans in 1970. Since 2005, those numbers have continued to rise.

Americans also tend to get far less exercise than they used to, with three out of four people failing to get the government-recommended amount of physical activity each week. The problem is most urgent in the young, with over twelve million American children classified as obese—nearly triple the obesity rate observed in 1980. The main health problems associated with obesity include diabetes, heart disease, and stroke. In 2008, obesity-related disorders cost Americans more than $100 billion.

The U.S. government has tried to combat the obesity epidemic in several ways. In 2005, the U.S. Department of Agriculture redesigned the "food pyramid" that illustrates the recommended quantity of different types of foods. The new chart emphasizes physical activity and natural food sources and offers different recommendations based on age and gender. In 2010, first lady Michelle Obama (1964–) launched a campaign aimed at reducing obesity among American children called "Let's Move!" At the local level, many school districts have banned the sale of soft drinks and candy bars in school vending machines. The impact of these changes is as yet unknown.

Greg Wilson

For More Information

"Learn the Facts." *Let's Move.* http://www.letsmove.gov/learn-facts/epidemic-childhood-obesity (accessed September 21, 2011).

Power, Michael L., and Jay Schulkin. *The Evolution of Obesity.* Baltimore, MD: Johns Hopkins University Press, 2009.

"U.S. Obesity Trends." *Centers for Disease Control and Prevention* (July 21, 2011). http://www.cdc.gov/obesity/data/trends.html (accessed September 21, 2011).

Smart Phones

Smart phones are mobile devices that perform functions far beyond those possible with a traditional phone. Smart phones often contain calendar and scheduling features, and many feature music player capabilities and built-in cameras. Smart phones are especially versatile because they allow users to download new applications—or apps, for short—that enhance the phone's functions.

Smart phones first became popular in the 1990s, but it was not until 2001 that Palm introduced a phone with the capability to perform scheduling, **e-mail** (see entry under 1990s—The Way We Lived in volume 5), and contact list functions, which were enough to eliminate the need for a separate personal data assistant (PDA). These smart phones functioned much like tiny **personal computers** (see entry under 1970s—The Way We Lived in volume 4), and even offered the ability to surf the **Internet** (see entry under 1990s—The Way We Lived in volume 5). The BlackBerry line of devices, created by Research in Motion (RIM), became dominant in the world of smart phones throughout the early and middle of the first decade of the 2000s.

It was the release of the Apple iPhone in 2007 that truly brought smart phones to mainstream consumers. The iPhone was rich in features, offering a multitouch screen, music playback, and advanced Web browsing abilities. The iPhone sold one million units in less than three months and was quickly followed by updated models that offered even more features for a lower price. In 2008, the iPhone was the first smart phone that allowed users to easily purchase additional application software through an online store. The purpose of these apps can range from productivity, such as the note-taking software Evernote, to entertainment, such as the casual physics-based game Angry Birds.

In 2008, **Google** (see entry under 2000s—The Way We Lived in volume 6) supported the development of an operating system designed specifically for smart phones, which the company named Android. The operating system was incorporated into new smart phone models created by HTC, Samsung, Motorola, LG, and Sony Ericsson. In 2010, Android-based smart phones sold more than sixty-seven million units, making Android the second most popular type of smart phone, trailing only Symbian from Nokia.

Greg Wilson

For More Information

Baig, Edward C., and Bob LeVitus. *iPhone 4S for Dummies.* 5th ed. Hoboken, NJ: Wiley, 2011.

Pogue, David. *iPhone: The Missing Manual.* 4th ed. Sebastopol, CA: O'Reilly, 2010.

Vogelstein, Fred. "The Untold Story: How the iPhone Blew Up the Wireless Industry." *Wired* (January 9, 2008). http://www.wired.com/gadgets/wireless/magazine/16-02/ff_iphone (accessed September 26, 2011).

Twitter

Twitter took social networking and made it quick, mobile, and, for some users, nearly constant. The free microblogging service, launched in the summer of 2006, allows users to upload text messages up to 140 characters in length—called "tweets"—to the Web site Twitter.com. Subscribers can then choose to "follow" the tweets of particular people or organizations via the Web site. Twitter users can read and send tweets on a computer, but more commonly use **Internet** (see entry under 1990s—The

Way We Lived in volume 5)-enabled **cellular phones** (see entry under 1990s—The Way We Lived in volume 5). This short, pulsed style of communication revolutionized social interaction within a few short years.

San Francisco–based Twitter was the brainchild of software engineer Jack Dorsey (1976–), who sent the world's first tweet in March 2006. After Twitter's public launch, its popularity grew—first quickly, then exponentially. Through late 2006 and 2007, Twitter users posted about twenty thousand total tweets per day. Twitter use surged dramatically during the South by Southwest Music, Film and Interactive Festival (SXSW) in Austin, Texas, in March 2007, when festival goers tweeted relentlessly to share their experiences, offer entertainment recommendations, or just to track each other's whereabouts. During SXSW, daily tweets jumped 300 percent to sixty thousand per day. By 2010, Twitter posted fifty million tweets per day. By the time the service celebrated its fifth birthday in 2011, it had an average of 140 million tweets per day and more than 200 million users.

Twitter users tweet for a wide variety of reasons. Some individuals simply share thoughts and experiences with their followers. Others microblog on particular topics of interest to themselves and others. Celebrities quickly embraced Twitter as a way to keep in touch with their fan bases. In fact, television and film star Ashton Kutcher (1978–) became the first Twitter user to attract one million followers in April 2009, reaching the milestone just ahead of a close rival: cable news network **CNN** (see entry under 1980s—TV and Radio in volume 5). Businesses lured by the burgeoning Twitter subscriber base also starting finding uses for Twitter in 2008 and 2009. Brand promotion, public relations, and customer service activities found a natural home on Twitter. Even local, state, and national governments joined the Twitter-verse in increasing numbers starting in 2009. Soon, Twitter had reached the White House: President **Barack Obama** (1961–; see entry under 2000s—The Way We Lived in volume 6) sent his first tweet—about disaster relief efforts following a massive earthquake in Haiti—in January 2010.

Cynthia Johnson

For More Information

Fitton, Laura, Michael E. Gruen, and Leslie Poston. *Twitter for Dummies.* 2nd ed. Hoboken, NJ: Wiley, 2010.

Kirkpatrick, David. "Twitter Was Act One." *Vanity Fair* (April 2011). http://www.vanityfair.com/business/features/2011/04/jack-dorsey-201104 (accessed May 15, 2011).

O'Reilly, Tim, and Sarah Milstein. *The Twitter Book.* 2nd ed. Sebastopol, CA: O'Reilly.

Twitter. http://twitter.com. (accessed May 15, 2011).

Wikipedia

Although the advent of the World Wide Web in the 1990s made sharing and accessing information on the **Internet** (see entry under 1990s—The Way We Lived in volume 5) more widely available than ever before, distribution of information was still limited to individual Web sites updated by the sites' owners. This paradigm changed dramatically in the early 2000s with the emergence of the Web 2.0, which introduced alternative information-sharing sites like **blogs** (see entry under 2000s—The Way We Lived in volume 6), social networks, and wikis.

The vanguard of the wiki movement was Wikipedia, launched in 2001. A wiki is a Web site that can be edited and updated by anyone. Wikipedia aimed to use that technology to build the world's biggest encyclopedia, one written by the global community, all presented to readers free of charge. By the end of 2001, Wikipedia was available in eighteen languages and boasted twenty thousand entries. Ten years later, Wikipedia was available in 282 language editions and boasted over 3.5 million articles.

Wikipedia's completely open system of article submission and editing has led to controversy surrounding the site's reliability and accuracy. Critics have accused Wikipedia of focusing too much on the arts and pop culture. There have also been serious doubts raised regarding the reliability of the site's overall content. In one well-publicized controversy, journalist and writer John Seigenthaler (1927–) discovered his Wikipedia biography contained erroneous information that had remained undetected for four months.

In general, however, Wikipedia's format allows for rapid correction of false information, particularly in egregious cases of what amounts to vandalism of certain entries. Over the course of its history, the Web site has also been steadily tightening its standards for submissions, particularly for articles discussing living people or ongoing events. Although Wikipedia does not yet carry the same level of authoritative citation as a printed encyclopedia, it is becoming increasingly accepted as a legitimate source of information. Comparisons between select Wikipedia articles and their printed counterparts often show little to no difference in depth or accuracy of coverage.

David Larkins

For More Information

Ayers, Phoebe, Charles Matthews, and Ben Yates. *How Wikipedia Works: And How You Can Be a Part of It.* San Francisco: No Starch Press, 2008.

Keen, Andrew. *The Cult of the Amateur: How Today's Internet Is Killing Our Culture.* New York: Crown Business, 2007.

Reagle, Joseph Michael, Jr. *Good Faith Collaboration: The Culture of Wikipedia.* Cambridge, MA: MIT Press, 2010.

"Wikipedia." *Wikipedia.* http://en.wikipedia.org/wiki/Wikipedia (accessed July 26, 2011).

YouTube

YouTube is a Web site where users can view and share videos. The site was launched in 2005 and quickly became a repository for everything from old commercial clips to the latest music videos. The site, owned by **Google** (see entry under 2000s—The Way We Lived in volume 6) since 2006, is especially popular for "viral videos"—short, memorable clips that are passed around through email, online forums, and social media. Prior to YouTube, sharing a viral video was a difficult process; by its very design, YouTube encourages its users to share existing videos and to create new videos for others to share. Individual users create "channels" that other users can subscribe to if they find the content on that channel to be entertaining. By May 2011, YouTube had become the third most popular Web site on the **Internet** (see entry under 1990s—The Way We Lived in volume 5), drawing more than three billion views each day. The site's success has also spawned similar video-sharing sites such as TeacherTube, which focuses on educational content.

YouTube's video playback system relies mainly upon the Adobe Flash platform, one of the most popular ways to add animation and interactive elements to Web pages. Although most Internet users have access to Flash in their web browsers, some **Apple Computer** (see entry under 1970s—The Way We Lived in volume 4) products such as the iPhone and iPad do not support Flash. During YouTube's early years, this left many Apple users unable to play or share videos through the site. In 2010, YouTube programmers developed a special version of the site that

YouTube is the third most popular site on the Internet. © KRT/ALAMY.

can be accessed without the need for Flash. YouTube has also advanced from fairly low-resolution videos to allowing users to upload full high-definition clips. In addition, YouTube content has become accessible through numerous television-based media devices such as **video game** (see entry under 1970s—Sports and Games in volume 4) consoles.

Many of the video clips found on YouTube were not created by the users that upload them—for example, clips from old television shows or films. This can create copyright issues, since the rights holder for the film or show may demand that the site remove an unauthorized work. Although YouTube warns users against uploading videos for which they do not own the rights, the site places much of the burden of policing videos to the rights holders themselves. Several major media organizations, most notably Viacom, the owner of **MTV** (see entry under 1980s—Music in volume 5), and Paramount Pictures, have sued YouTube in an attempt to be reimbursed for the unauthorized use of their material.

With its emphasis on creativity and sharing, along with its ease of use and free access, YouTube has become a vital tool for aspiring artists of all stripes. Perhaps the most famous example of success achieved through YouTube is Canadian pop star Justin Bieber (1994–). When Bieber was just twelve years old, his mother uploaded some of his local performances to YouTube, where they quickly became popular. An American talent manager saw the videos and flew to Canada to meet Bieber and was so impressed that he brought the talented young musician back to Atlanta to record his first studio tracks. Within two years, Bieber had become a platinum-selling artist, thanks to that initial exposure provided by YouTube.

Greg Wilson

For More Information

Cloud, John. "The YouTube Gurus." *Time* (December 16, 2006). http:// www.time.com/time/magazine/article/0,9171,1570795,00.html (accessed September 25, 2011).

Rowell, Rebecca. *YouTube: The Company and Its Founders.* Edina, MN: ABDO, 2011.

Sahlin, Doug, and Chris Botello. *YouTube for Dummies.* Hoboken, NJ: Wiley, 2007.

Where to Learn More

The following list of resources focuses on material appropriate for middle school or high school students. Please note that the Web site addresses were verified prior to publication, but are subject to change.

Books

America A to Z: People, Places, Customs and Culture. Pleasantville, NY: Reader's Digest Association, 1997.

Beetz, Kirk H., ed. *Beacham's Encyclopedia of Popular Fiction.* Osprey, FL: Beacham, 1996.

Berke, Sally. *When TV Began: The First TV Shows.* New York: CPI, 1978.

Blum, Daniel; enlarged by John Willis. *A Pictorial History of the American Theatre, 1860–1985.* 6th ed. New York: Crown, 1986.

Brinkley, Douglas. *The Great Deluge: Hurricane Katrina, New Orleans, and the Mississippi Gulf Coast.* New York: Morrow, 2006.

Brooks, Tim, and Earle Marsh. *The Complete Directory to Prime Time Network and Cable TV Shows, 1946–present.* 9th ed. New York: Ballantine, 2007.

Cashmore, Ellis. *Sports Culture: An A to Z Guide.* New York: Routledge, 2000.

Condon, Judith. *The Nineties (Look at Life In).* Austin, TX: Raintree Steck-Vaughn, 2000.

Craddock, Jim. *VideoHound's Golden Movie Retriever.* Rev. ed. Detroit: Gale, 2011.

Daniel, Clifton, ed. *Chronicle of the Twentieth Century.* Liberty, MO: JL International Pub., 1994.

Dunning, John. *On the Air: The Encyclopedia of Old-Time Radio.* New York: Oxford University Press, 1998.

Dunning, John. *Tune in Yesterday: The Ultimate Encyclopedia of Old-Time Radio 1925–1976.* New York: Oxford University Press, 1998.

Ehrenreich, Barbara. *Nickel and Dimed: On (Not) Getting By in America.* New York: Metropolitan Books, 2001.

Epstein, Dan. *20th Century Pop Culture.* Philadelphia: Chelsea House, 2000.

Finkelstein, Norman H. *Sounds of the Air: The Golden Age of Radio.* New York: Charles Scribner's, 1993.

Flowers, Sarah. *Sports in America.* San Diego: Lucent, 1996.

Friedman, Thomas L. *Hot, Flat, and Crowded: Why We Need a Green Revolution—and How It Can Renew America.* New York: Picador, 2009.

Gilbert, Adrian. *The Eighties (Look at Life In).* Austin, TX: Raintree Steck-Vaughn, 2000.

Godin, Seth. *The Encyclopedia of Fictional People: The Most Important Characters of the 20th Century.* New York: Boulevard Books, 1996.

Gore, Al. *An Inconvenient Truth.* Emmaus, PA: Rodale Press, 2006.

Grant, R. G. *The Seventies (Look at Life In).* Austin, TX: Raintree Steck-Vaughn, 2000.

Grant, R. G. *The Sixties (Look at Life In).* Austin, TX: Raintree Steck-Vaughn, 2000.

Green, Joey. *Joey Green's Encyclopedia of Offbeat Uses for Brand-Name Products.* New York: Hyperion, 1998.

Green, Stanley. *Encyclopedia of the Musical Theatre.* New York: Da Capo Press, 1976.

Hischak, Thomas S. *Film It with Music: An Encyclopedic Guide to the American Movie Musical.* Westport, CT: Greenwood Press, 2001.

Katz, Ephraim. *The Film Encyclopedia.* 6th ed. New York: Collins, 2008.

Kirkpatrick, David. *The Facebook Effect: The Inside Story of the Company That Is Connecting the World.* New York: Simon & Schuster, 2011.

Lackmann, Ron. *The Encyclopedia of American Radio: An A–Z Guide to Radio from Jack Benny to Howard Stern.* New York: Facts on File, 2000.

Lebrecht, Norman. *The Companion to 20th-Century Music.* New York: Simon & Schuster, 1992.

Levitt, Steven D., and Stephen Dubner. *Freakonomics: A Rogue Economist Explores the Hidden Side of Everything.* Rev. ed. New York: Harper, 2009.

Lissauer, Robert. *Lissauer's Encyclopedia of Popular Music in America: 1888 to the Present.* New York: Facts on File, 1996.

Lowe, Denise. *Women and American Television: An Encyclopedia.* ABC-CLIO: Santa Barbara, CA, 1999.

Maltin, Leonard, ed. *Leonard Maltin's Movie Encyclopedia.* New York: Dutton, 1994.

Martin, Frank K. *A Decade of Delusions: From Speculative Contagion to the Great Recession.* Hoboken, NJ: Wiley, 2011.

McNeil, Alex. *Total Television: The Comprehensive Guide to Programming from 1948 to the Present.* 4th ed. New York: Penguin, 1996.

National Commission on Terrorist Attacks. *The 9/11 Commission Report: Final Report of the National Commission on Terrorist Attacks Upon the United States.* New York: Norton, 2004.

Newcomb, Horace, ed. *Encyclopedia of Television.* 2nd ed. Chicago: Fitzroy Dearborn, 2004.

Packer, George. *The Assassins' Gate: America in Iraq.* New York: Farrar, Straus, and Giroux, 2005.

Rosen, Roger, and Patra McSharry Sevastiades, eds. *Coca-Cola Culture: Icons of Pop.* New York: Rosen, 1993.

Schlosser, Eric. *Fast Food Nation.* New York: Houghton Mifflin, 2001.

Schwartz, Herman M. *Subprime Nation: American Power, Global Capital, and the Housing Bubble.* Ithaca, NY: Cornell University Press, 2009.

Schwartz, Richard A. *Cold War Culture: Media and the Arts, 1945–1990.* New York: Facts on File, 1997.

Sennett, Richard. *The Culture of the New Capitalism.* New Haven, CT: Yale University Press, 2007.

Sies, Luther F. *Encyclopedia of American Radio, 1920–1960.* 2nd ed. Jefferson, NC: McFarland, 2008.

Slide, Anthony. *Early American Cinema.* Rev. ed. Metuchen, NJ: Scarecrow Press, 1994.

Tibbetts, John C., and James M. Welsh. *The Encyclopedia of Novels into Film.* 2nd ed. New York: Facts on File, 2005.

Tibbetts, John C., and James M. Welsh. *The Encyclopedia of Stage Plays into Film.* New York: Facts on File, 2001.

Vise, David A. *The Google Story.* Updated ed. New York: Delacorte Press, 2008.

Weisman, Alan. *The World Without Us.* New York: St. Martin's Press, 2007.

Wilson, Charles Reagan, James G. Thomas Jr., and Ann J. Abadie, eds. *The New Encyclopedia of Southern Culture.* Chapel Hill: University of North Carolina Press, 2006.

Woodward, Bob. *Bush at War.* New York: Simon & Schuster, 2002.

Web Sites

Bumpus, Jessica. "The Noughties' Fashion Highlights." *Vogue* (December 22, 2010). http://www.vogue.co.uk/spy/celebrity-photos/2010/12/22/the-noughties (accessed September 23, 2011.)

Markowitz, Robin. *Cultural Studies Central.* http://www.culturalstudies.net/ (accessed August 7, 2011).

"The Noughties: Year by Year." *The Sunday Times,* October 20, 2009. http://women.timesonline.co.uk/tol/life_and_style/women/the_way_we_live/article6881549.ece (accessed September 23, 2011).

"100 Songs That Defined the Noughties." The *Telegraph,* September 18, 2009. http://www.telegraph.co.uk/culture/music/rockandpopfeatures/6198897/100-songs-that-defined-the-Noughties.html (accessed September 23, 2011).

"Pictures of the Decade." *Reuters.* http://www.reuters.com/news/pictures/slideshow?articleId=USRTXRYG2#a=1 (accessed September 23, 2011.)

"A Portrait of the Decade." *BBC News,* December 14, 2009. http://news.bbc.co.uk/2/hi/8409040.stm (accessed September 23, 2011).

Washington State University, American Studies. *Popular Culture: Resources for Critical Analysis.* http://www.wsu.edu/%7Eamerstu/pop/tvrguide.html (accessed August 7, 2011).

Yesterdayland. http://www.yesterdayland.com/ (accessed August 7, 2011).

Zupko, Sarah. *Popcultures.com: Sarah Zupko's Cultural Studies Center.* http://www.popcultures.com/ (accessed August 7, 2011).

Index

Italic type indicates volume number; **boldface** indicates main entries; (ill.) indicates illustrations.

B

C

Gelatin dessert (Jell-O), *1:* 66–68, 67 (ill.)

Gelb, Lawrence M., *2:* 398

Gelbwaks, Jeremy, *4:* 1150

Geldof, Bob, *5:* 1248

Gemayel, Bashir, *5:* 1265

"Gene, Gene, the Dancing Machine," *4:* 1132

General Foods, *2:* 451

General Lee (car), *4:* 1128

General Mills, *2:* 262–63

General Motors (GM), *1:* 140 (ill.), **140–41,** 158

General reference books, *1:* 212–13

Generation X (X-ers), *5:* **1318–20,** 1336, 1349, 1416

 extreme sports, *5:* 1392

 Friends, 5: 1338, 1415–16, 1416 (ill.)

Genital herpes and warts, *4:* 1191

"Genius Bar," *6:* 1472

Gentlemen Prefer Blondes (Loos), *2:* 251

George, Peter, *4:* 899

The George Burns and Gracie Allen Show, 3: 832

George Olsen and His Music, *2:* 282

Georgia Jazz Band (Ma Rainey's), *1:* 158

"Georgia Peach," *1:* 104

Gerber, Daniel Frank and Dorothy, *2:* 304

Gerber baby food, *2:* **304–5,** 305 (ill.)

Geritol, *3:* 823

German measles epidemic, *4:* 1189

Germanotta, Stefani Joanne Angelina, *6:* 1542

Germany, Volkswagen Beetle, *3:* 718 (ill.), 718–20

Gershwin, George and Ira, *2:* 255, 311; *3:* 610

Gertie the Dinosaur, *1:* 157, **185–87,** 186 (ill.)

"Get a clue!," *4:* 1040

Get Crunk: Who U Wit: Da Album, 6: 1529–30

Get Rich or Die Tryin', 6: 1464

Get Smart, 3: 682, 835

"Get Your Kicks on Route 66," *2:* 385

Getz, Stan, *1:* 74

Ghettos, *4:* **1017–19**

Ghostbusters, 5: **1230–32,** 1231 (ill.)

G.I. Bill, *3:* 556

G.I. Joe, *3:* 553; *4:* **877–78,** 878 (ill.)

G.I. Joe: Rise of Cobra, 4: 878

Giant (film), *3:* 728

Gibb, Andy, *3:* 612

Gibbons, Tom, *2:* 348 (ill.)

Gibson, Althea, *3:* 785–86

Gibson, Charles Dana, *1:* 84, 85 (ill.); *2:* 485

Gibson, Debbie, *3:* 612

Gibson, Dorothy, *1:* 246

Gibson, Henry, *4:* 1001

Gibson, Josh, *1:* 115

Gibson, Mel, *6:* 1507–9

Gibson, Walter Brown, *2:* 494

Gibson Girl, *1:* **84–85,** 85 (ill.)

Gibson Guitar Company, *3:* 755

Gibson Man, *1:* 85

Gifford, Chris, *6:* 1598

Gifford, Frank, *4:* 1108 (ill.), 1109

Gifford, Kathie Lee, *4:* 987, 1136

Gift-giving, on Mother's Day and Father's Day, *1:* 232, 237–38

Giggle water, *2:* 250

Gilbert, A. C., *1:* 217

Gilbert, Melissa, *4:* 1137

Gilbert, Sara, *5:* 1298 (ill.)

Gillespie, Darlene, *3:* 827

Gillespie, Dizzy, *1:* 73

Gillespie, Leonard, *4:* 988

Gilliam, Terry, *4:* 1146, 1146 (ill.), 1147

Gilligan's Island, 3: 833; *4:* 992 (ill.), **992–93**

Gillis, Dobie, *3:* 810 (ill.), **810–11**

Gilpin, Peri, *5:* 1414

Gilroy, Zelda, *3:* 810

Gimble's department store, *2:* 270; *3:* 648

Gingrich, Arnold, *2:* 480

Ginsberg, Allen, *3:* 765, 766, 776

Ginzburg, Ralph, *2:* 481

Girdles, Spanx, *6:* 1490–91

Girl Guides (Britain), *1:* 244

Girl Scouts, *1:* **243–45**

The Girl with the Dragon Tattoo, 6: **1554–55**

"The Girl without Fear," *1:* 157

Girls. *See also* Children's life and culture; Teenagers; Young women; Youth culture

 Barbie, *3:* 708–10, 709 (ill.)

 Cassidy, David, *4:* 1149 (ill.), 1150

 Sassy, 5: 1263–64

 teen idols, *3:* 693 (ill.), 693–95

"Girls Just Want to Have Fun," *5:* 1200

Gish, Dorothy, *1:* 181; *2:* 251

M

(W)

X

Y